THE FRENCH THEORY OF
THE NATION IN ARMS
1866-1939

THE FRENCH THEORY OF
THE NATION IN ARMS
1866-1939

By

RICHARD D. CHALLENER

NEW YORK

RUSSELL & RUSSELL · INC

1965

NUMBER 579

Columbia Studies in the Social Sciences

PRINTED IN THE UNITED STATES OF AMERICA

TO MY PARENTS

William Albert and Winifred Delo Challener

Acknowledgments

IT IS A PLEASURE to record my indebtedness to the many persons who have encouraged and advised me during the course of this work. I am particularly grateful for the friendly criticisms and helpful suggestions of Professors John Wuorinen, Carleton J. H. Hayes, and Garrett Mattingly, all of Columbia University. Likewise, I am deeply grateful for the advice given me by Professors Robert R. Palmer, Gordon A. Craig, and Joseph R. Strayer, all of Princeton University; by Mr. Donald J. Harvey of Great Neck, Long Island; by Mr. Shelby Cullom Davis of New York City; and by Professor Arpad Kovacs of St. Johns University. I also wish to thank the staffs of the libraries of the National War College and the Industrial College of the Armed Forces, Washington, D. C., for extending facilities for research in the summer of 1950. For the same reason I wish to thank Colonel Willard Webb of the Library of Congress. I am especially grateful for financial help given to me by the Research and Publication Fund of Princeton University. I wish also to thank Berger-Levrault for permission to quote from Charles de Gaulle, *Vers l'armée de métier,* and M. A. Fournier Foch for permission to quote from *The Memoirs of Marshal Foch.*

Above all, I would like to express my appreciation for the assistance given to me by Professor Shepard B. Clough of Columbia University. It was he who first suggested this topic to me and who guided me through my research and the writing of this work. Without his advice, criticisms, and encouragement this book could never have been completed.

RICHARD D. CHALLENER

Princeton University
July, 1954

Contents

THE FRENCH THEORY OF
THE NATION IN ARMS
1866-1939

Introduction

THE CONCEPT OF THE NATION IN ARMS, like so many of the theories and institutions on which modern France has been built, originated in the war-torn years of the Revolution. Universal and compulsory military service—a more accurate if prosaic equivalent for the revolutionary phrase "the nation in arms"—was, to be sure, an unexpected and unwanted consequence of the events which followed from the meeting of the Estates General in 1789. Many of the *cahiers de doléances* compiled in preparation for this meeting had in fact called for the abolition of the royal practice of recruiting provincial militias, and many a revolutionary bourgeois had fondly imagined that the creation of a constitutional regime would usher in an era of permanent peace. Yet within a few short years conscript soldiers formed the rank and file of the French forces defending *la patrie* from the armies of the First Coalition, and the National Convention had, with a patriotic flourish, decreed that "the battalion organized in each district shall be united under a banner bearing the inscription: The French people risen against tyranny." [1] This same assembly had, in August of 1793, laid down both the theory and practice of what the twentieth century was to call "total war": the young men were to go forth to battle, the married men would forge arms, the women were to make tents and clothing, and the aged were "to preach hatred of kings and the unity of the Republic." [2]

[1] Jean B. Duvergier, ed., *Collection complète des lois, décrets, ordonnances, réglemens, avis du conseil d'état . . . de 1788 à 1830 . . .* (30 vols., Paris: Guyot, 1834-38), VI, 108.
[2] *Ibid.*, p. 107.

Many events and forces united to kill the hopes of 1789 and create the realities of 1793. National guard units, arising spontaneously, had seemed to prove that an armed citizenry could safeguard the bourgeoisie from both the real and the assumed threats of counterrevolutionary action. At the same time the "old army," in which the purchase of commissions was a zealously guarded prerogative of the rich and well-born, appeared as a legitimate object for the reforming ardor of the Third Estate.[3] French liberal thought of the prerevolutionary years had itself foreshadowed the coming of conscription. Had not Rousseau advised the Poles as early as 1772 that only a well-trained militia, in which it was the duty of every citizen to serve as a soldier, would assure the defense of a free nation?[4] But above all the harsh realities of military necessity demanded the creation of armies far greater in size than the professional forces employed in the dynastic warfare of the earlier part of the eighteenth century. Both patriotism and egalitarianism, vital attributes of the revolutionary ideology, affected this development; patriotism demanded that all the sons of France be enrolled in her defense, and egalitarianism insisted that the burden of sacrifice must be equally shared. The result was the nation in arms.

The citizen turned soldier—indeed, conscript service as both the badge and moral consequence of citizenship—was one of the major results of the French Revolution. It was by no means the least important legacy bequeathed by the revolutionary age to the generations of the modern world.

Since the decade of revolution the concept of the nation in arms has been an integral part of the French military heritage and has served as a focus around which the French have elabo-

[3] Georges Lefebvre, *The Coming of the French Revolution,* trans. R. R. Palmer (Princeton: Princeton University Press, 1947), pp. 16-17, 97, 124.

[4] Jean Jacques Rousseau, *Considérations sur le gouvernement de Pologne et sur sa réformation projetée,* full French text in C. E. Vaughan, ed., *Political Writings of Jean Jacques Rousseau* (2 vols., Cambridge: Cambridge University Press, 1915), II, 422 ff.

rated theories for military organization as well as for the conduct of warfare. Yet however interesting and important the concept was in the years of the First Republic and the First Empire, it has played an even greater role in the more recent military history of the French nation. Especially since the closing years of the Second Empire and throughout the entire life-span of the Third Republic—roughly, from 1866 to 1940—the theory has been of major importance in the determination of French military policies.

The aim of the chapters which follow is, then, to discuss French thought on the nation in arms from the time when Napoleon III initiated military reform after the Austro-Prussian War of 1866 until the outbreak of the Second World War. These pages will deal with the various opinions and programs advanced by both military writers and political spokesmen, but they will concentrate upon the development of theory. That is, an attempt will be made to show how the idea of the nation in arms changed from an essentially political concept centering upon endless arguments over divergent conscription policies to a body of doctrine which by 1939 imposed upon France a consistent, detailed set of regulations for the total exploitation of her human and economic resources in time of war.

A secondary but no less important aspect of this book is to point out some of the consequences of this evolving military theory. One of the principal assumptions of the following pages is that the concept of the nation in arms provides a logical frame of reference for a better understanding of the success or failure of French arms in the wars of 1870, 1914, and 1939. The fact that army leaders had no faith in the conscript soldier and that the French people were unwilling to accept the rigors of compulsory military service is a significant aspect of the defeat of 1870. Likewise, the prevailing interpretations of the concept of the nation in arms in 1914 and in 1939 led the French to expect and plan for a particular type of warfare which never materialized, and thus had a marked effect upon the military outcome.

There are several problems concerning the evolution of the nation in arms which must be mentioned in advance of the main body of the narrative.

The first of these is the question of definition. For while the Jacobin origin of the theory is both clear and well established, it is a difficult task to give precise meaning to the phrase "the nation in arms." For this there are two main reasons. The first is simply that the political outlook of an individual has always affected his definition of the nation in arms; a Socialist follower of Jaurès, for instance, would describe the concept in words that no marshal of the Second Empire could ever have used. The second reason is that the concept of the nation in arms has itself changed in the course of time; no Frenchman writing in 1939, whether a left-wing politician or a hidebound military officer, would have defined it in the same way as he would have twenty-five years earlier.

At the level of basic meaning—a sort of lowest common denominator of accepted belief—"the nation in arms" implies perhaps nothing more than the principle of universal and compulsory military service. Yet even this definition carries with it the important corollary that one of the primary moral obligations of the French citizen is to fulfill his conscript duties.

But the range of individual definitions is great. Republican heirs of the Revolution, devoted to egalitarian principles, have consistently made the concept of the nation in arms into a moral touchstone with which to judge the virtue of all succeeding French military institutions; conservative enemies of that Revolution, no less devoted to principle, defined it as an open invitation to anarchy and the social disorders produced by undisciplined armed mobs. A generation of French military officers after 1870, impressed by both the quantity and the quality of the German army, thought of the nation in arms in purely military terms; for them it was the most rational principle on which to build the mass armies demanded by mass warfare. On the other hand, the militia-minded political reformers of the Dreyfus era, desiring to weaken the influence of the military hierarchy in French society, emphasized the role of the citizen-soldier in their definitions. In their view, a young Frenchman should be a citizen first, a soldier second, so that, through the mysterious workings of patriotic devotion, he would be a better guardian of the nation.

The passage of time has had an even greater effect upon definitions of the nation in arms. Prior to the war of 1914 French thought on the nation in arms concerned itself only with the military relationship between the state and its male citizens; it dealt with the human resources of the nation and not at all with the economic or industrial potential of France. But after four years of relentless struggle had revealed the expanded and altered character of modern war, the concept of the nation in arms became a body of ideas which dealt with the organization of every phase and every aspect of French life in time of war. Before 1914 the concept was political in content; thereafter it became a theory of total war.

In addition to the problem of changing definition there is a second aspect of the history of the nation in arms which must be noted in advance. This is the fact that much of the story is narrowly political and can be explained only by reference to the complicated and often exasperating network of French party politics. This orientation arises from the fact that the army has played a vital role in French domestic affairs ever since 1789. National guards, popular militia, and disgruntled regulars were in large measure responsible for the success of revolutionary and insurrectionary movements from the storming of the Bastille to the creation of the short-lived Commune of 1871; on the other hand, the two most famous crises of the young Third Republic —the "affairs" of Boulanger and Dreyfus—seemed to many to be manifestations of a plot by reactionary military officers to dominate if not destroy parliamentary institutions.

Because of the importance of the army in the life of the nation French political parties have always held strong, even violent opinions on military affairs. The Right, fearful that conscription would put guns into the hands of the politically unreliable, long maintained that only a large regular army would guarantee social stability and the preservation of law and order; the republicans and their allies, afraid lest "the military" achieve an undue influence over civil institutions, were equally insistent that only an army of citizen-soldiers satisfied the needs of a democratic nation. The concept of the nation in arms has thus always been an issue of political life in France—in fact, as early as 1789 the Revolutionary leader Dubois-Crancé indicated the political overtones lurking behind the theory when he told the Constituent Assembly that "each citizen should be a soldier, and each soldier a citizen, or we shall never have a constitution." As a result, the concept of the nation in arms, involving as it does such fundamental questions as the recruitment, organization, effectiveness, and loyalty of the army, cannot be discussed outside the framework of French political life.

The third and final preliminary consideration is of the nature of a paradox. Although the French, as has been said, originated the concept of the nation in arms during the Revolution, there was a gap in both theory and practice which stretched from the Bourbon restoration to the latter days of the Second Empire. Furthermore, it was an event in the history of Central Europe —the crushing victory over Austria of the Prussian conscript army at Sadowa in 1866—which produced a revival of French thought on the nation in arms. The impetus to reconsider the problems of military structure and organization was the result of foreign rather than domestic events, and it came after many long years in which both theory and practice had been neglected. The reasons for this—a few of which will be mentioned in Chapter I—are perhaps less important than the fact. Consequently, despite the fact that the nation in arms was born in the years immediately after 1789, the essential starting point for this book is the year 1866 when the unexpectedly decisive victory of the Prussian war machine forced the France of Napoleon III to begin re-examination of its military institutions and the theories on which they were founded.

I

The Influence of Sadowa and Sedan

THE OVERWHELMING TRIUMPH of Prussian arms in the war with Austria, a victory decisive in the affairs of Germany, was an event of major significance in the history of the empire of Napoleon III. Not only did the Prussian success reveal the bankruptcy of an unrealistic French foreign policy founded on the dubious assumption that Napoleon could still play the role of European territorial arbiter, but it also indicated that the imperial army, though but recently victorious in Italy and in the Crimea, was ill-prepared to make any effective intervention beyond the Rhine.[1]

Coming at a time when the once-powerful Second Empire was already beginning its slow slide into the trough of futility, the Prussian victory produced an angry response of French public opinion.[2] Of greater significance than the outcry of outraged journalists and deputies, however, was the reaction of Na-

[1] For discussion of French foreign policy and the possibility of military intervention, see Émile Bourgeois, *Manuel de politique étrangère* (4 vols., Paris: Belin, 1900-26), III, 689 and Herman Oncken, *Napoleon III and the Rhine*, trans. Edwin H. Zeydel (New York: Knopf, 1928), pp. 59 ff. A thorough critique of military plans and potentialities is Pierre Lehautcourt, "La Réorganisation de l'armée avant 1870," *Revue de Paris*, IV (Aug. 1901), 525-52. Lehautcourt insisted that the army could not have acted in 1866. Germain Bapst, *Le Maréchal Canrobert* (6 vols., Paris: Plon, 1898-1909), IV, 53, claimed that on August 20, 1866, General Castelnau submitted a note to the Emperor which pointed out that France had a total of but 288,000 men available and that they were scattered in Africa, Mexico, and Rome as well as in metropolitan France.

[2] For newspaper reactions and the demand for army reform see Émile Ollivier, *L'Empire libéral* (18 vols., Paris: Garnier Frères, 1895-1918), X, 312-15. A good example of this outcry was the column of political commentary by Forcade in the *Revue des deux mondes.* In his "Chroniques de la quinzaine," Forcade flatly stated that France was in real military danger, called for the recruitment of a million men, and insisted that it was necessary to model French military institutions upon the Prussian pattern. *Revue des deux mondes,* LXV (Sept. 1, 1866), 238-44.

poleon III. The Austrian defeat at Sadowa prodded the Emperor into opening a searching inquiry into the state of the French army and into suggesting reforms in its recruitment and composition. As early as late August, 1866, Napoleon began to invite a few select military leaders to dinner at the imperial residence. Once the marshals and generals were well fed and presumably better disposed, he outlined to them a scheme for military reform based upon the adoption of compulsory service for French youth, and requested his guests to submit memoranda on the best methods for achieving his proposed reform. Soon the Emperor informed the French public that, on the sixth of November, a great military commission composed of three civil ministers, four generals, and all the marshals and admirals would meet at Saint Cloud to discuss the reorganization of the French army.[3]

The French military system which Napoleon III proposed to revise was not even a pale image of the Jacobin ideal that every citizen should be a soldier and every soldier, a citizen. The army was the product of basic legislation which had been enacted in 1818 and which, with modifications made in 1832, was

[3] The best discussion of the reform attempt is Arpad Kovacs, " French Military Institutions before the Franco-Prussian War," *American Historical Review*, LI (Jan., 1946), 217-35. The standard account, though biased in view of its admiration for the military policies of the Left, is Joseph Monteilhet, *Les Institutions militaires de la France (1814-1932)* (Paris: Alcan, 1932, 2d ed.), a work which has been of invaluable assistance in the preparation of this study. Valuable though abbreviated accounts of the army and the reforms of the sixties are to be found in such standard accounts as Colonel Joseph Revol, *Histoire de l'armée française* (Paris: Larousse, 1929); General Maxime Weygand, *Histoire de l'armée française* (Paris: Flammarion, 1938); Gabriel Hanotaux, General Charles Mangin, and Marshal Louis Franchet d'Esperey, *Histoire militaire et navale* (*L'Histoire de la nation française*, ed. Gabriel Hanotaux, 15 vols., Paris: Plon, 1920-29; Part II, Vol. VIII); and Charles de Gaulle, *La France et son armée* (Paris: Plon, ed. of 1945). Useful contemporary sources are Le Duc Henri d'Aumale, *Les Institutions militaires de la France* (Paris: Lévy Frères, 1867) and General Louis Trochu, *L'Armée française en 1867* (Paris: Amyot, 1867). By far the most comprehensive general history which discusses the military situation is Pierre de la Gorce, *Histoire du Second Empire* (7 vols., Paris: Plon, 1899-1905), Vol. V. There is also a wealth of information on the military affairs of the Second Empire, material which ranges from the writings of Ollivier and Lehautcourt, already cited, to the biographical studies and memoirs of such military figures as Randon, Castellane, and Canrobert.

still in force during the Second Empire. At the time of passage of the law of 1818, the French people, exhausted by long years of warfare, were in no mood to accept compulsory military service. Almost everyone had heartily welcomed that part of the Bourbon charter of 1814 which abolished conscription, and Chateaubriand summed up the popular attitude when he wrote that most Frenchmen, after living through the wars of the First Republic and the First Empire, believed conscription to be an evil, whether it was the policy of a democracy or of a despot.[4] To be sure, by 1818 the flow of volunteers had been so meager that even the first Restoration government found it necessary to hedge a bit, and the resulting military legislation provided for at least a semblance of conscription. But the terms of the 1818 law were such that it established little more than a recruiting system which paid only lip service to the principle of compulsory service.

The legislation of 1818 established an annual contingent; the size of this, according to a later law, passed in 1830, was determined each year by the legislature. An elaborate lottery system was set up to determine which young men should form the annual contingent and who would serve in the active army.[5] The young man who was fortunate drew a "good number," and was exempted from all military obligations for the remainder of his life, but the individual whose lot was a "bad number" soon found himself subject to seven years of service with the regulars. The harshness of this system, however, was mitigated by the provisions which enabled any man drawing a "bad number" to hire a substitute to serve in his place. In 1855 the Emperor added a new feature: instead of hiring a substitute, the man eligible for active duty could fulfill all of his military obliga-

---

[4] Monteilhet, *Institutions militaires*, pp. 4-5.

[5] The lottery, with its notorious system of "good" and "bad" numbers, was of venerable age, and its operation on a formalized basis dated from the years of Louis XIII when it had been used to determine the enrollment in provincial militias. Édouard Gachot, "Histoire du tirage au sort," *Nouvelle Revue*, XXVI (Jan.-Feb., 1904), 22 ff.

tions by making a direct money payment to the state of between 2,000 and 2,500 francs. The money thus accumulated was to be used to encourage re-enlistments and to pay bounties to professional soldiers.[6]

Under such legislation, with its provisions for substitution and its reliance upon a seven-year term of service, conscription played a distinctly secondary role in the formation of French armies. The number of actual conscripts, never large after 1818, soon dwindled to no more than 20,000 per year. And, by the very nature of the system, these men came almost exclusively from the ranks of the poor and the peasantry who could not afford the luxury of a paid substitute or a direct payment to the state. Conscription, then, furnished but a fraction of the men in service and, as practiced, operated in no egalitarian fashion but served rather to mark the distinction between rich and poor.

Although in more recent times many liberals have denounced the military system which was in practice after 1815, the conscription policies followed by successive French governments were approved by the vast majority of Frenchmen and had become an established part of the social order. Indeed, there were even insurance companies which issued policies against the calamity of military service and which found substitutes for policy-holders whose premiums were up-to-date. Obviously the provisions of the 1818 law suited the wealthy, but they also pleased the poor because, even if cash for a substitute or an insurance policy was lacking, there was always the fact that in the conscription lottery the odds were good. Doctrinaire liberalism warmly approved the system. Adolphe Thiers, certainly a paragon of bourgeois respectability, expressed the dominant at-

---

[6] For a defense of the system, see *Mémoires du Maréchal Randon* (2 vols., Paris: Lahure, 1875-77), II, 250 ff. Statistics which indicate the harmful effects of this policy on the composition of the army are to be found in Pierre Lehautcourt, "La Réorganisation de l'armée avant 1870," *Revue de Paris*, IV (Aug., 1901), 542. There was also considerable contemporary criticisms by men who were by no means ardent reformers of the military establishment. See Trochu, *L'Armée française*, p. 318 ff. and d'Aumale, *Institutions militaires*, pp. 189-90.

titude of the leaders of the era of the *juste milieu* when he said,

If you want to impose the same conditions and the same sort of life on individuals who are entirely different, you are the one who wounds equality. . . . What harm is done to the peasant? Transported into the ranks of the army, he finds there a way of life superior to that which he had at home. But military service is an intolerable tyranny to the man destined for a civil career.[7]

How far the French had strayed from the path of Revolutionary "virtue" was further indicated during the course of the short-lived Second Republic. The men of '48, despite their warm devotion to republican principles, nonetheless specifically authorized the practice of replacement and substitution in the constitution of that year, and the vote in favor of these arrangements was an overwhelming 663 to 140.[8] Indeed, the obligation to serve in the army, regarded a half century earlier as the fulfillment of high civic and patriotic duties, had become known by the mid-nineteenth century as "the blood tax"—the *impôt du sang*.[9]

The military leaders of France gave strong approval to the prevailing system of military organization and recruitment. They unanimously averred that it took years to make a good soldier and that no individual could be properly trained in less than seven years. The short-term conscript, they said, did not

---

[7] As quoted in Monteilhet, *Institutions militaires*, p. 30. For similar opinions of Thiers, see also Nassau Senior, *Conversations with M. Thiers, M. Guizot, and other Distinguished Persons during the Second Empire*, (2 vols., London: Hurst and Blackett, 1878), II, 324. That other pillar of Orleanist society, Guizot, expressed warm approval of current conscription practices when he, too, had the chance to talk with Senior. See *Conversations with Distinguished Persons during the Second Empire* (2 vols., London: Hurst and Blackett, 1880), II, 269-70.

[8] Monteilhet, *Institutions militaires*, p. 28 ff.

[9] According to the Duc d'Aumale, the phrase was coined by General Foy in 1824 and because it so accurately and concisely expressed the public feeling quickly became a part of popular speech. d'Aumale, *Institutions militaires*, p. 31. He himself felt that "The phrase contains a proper and striking image, and all those persons who have any control over the destinies of our armies should repeat it every day; but, reduced to its mathematical value, it has led to some conclusions which are not exact—to consider recruiting as a tax, to materialize a moral obligation, to treat the malingerer as merely a loiterer and the deserter as a bankrupt."

have and could not acquire the requisite knowledge, discipline, and spirit. Indeed, the French army of these years placed its faith in the "old soldier"—a man so thoroughly purged of his previous attachments and so completely habituated to the military way of life that his one and only loyalty was to the colors of his regiment.[10] And such a soldier was valued precisely because he would obey orders almost by reflex action.

Military writers based their opinion on the assumption that only the old soldier possessed a true military spirit—*l'esprit militaire*, a phrase much in favor—and that it was this quality which produced victory on the battlefield. A whole system of values revolved around the idea of *l'esprit militaire*. It was believed that only when a soldier had served long years in his regiment and developed an automatic response to commands did he possess this quality; then when he was engaged in battle he emerged the victor because, again, he was the possessor of this supreme military virtue. It followed from this assumption that the French military theorists believed that the quality of their soldiers was far more important than the number of men under arms. One of the reasons why the French army hierarchy was shocked by the Prussian victory of 1866 was because the official French doctrine, as taught in the military schools, maintained that the German army, composed of short-term conscripts, was by definition deficient in military spirit and, hence, in fighting ability.[11] Colonel Ardant du Picq, the principal French theorist of the sixties, resolutely challenged anyone who suggested that quantity was as important as quality. To believe in the value of mere numerical strength, he wrote, was a "shameful

[10] A particularly moving description of the plight of the old soldier is to be found in de la Gorce, *Histoire*, V, 321 ff. in which much attention is paid to the inability of such a man to adjust himself to civilian life and standards after discharge. Equally interesting is the account of the Academician Étienne Lamy, "Les Ennemis de l'armée," *Revue des deux mondes*, CXXII (Mar. 15, 1894), 433 ff.

[11] General Trochu wrote that prior to 1866 the French officers had considered the Prussian system of universal service feeble and lacking the equilibrium necessary for war. This, he said, was the official school doctrine (*L'Armée française*, pp. 8-9).

theory" because it did not "reckon on courage but on the amount of flesh." In his eyes the American Civil War furnished abundant evidence of what "will become of modern battle with armies immense but without cohesion."[12] In du Picq's analysis, the essential factors for military victory were courage, moral force, cohesion, discipline, and military spirit. And, of course, these were qualities never found in the conscript but only in the old soldier who was a veteran of long years in the ranks.

Whatever the advantages of these practices may have been, the fact remains that the French recruitment system had one grave weakness which became more and more apparent as Europe, all unknowing, began in 1859 the sudden descent into an era of national wars. Existing legislation had failed to produce a supply of trained reservists. To be sure, the reserves had been intentionally eliminated from the calculations of the planners and theorists because some questioned their political reliability, some doubted if men returned to civil life could ever regain their lost military spirit, and others felt that any ex-soldier recalled to duty would be a particularly reluctant and disgruntled fighter.[13] But the Italian war, in which the shortage of trained reserves was painfully apparent, pointed up the errors in much of this reasoning. Before long Napoleon III was himself moved to decree that the heretofore exempted members of the second portion of the annual contingent were to undergo five months' basic training. Although this step was proclaimed in 1861, a

---

[12] Colonel Ardant du Picq, *Études sur le combat* (Paris: Chapelot, ed. of 1904), p. 102. See also the chapter "Théorie des gros bataillons," pp. 129-34. See also Alfred Vagts, *Militarism: Romance and Realities of a Profession* (New York: Norton, 1937), p. 222. The best analysis of du Picq's theories and his influence on French military thought is Stefan T. Possony and Etienne Mantoux, "Du Picq and Foch: the French School," in E. M. Earle, ed., *Makers of Modern Strategy* (Princeton: Princeton University Press, 1943), Chap. IX.

[13] Marshal Soult, the Algerian veteran, pointed out that "When, at the moment of war, we call to the colors those who have not as yet served, they will come more voluntarily than those who know the boredom of the barracks, the inconveniences of the profession." Cited in Pierre Lehautcourt, *Histoire de la guerre de 1870-71* (7 vols., Paris: Berger-Levrault, 1901-08), II, 55.

chronic lack of both funds and interest kept the decree from being effective.[14] The crisis of the summer of 1866 provided additional evidence that the shortage of trained reserves was one of the conspicuous failures of the French military recruitment system.

When the Emperor proposed the Saint Cloud conferences and spoke of the need for a return to compulsory service, it was the lack of reservists and the question of the numerical size of the army which were paramount in his mind. As he later pointed out to the *corps législatif,* he firmly believed that "the influence of a nation depends upon the number of men she can put under arms." [15] While the Emperor was skilled in the usage of republican-sounding formulae which associated compulsory service with traditional principles of equality, his basic objective was more men for his army. Significantly, he opened a session of the Saint Cloud meeting with two questions: "Do we need a million men?" and " How are we going to get them?" [16] And to his friend Émile Ollivier he wrote, "Numbers are going to be the decisive thing this time. We must make absolutely certain of them." [17]

Nevertheless there was still in the Man of Destiny a reflection of the Prisoner of Ham. In his younger days, when he had been engaged in writing high-sounding pamphlets linking his name with that of his more famous uncle, Louis Napoléon had

[14] For a discussion of the conferences which led to this change of policy as well as evidence that the Emperor was the one who most desired it, see Esprit V. Castellane, *Le Journal du Maréchal Castellane, 1804-1862,* (5 vols., Paris: Plon, 1896-1930), V, 278, 327-31. Pertinent information on the shortage of reserves is in Arpad Kovacs, "French Military Institutions before the Franco-Prussian War," *American Historical Review,* LI (Jan., 1946), 223. In the mid-sixties the Prussians were training 63,000 men each year under the newly established three-year system of Von Roon and, in addition, maintained them for a period of sixteen years in the reserves. In France all military obligations ceased after a man had served seven years in the active army.

[15] *Le Moniteur universel,* Feb. 15, 1867.

[16] Bapst, *Canrobert,* IV, 54.

[17] Octave Aubry, *Le Second Empire* (Paris: Fayard, 1938), p. 487.

written in enthusiastic vein of the Prussian system of compulsory service. In one of these pamphlets, for instance, after applauding the dictum that the citizen and the soldier must be one, the future emperor had predicted that all the European powers would ultimately adopt the Prussian system of military organization because it alone responded to the new demands of the European peoples.[18] Hence, when Napoleon III took up the question of military reform in the summer and autumn of 1866, his scheme was in a very real sense a return to the ideas of his youth.

The November meetings of the top military and civilian leaders at Saint Cloud, and later ones at Compiègne, produced the first setback for the Napoleonic program. Many of the military officials showed themselves hostile to any return to compulsory service, and, above all, the Emperor's political advisers were opposed. These, fearful of an unfavorable reaction by the *corps législatif,* insisted that universal service was unconstitutional and that the chamber could not be deprived of its right to vote the annual contingent. Among the military officials, the opposition of Napoleon's Minister of War, Marshal Randon, was so unyielding that even before he could present his program to the French public, the Emperor found it necessary to replace Randon with an officer less intractable.[19]

The proposal which emerged from the long series of meetings was essentially a compromise. The work of General Niel, the officer who soon replaced Randon at the War Ministry, this project was designed to satisfy Napoleon's demands for compulsory service, a sufficient quantity of trained reserves, and an

---

[18] *Oeuvres de Napoleon III* (5 vols., Paris: Plon, 1856-69), I, 423. See also articles he wrote for the *Pas de Calais* in 1843, reprinted in *Oeuvres de Louis-Napoléon Bonaparte* (2 vols., Paris: Librairie Napoléonienne, 1848), I, 50.

[19] For accounts of the Saint Cloud and Compiègne meetings, see General Louis Trochu, *Oeuvres posthumes* (2 vols., Tours: Alfred Mame, 1896), I, 74-75; Bapst, *Canrobert,* IV, 57-66; and Ollivier, *Empire libéral,* X, 318. For a good example of Randon's continued adherence to the established military system, see his letter of October, 1866 to the Emperor in Randon, *Mémoires,* II, 180 ff.

army of a million men and, at the same time, to appease all the imperial advisers who believed the existing military structure to be basically sound. A notice, written by the Emperor himself, appeared in *Le Moniteur universel* on December 12, 1866, and announced the broad outlines of the projected reform. All Frenchmen were to be subject to some form of military service in one of three proposed categories: active, reserves, or *garde mobile*. Since every young man owed a total of nine years' service in one or more of these categories, the Napoleonic principle of universal military service was maintained. But at the same time many of the salient features of the old order remained. A lottery was to decide which men went into the active army and which men were assigned to the reserves. And if a man was selected for the actives, his period of service was to be a full six years. These, obviously, were provisions designed to preserve the "old soldiers" so beloved by the army hierarchy.

Moreover, any man selected for the active army could still obtain a substitute; this provision was a concession made to those who felt that the French public would not accept a rigorous application of the principle of universal service. The Emperor himself realized that he had to bow before necessity, for while his initial statement looked toward the coming of the day when all Frenchmen would defend their country in time of war, he also indicated a willingness to compromise. The *Moniteur* stated:

At the same time, while we proclaim the obligation of each individual to defend the nation in case of war as a principle of equality and of justice, it is important not to crush established customs too brusquely and not, in time of peace, to thwart the vocations of young men destined for liberal careers.

Nonetheless, no Frenchman totally escaped, and the proposed law was in fact a step towards the re-establishment of the nation in arms. The individual who was initially assigned to the reserves was to receive military training although, to be sure, his burden was far less than it would have been had the lottery consigned him to the actives instead. Likewise, the young man who hired a substitute was not completely free of all military obligations; he was to belong to the *garde mobile* for nine years, would receive some military instruction, and could be mobilized in time of war. While the Niel project did maintain the existing structure of an active army based on long-term service, the fact that it added a superstructure of reserves and obligated all young men to fulfill some form of military service over a period of nine years established French military recruitment upon a broader basis. Moreover, in view of Napoleon's estimate that the reform would more than double the wartime strength of his armies, the Niel project indicated that in the proposed organization the numerical strength of the army would be considered as important as the quality of its individual soldiers.

Napoleon and Niel, however, soon discovered that their compromise was far in advance of both public and military opinion. When the Emperor instructed his prefects to submit special reports on the popular attitude toward the proposed military reform, the response from all parts of France was unanimous: all classes and ranks of French society opposed any change which would eliminate "good numbers" and put an end to all total exemptions. The primitive yet frequently efficient polling techniques of the Second Empire clearly indicated that the French people strongly disapproved any and all schemes to return to a military system founded upon the principle of the nation in arms.[20] Likewise, the imperial proposals encountered further opposition in army circles. While there were quite a few members of the officer corps who were willing to sanction some moderate change, such as the abolition of complete exemptions and the addition of reserve organs, these same men insisted that the military role of the reserves should be sharply limited,

---

[20] Based upon Gordon Wright, "Public Opinion and Conscription in France, 1866-70," *Journal of Modern History*, XIV (Mar., 1942), 28-31.

that the long-service regulars should remain predominant, and that the Niel recruitment system was too extreme. General Nicolas Changarnier, one of the members of the Saint Cloud commission, was willing to tolerate the reserves and *garde mobile* only if the law expressly stipulated that these units should never be convoked or trained in time of peace.[21] And Randon, in a final appeal to the Emperor, warned that any military system which relied upon reserves was the denial of the military wisdom of the ages.[22]

Nor was the French legislature disposed to accept the imperial project in its original form. Though the Emperor exerted pressure and even toyed with the idea of dissolving the assembly and appealing to the people, he abandoned this policy when his advisers emphasized the strength of the opposition and the hostility of the public. Napoleon was indeed never able to convince the reluctant deputies that the project should be enacted without drastic alterations.[23] These men, after all, were fully aware that the public opposed Napoleon's desires; when two supposedly "safe seats" were lost in by-elections to candidates who bitterly attacked the conscription law, the panic was on.[24] As one deputy pithily remarked, "Of course we shall be obliged to pass this bill, but we shall fix it up in such a way that it will never work."

The report submitted by the deputy Gressier in the name of the eighteen-man commission which examined the Niel project was a typical example of the attitude of the *corps législatif.*

---

[21] An extensive summary of Changarnier's views, typical of the stand-pat attitude of many high officers, is his article, " Un Mot sur le projet de réorganisation militaire," *Revue des deux mondes,* LXVIII (Apr. 15, 1867), 874-90. "Evil will come to France, if, breaking the chain of her glorious traditions, she permits herself to have an army more powerful in number than in organization" (p. 878).

[22] Randon, *Mémoires,* II, 179. "No reserve can prepare men for the cadres nor make up for the training, the discipline, or the solidity of soldiers broken to military life."

[23] Bapst, *Canrobert,* IV, 69; Ollivier, *Empire libéral,* X, 347.

[24] Gordon Wright, "Public Opinion and Conscription in France, 1866-70," *Journal of Modern History,* XIV (Mar., 1942), 38.

Gressier was willing to concede the need for a larger army and the organization of reserve complements, but he feared that the law would impose a far too heavy burden upon the nation. The government project, he wrote, bore too great a resemblance to the conscription laws of the revolutionary era and set aside all of the post-1814 legislation which had become established in French custom. It appeared to Gressier that the Emperor desired to create a military system which would not only escape legislative control but which would also militarize the youth of France.[25]

The result was that the *corps législatif* drastically revised the military reform bill and removed most of the provisions which timid deputies feared would offend the French voter. The length of service in the actives was reduced from six to five years. More important, the size of each annual contingent was to be determined each year by a vote of the legislature; thus the execution of the law was at the mercy of a parliamentary majority. The greatest alterations, however, were in the organization of reserve formations and the *garde mobile*. The obstinate assembly removed control of the reserves from the hands of the Minister of War and decided that the *garde mobile* was never to receive more than fifteen days of training per year, could never be subjected to military discipline, and might never be sent on any training maneuvers which lasted longer than from sunrise to sunset.

The enactment of such restrictive provisions achieved the legislative goals and eventually made it possible for the deputies to approve the new recruitment law. Gressier, for instance, found that the modifications were sufficient to keep the legislation from being a danger to French society and reached the conclusion that, even with the new law, the familiar post-1815 military structure remained essentially unchanged.[26] But de-

25 *Le Moniteur universal*, June 19, 1867, Report No. 176, pp. 767-68.
26 *Ibid.*, p. 769.

spite all his efforts to make conscription less rigorous, Gressier himself was not permitted to be a candidate in the next election. Although he had long been a favorite, his constituents believed that he was responsible for the attempt to put their sons in uniform.[27]

Although deputies like Gressier did nothing to advance French military thinking, the principle of the nation in arms received thorough exposition in the speeches and writings of the small but ardent group of republicans just then beginning to emerge as a force in French public life. These republicans, to be sure, formed but a highly vocal minority and were in no sense representative of French public opinion. Moreover, as a nonconformist and diverse group—as indicated by their widely differing roles in the Third Republic—they advocated military concepts which, at best, were little more than the opinions of individual republicans. Nevertheless, their ideas marked a revival of French interest in the revolutionary principles of military organization and indicated the path which republican politicians would follow in the decades after 1870.

Whereas in advocating conscription Napoleon III focused primarily upon the goal of a larger army and paid limited attention to egalitarian ideals, French republicans had a broader vision which subordinated purely military needs to political and social consequences. Republicans, of course, believed that universal military service furnished the only effective means of national defense. But their theories, centering around such ideas as the absolute equality of military service and the identification of the soldier and the citizen, aimed ultimately at establishing a working harmony among the military, social, and political institutions of France. The concept of the nation in arms, then, was prized by French republicans because to them it represented the only legitimate form of military organization capable of doing full justice to the needs and demands of a democratic society.

[27] Ollivier, *Empire libéral*, X, 381.

When the conscription bill of Niel and Napoleon came before the legislature, the republicans faced a genuine dilemma. This project, after all, was sponsored by a government they distrusted, and it was designed to benefit an army they feared. To approve the measure meant that a hated political regime would be strengthened; it might well provide the government with the military means to continue such detested policies as the Mexican intervention or the maintenance of French troops in Rome. Yet, on the other hand, despite their antimilitarism and hatred of the Napoleonic order, French republicans were essentially patriotic. They were, after all, the heirs of the Jacobins, who had not only rallied Frenchmen to the defense of *la patrie* in the Revolution but had also attempted to spread the republican gospel throughout all Europe by force of arms. Patriotism thus prevented republicans from being indifferent to the problems of national defense. Hence their problem was to develop a military theory which would reconcile their hatred of the Second Empire with their concern for the defense of France.[28]

The answer to their dilemma was to insist that the army of France must be a "republican army." A genuine citizen army —in which the emphasis was upon the word *citizen*—appeared to be a satisfactory guarantee of both the political and military future of France. An army of citizen-soldiers, it was reasoned,

[28] For typical republican arguments that the Niel project would aid and abet Napoleon's domestic despotism and reactionary foreign policies, see speeches by such deputies as Magnin and Glais-Bizon, *Le Moniteur universal*, December 21, 1867, p. 1592, and December 25, pp. 1617-18. The best available source is, however, Jules Simon, *La Politique radicale* (Paris: Librairie Internationale, 1868), pp. 177 ff. An interesting and perceptive discussion of the pacifist orientation of much republican thought in these years is D. W. Brogan, *French Personalities and Problems* (New York: Knopf, 1947), pp. 50-52. Evidence of the continuance of the patriotic tradition is likewise readily available. See, for instance, Jean Dietz, "Les Débuts de Jules Ferry," *Revue de France*, XII (Oct. 15, 1932), 613 ff. When Ferry tried to get Gambetta to approve his program for the abolition of standing armies, the latter insisted that in the present condition of Europe such a policy would be madness. And if Juliette Adam, the *grande dame* of French republicanism, is to be believed, those patriotic republicans like Favre and Simon who frequented her salon found the military debates a torture for their consciences (Juliette Adam, *Mes Sentiments et nos idées avant 1870* [Paris: A. Lemerre, 1905], p. 191).

would never be the willing tool of a political despot. Its creation would thus satisfy the republican demand for a military force which would not, unlike the army of the Second Empire, be the obedient servant of the Man of Destiny. An army composed of the peace-loving masses would, by definition, never permit itself to be employed in an unjust cause. It was therefore a military force which antimilitarist republicans could approve. And, equally important, an army of citizens fighting to defend their homes would be a more certain guardian of the nation than a body of mercenaries whose primary interests were career, salary, and eventual pension. It was thus an army which satisfied the patriotism of French republicans.

Of no less importance is the fact that the republicans believed that the concept of the nation in arms provided them with a political weapon of great utility. In the first place, they felt that their theories of military organization could be used to discredit the imperial government and the army of the Second Empire. Secondly, the republicans were convinced that their schemes for military reorganization, if actually adopted, would in fact prevent the army from being used as an agent of internal repression and would, in addition, serve to check the ambitions of the Emperor. Hence, however much the republicans surrounded their military theories with the hallowed phrases of the Revolution, however much they insisted that only free citizens could provide an effective means of national defense, in the last analysis they were firm advocates of the nation in arms because they believed that there were political advantages and values in the idea of an army based upon republican concepts. And, at a later date and for similar reasons, another group of republicans was to find these same principles of value in their political struggle against the army that had condemned Captain Dreyfus, while French Socialists were to adapt these theories to serve in their own battle against the institutions of the Third Republic.

During the actual parliamentary debate on the Niel conscription project, republican spokesmen presented widely varying plans for the achievement of their program. There was actually no one single theory of the nation in arms upon which all republicans were agreed. At one extreme was Garnier-Pagès, one of the few remaining "men of 1848." He believed in complete disarmament and, if war broke out, wanted to rely upon a spontaneous *levée en masse* of all the able-bodied men. To him it was an axiom that "when a vigorous *élan* is needed to save the country, in all parts of France men will rise as a single man, and each citizen will expose his breast to the enemy. . ."[29] At the other pole was Émile Ollivier, soon to become a minister of the so-called "liberal empire." He offered a project which closely resembled the then-existing Prussian military legislation and which in fact anticipated the recruitment law that France herself adopted a generation later. His proposal would have subjected every young man to three years' service and would have organized strong reserve formations. "From whom can we learn better than from the victors of Sadowa?" asked Ollivier. "In any event they have taught us that soldiers who, for the most part, have spent but two or three years under the colors were able to defeat troops with up to eleven years of service."[30]

Most representative of "advanced" republican theory was the *projet de loi* introduced by Jules Simon and Jules Favre.[31] It was a perfect example of the republican endeavor to organize an army which would not only guarantee national defense but also serve as a check upon imperial policies. It was also a good specimen of the radicalism of republican military thought in the sixties. Favre and Simon, for instance, demanded the abolition

[29] *Le Moniteur universel*, December 25, 1867, p. 1618.

[30] *Ibid.*, December 24, 1867, p. 1612. See also the scheme of Glais-Bizon, another republican who advocated imitation of Prussia, *ibid.*, December 25, 1867, p. 1617.

[31] See the speeches of Simon reproduced, in *La Politique radicale*, or the *Moniteur*, December 24, 1867, pp. 1609-10.

of the standing army and its replacement by a militia system under which each citizen would be a member of the militia but none would ever spend more than three consecutive months on active duty. Indeed, under this plan, French militiamen apparently would have received the bulk of their military instruction in two-hour training periods held on alternate Sundays in their home districts. With such a system, in which the recruit would be subject to military life for no more than three months, it was felt that there was no danger that he would lose his civilian outlook or become so thoroughly militarized that he would willingly fight in an unjust war. The plan's authors claimed, "We would have an army, but an army of citizens and of soldiers, invincible at home and incapable of waging war abroad; an army without military spirit. . . ." [32]

None of the various republican projects, it must be admitted, achieved any success. The legislation ultimately enacted in 1868 by the assembly was untainted by republican heresies. That law, however, remained a dead letter in the few years of peace before the Franco-Prussian War, which began in 1870. Though Niel and Napoleon were not without hope that the watered-down law of 1868 could be put to some use, in actual practice almost nothing was done. In 1870 the French sent to war an army virtually identical with the military force which, four years earlier, the Emperor had recognized as inadequate.[33]

Once Napoleon III had been captured and the Second Empire had been toppled by angered Parisians, the republican-dominated Government of National Defense set out to repel the Prussian invader with the methods and ideas of the Republic of 1792. When the first proclamation of the new government began with the encouraging words, "The Republic was victorious

[32] Simon, *Politique radicale,* pp. 222-23.

[33] On the immediate hopes of Niel and Napoleon, see Bapst, *Canrobert,* IV, 72; on the ultimate failure of the legislation see Pierre Lehautcourt, "La Réorganisation de l'armée avant 1870," *Revue de Paris,* IV (Aug., 1901), 550-52 and Colonel Nathanaël Fix, *Souvenirs d'un officier d'état-major (1846-1870)* (Paris: Juven, n.d.), p. 6.

over the invasion of 1792. The Republic is proclaimed," the republicans expressed in these few words the sum and substance of their entire wartime program. Viewing the military ventures of the First Republic through the rose-colored glasses of republican legend, the men of the Government of National Defense firmly believed that a repetition of past policies would save the endangered nation.[34]

It was a crazy-quilt military organization which then developed in the fact of ever-increasing emergencies. From Tours, Léon Gambetta attempted to organize and direct a great *levée en masse* to rescue beleaguered Paris; within that city radicals called for a *sortie torentielle*, a mass assault on the Prussian lines by the entire population, to save the French capital. From volunteers and conscripts a great mass army was created, indeed, an army too large for the nation's available resources to equip. Once more alongside the regular military formations there appeared a politically conscious National Guard, an organization more adept at spreading propaganda and interfering with the conduct of government than at waging war. France, in short, again became a nation in arms.[35] But the essence of the entire organization, from top to bottom, was improvisation—improvisation which, however brilliant, could never lead to victory.

Gambetta, a brilliant military amateur who, like Danton, believed that audacity was the key to victory, followed policies

[34] An excellent summary of these points is J. P. T. Bury, *Gambetta and the National Defense* (London: Longmans, Green, 1936), Chapter IX. Gambetta's Tours dispatch—so expressive of his attitude—calling for a *levée en masse* which, by tapping the resources and skills of the nation, could not fail to bring victory is in Charles de Freycinet, *La Guerre en province pendant le siège de Paris* (Paris: Michel Lèvy, 1871), pp. 8-11.

[35] It must be observed, however, that neither Gambetta nor the Paris provisional government was solely responsible for the *levée en masse*. The imperial government had in fact already started the process. On August 13th the government had called upon all citizens of Paris who were over twenty-one and who had resided in the city for a year to become members of the National Guard (Trochu, *Oeuvres*, I, 247-8). Moreover, the decrees and laws of Napoleon III obtained 750,000 men for the army —far more soldiers than Gambetta was ever able to make use of (Bury, *Gambetta*, pp. 142-44).

which were a curious amalgamation of orthodox republican military theory and ideas derived from the wartime experiences of the "United States of the North." With the example of Lincoln's armies in mind, Gambetta organized the so-called auxiliary army, a force created out of the raw levies furnished by the draft. Its soldiers were trained in regional camps scattered throughout France and enjoyed equality of pay with the regulars for the duration of hostilities.[36] On the other hand, Gambetta and his followers declared that the same auxiliary army was the fulfillment "of a frankly republican program inspired by the traditions of 1792." When its ranks were opened, the official announcement began with the words, "It is important to excite emulation in all ranks of the army and make an appeal to young talent, in view of the fact that it was by resolutely breaking with tradition that the First Republic was able to sustain the prodigies of 1792." [37]

This was a point of view on national defense in which the civilian outlook was dominant. The leaders firmly believed that the military hierarchy had clearly revealed its incompetence and that only civilian rule could produce victory. When with fiery rhetoric Gambetta called for a rallying of the people, he was inspired by the belief that an army of citizens was superior to an army of professionals and long-term soldiers. Nearly a half century later, it was not without pride that his principal lieutenant, Charles de Freycinet, wrote in his memoirs that such an innovation as the policy of granting commissions to qualified civilians was a valuable practice which only a civilian-controlled ministry could have envisaged.[38]

Throughout the war the republicans never forgot that one of their principal objectives was to establish a strong and lasting republic. The dual role of the Government of National De-

[36] Freycinet, *Guerre*, pp. 52-53; Bury, *Gambetta*, p. 137.
[37] Freycinet, *Guerre*, p. 369.
[38] Charles de Freycinet, *Souvenirs, 1848-1878* (Paris: Delagrave, 1912), p. 148.

fense was to save the nation from invasion and to establish a republican form of government. An important aspect of Gambetta's program was his firm belief that the *levée en masse* and obligatory military service, regardless of their purely military value, would aid in the establishment of a republic. He reasoned that such policies would identify every citizen with the national defense and, hence, would at least indirectly bind each and every individual to the republican cause.[39]   Once again, as in the latter years of the Second Empire, the concept of the nation in arms was found particularly adaptable to republican political aims and was held in high esteem because it served political as well as military interests.

But while Gambetta was failing to convince his compatriots of the necessity of "war to the knife" and while the country, exhausted by military defeat, was suing for peace and electing a royalist, conservative assembly, the last act of the Franco-Prussian War took place in Paris—the violent birth and more violent death of the Commune. In both military theory and practice the Commune was sterile; the Communards had nothing to contribute but an extremist faith in the military qualities of an armed citizenry. Indeed, from one point of view the only lasting result of the Commune was that its suppression led, in turn, to the abolition for all time of the National Guard, an institution which had once occupied a central position in republican theories of citizen armies. The Commune had originated in the ranks of the poor and disaffected members of the Guard; its elimination was, after all, but a matter of common prudence on the part of the victors.[40]

---

[39] Bury, *Gambetta*, p. 146 presents the best evidence for this. Adolphe Thiers, soon to become head of the French state, definitely felt this to be the governmental objective and was quite critical of it. Charles Chesnelong, *Les Derniers Jours de l'Empire et le gouvernement de M. Thiers* (Paris: Librairie Académique Perrin, 1932), p. 72.

[40] A recent historian of the Commune has gone so far as to write that the most important accomplishment of the insurrectionaries was that they brought about the ending of the Guard. E. S. Mason, *The Paris Commune: An Episode in the History of the Socialist Movement* (New York: Macmillian, 1930, p. 85.

The Communard conception of the people in arms—obviously, the city of Paris, however highly it regarded itself, could scarcely constitute a "nation"—was nothing more than an extreme Jacobin faith in the military value of armed citizens. The Communards were convinced, as Thomas Carlyle once phrased it, that the rifle made all men tall. Their club orators incessantly demanded a universal arming of Parisians, and there were frequent calls for a *sortie torentielle* to crush the government troops which ringed the city. And in its final death agonies the Commune produced a theory of the people in arms so extreme that it was a denial of all theory:

Enough of militarism, no more staff officers bespangled and gilded! Make way for the people, the fighters, the bare arms! The hour of revolutionary warfare has come! The people knows nothing of scientific maneuvers, but when it has a musket in its hand, paving stones under its feet, it fears not all the strategists of the monarchist school.[41]

The Franco-Prussian War and the Paris Commune were decisive factors in the history of the nation in arms. It is, of course, arguable that the defeats of 1870-71 were due as much to faulty military leadership as to other causes, but the French were convinced that their downfall could largely be explained in terms of the failings of their military organization as a whole. It seemed to them that the events of the war provided convinc-

---

The commanders of the 1870-71 Paris garrison, Trochu and Ducrot, held strong opinions about the *garde*. Ducrot flatly stated, "It [the Guard] was the unconscious mob, it was what M. Thiers called with reason 'the vile multitude' which was armed and equipped . . . capable of doing everything for evil purposes, incapable of lending any serious assistance to the regular army." One of the reasons why Paris had not broken the Prussian siege was, according to Ducrot, that it had been as necessary to stand watch over the National Guard, "the enemy within," as over the Prussians, "the enemy without" (General Auguste Ducrot, *La Défense de Paris* [4 vols., Paris: Dentu, 1877-83], IV, 369-70). Trochu, whose views were not as harsh, nonetheless characterized the Parisian military forces as four-fifths an "armed mob" (Trochu, *Oeuvres*, I, 246).

41 Frank Jellinek, *The Paris Commune of 1871* (New York: Oxford University Press, 1937), p. 314. As luck would have it, the commander of the Communard military forces was a military adventurer named Cluseret who trusted only professional soldiers. The anarchy of the Paris Guard, he later wrote, was "perfect of its kind."

ing evidence that the Prussian military organization, based upon a rigorous system of obligatory service, produced an army which was superior in both quantity and quality to their own military machine. Nor could thoughtful Frenchmen draw any conclusion from the Gambetta experience except that it was rank folly to improvise an army after the outbreak of war. The nation in arms, however revered the tradition of the *levée en masse* might be, was not something which, like Gambetta's armies, could be created "out of the earth." And when the enemy was not the bumbling Duke of Brunswick but a highly specialized Prussian army with a skilled general staff, the only safety lay in a military machine thoroughly organized in time of peace. On the other hand, the Commune had filled both moderates and conservatives with a not unjustified fear of popular military insurrections and of trusting the populace with arms. All post-1870 military theories would thus have to reconcile the obvious need for conscription with the dread of social and political disorder. But the experience of *l'année terrible* did, in the long run, accomplish much in focusing and clarifying French military thought as well as in purging it of many of its radical attributes.

As soon as her domestic affairs had been set in something roughly resembling order, France, with surprising haste, began the reconstruction of her shattered military institutions. Though conservatives and monarchists controlled the assembly and had been elected because they favored peace with Bismarck, the vast majority of the deputies believed that compulsory service must form the basis for any new military order. There was so little doubt of this that, as Jules Simon wrote, "The difficulty was not to establish personal, obligatory service but how to organize it." [42] Moreover, the goal of compulsory service was achieved despite the fact that the head of the state, Adolphe Thiers—the one truly indispensable man of the postwar years—

[42] Jules Simon, *Le Gouvernement de M. Thiers, 8 février 1871-24 mai 1873* (2 vols., Paris: Calmann-Lévy, 1879), II, 59.

was one of the very few who remained unconvinced that the pre-1870 military institutions needed reform. Despite Thiers the law of July 27, 1872, carried at its head the flat and simple statement that, henceforth, military service in France was personal and obligatory for the entire male population. Whatever else the deputies wrote into the law, they at least provided legal sanction for the basic principle of all concepts of the nation in arms.

Enactment of obligatory military service was made less difficult by the very nature of the defeat of 1870. Both the "old soldiers" beloved by the military hierarchy and the citizen levies equally dear to republicans had suffered battlefield reverses.[43] As the moralist Ernest Renan observed, 1870 had destroyed two of the most cherished of all French legends: the legend of the victorious Empire, lost in the rout of Napoleon III, and the legend of 1792, lost by Gambetta and the Commune.[44] Despite the oversimplification involved in such a dualism, it is true that both the fanatic defender of the *levée en masse* and the equally intractable advocate of the professional soldiery were conspicuous by their absence in the 1872 debates. A fairly extensive middle ground remained on which to base compromise.

The work of the legislators was made easier by the prevailing spirit of the immediate postwar years, an era in which there appeared to be both a semireligious quest for moral regeneration and a hope for a new and purified nation to arise phoenixlike from the ashes of the Second Empire. The mood of the military discussions was established when the reporter for the National Assembly, the Marquis de Chasseloup-Laubat, opened his report with these sentences: "Gentlemen, great disasters produce great lessons. Wisdom consists in understanding them; cour-

[43] For discussion of the point that there was a "double defeat" in 1870-71, see E. L. Katzenbach, Jr., *Charles-Louis de Soulces de Freycinet and the Army of Metropolitan France* (Unpublished dissertation, Princeton University, 1953), pp. 22 ff.

[44] Ernest Renan, *La Réforme intellectuelle et morale* (1871), reprinted in *Oeuvres complètes de Ernest Renan* (5 vols., Paris: Calmann-Lévy, 1947-52), I, 334-35.

age, in profiting from them."[45]   The war, he wrote, had been
the work of Providence, which had acted so as to teach Frenchmen to do better.   And in debate after debate the example of
Prussia's actions after the battle of Jena was cited for the
French to follow in producing a similar regeneration of their
own military institutions.[46]

Equally characteristic of the military discussions and theories
of 1872 was their essential conservatism.   An assembly dominated by monarchists and conservatives who vividly remembered the events of the Commune was obviously not a parliamentary body which would tolerate extremist views about a
citizen-army.   The army, like the Third Republic these deputies
were about to create, was to be a conservative institution.
Moreover, the Left, temporarily chastened by defeat, at least
momentarily realized the political wisdom of eschewing radicalism, and even those republicans whose loyalty to the citizen-

[45] *Journal officiel de la République française,* March 12, 1872, *annexe 975,* p. 2380.
This document is not only one of the best summaries of the pre-1870 French military institutions but furnishes in addition the best indication of the aims and objectives of the legislator of 1872.   For French military affairs after 1870, aside from
the writings of Monteilhet and the military histories already cited, the best source
remains the *Journal officiel.*   A recent and excellent summary which carries the story
down to the Second World War is Arpad Kovacs, "French Military Legislation in
the Third Republic, 1871-1940," *Military Affairs,* XIII (Spring, 1949), 1-13.   Helpful as a guide through the seemingly endless volumes of the *J. O.* is a semi-official
publication of the French government which carries the legislative projects and debates in abbreviated form down to the beginning of the twentieth century, *Historique des diverses lois sur le recrutement depuis la Révolution jusqu'à nos jours*
(Paris: Imprimerie nationale, 1902).

[46] See, for example, Renan, *Réforme intellectuelle,* I, 370-74; Trochu, *Oeuvres,* II,
93 ff.; Colonel J. Paixhans, "La Loi militaire et le service militaire," *Correspondant,*
LI (May 10, 1872), 394 ff; and the commentaries of Charles de Mazade in the
Revue des deux mondes, XCIX (Jun. 1 and 15, 1872), 704-07 and 943-51.   According to M. Mazade, "This principle of compulsory service was imposed upon us
by our misfortunes; it was born in much the same fashion for us in the recent war
as it was formerly born for Prussia in the blood of Jena" (p. 945).   Innumerable
examples of the prevalent moral approach as well as of the hope of imitating the
Prussian regeneration are to be found in the parliamentary debates of 1872.   For
example, when M. le Duc d'Aumale came to cast his vote for conscription, he justified his action on the ground that compulsory service would complete "the work of
reorganization and regeneration to which you consecrated yourselves at Bordeaux."
AAN, May 28, 1872, p. 32.

soldier ideal remained unchanged tended for tactical reasons to express moderate opinions. This atmosphere of conservatism and restraint was not without influence upon the establishment of the new nation in arms. Obviously it made basic agreement easier to achieve, but at the same time it led the deputies to retain more than a little of the pre-1870 military order. Because most of the deputies were convinced of the political unreliability of the masses, they stipulated that the term of military service must remain lengthy so that France would possess not merely a well-trained army but one also obedient and disciplined. The pronounced conservatism of the 1872 legislature made it possible, at a later date, for a new group of republicans to argue with some plausibility that their predecessors enacted a conscription law specifically designed to produce an army blindly obedient to orders and subservient to the rulers of the state.

In the 1872 military debates there was, indeed, none of the optimistic egalitarianism which a Jules Simon had exhibited only a few years earlier. Rather, it seemed as if many of the advocates of compulsory service considered that conscription would be a moral antidote for the anarchy of the times. The Marquis de Chasseloup-Laubat, revealing the extent to which the army committee of the National Assembly was motivated by a desire to solve domestic French problems, at times seemed a warm admirer of conscription simply because he believed it would be beneficial for French youth to endure the rigors of military discipline.[47] Moreover, he felt that a truly national army established upon a basis of universal service would be a powerful solvent of social discontent. In an age when so many "detestable doctrines" aimed at destroying the bonds of society, the Marquis wrote, compulsory military service for all would make it clearly apparent that there was no social discrimination in French military policies.[48] Other advocates of universal

[47] *J. O.* No. 975, March 12, 1872, p. 2383.
[48] *Ibid.*, p. 2385.

service argued their case on the grounds that within the ranks of a conscript army members of different social classes would have the opportunity to mingle together, to learn to know one another, and to develop a common solidarity. For instance, a General Guillemaut claimed that conscription would benefit the whole nation because "in a country as avid for equality as ours . . . the army must not be composed solely of the disinherited, and to lessen the peril of future civil war, the rich must not let the poor do their fighting. Further, if rich and poor associate together in the ranks, they will develop mutual esteem and reciprocal feelings—and out of this union and solidarity will emerge a firmly established social order." [49] Conscription thus appeared to be not only a means of restoring national morale and social concord but also a valuable way of suppressing the class struggle.

Although agreement on broad principles was relatively easy to achieve, the concrete application of military theories was a more difficult problem. Determination of the specific length of military service was, as always, a particularly complicated question. While the deputies, the government, and the ranking military leaders agreed that conscription was necessary and that France must have more trained soldiers, there were few who advocated a short-term service. For a variety of reasons most men favored a four- or five-year tour of duty. To some, in-

---

[49] *AAN*, May 28, 1872, p. 35. Both within and without the National Assembly such opinions were frequently expressed. See General Jean Chareton, *Projet motivé de réorganisation de l'état militaire de France* (Paris: Plon, 1871). "The army must not be composed solely of poor devils who have nothing to defend and who are soldiers only because their families didn't have the money necessary to buy them back from what they considered a form of slavery" (p. 47). Mazade believed universal service would fortify "the whole society by cementing the moral unity of the nation under the colors" (Charles de Mazade, "Chroniques de la quinzaine," *Revue des deux mondes*, XCIX [Jun. 15, 1872], 946). General Temple concluded a parliamentary address with the remark that he had learned one lesson from the Commune. When the Versailles troops re-entered Paris, he said, they found placards addressed to them which read, "Soldiers, don't fire on your brothers. It would be fraticide, for you are proletarians like us." Compulsory service, Temple concluded, was the sole remedy for such sentiments (*AAN*, June 10, 1872, p. 234).

cluding not a few of the republicans, it seemed that such a
length of service was essential if France was to have a well-
disciplined army which would be immune to political passions,
while to others it was an axiom that it took years to train a
good soldier.[50] The majority of French legislators and military
men continued to believe that the quality of the individual soldier was of primary importance and that true military virtue
could be attained only by the conscript who had the benefit of
years of training.[51] There were, to be sure, a few individuals,
particularly General Trochu, the onetime military governor of
Paris, who advocated direct imitation of the three-year conscription system of Germany. But such opinions were countered with the argument that the French social structure prevented the adoption of Prussian practices. The German conscript, it was averred, was the product of a disciplined, orderly
society and had already acquired habits of obedience in civil
life; the French recruit, on the contrary, came from a nation
without social stability, lacked a sense of discipline, and therefore could not become a good soldier in less than four or five
years.[52]

---

[50] On the strong desire to establish an army immune to domestic political quarrels, see the discussions concerned with the clauses of the conscription bill which
abolished the voting privileges of members of the active army. *J. O.* No. 975, pp.
2384-85 (opinions of Chasseloup-Laubat) and *AAN*, May 30, 1872, p. 70 (speech by
General Ducrot). For evidence that the republicans at that time endorsed the prohibition on the soldier vote, see the speech by Gambetta, *ibid.*, May 30, 1872, p. 66.
Even an officer like General Vinoy, a man quite skeptical of the over-all value of
compulsory military service, agreed that one of the happiest provisions of the 1872
legislation was the one which prohibited members of the active army from voting.
General Joseph Vinoy, *L'armée française en 1873* (Paris: Plon, 1873), p. 98.

[51] *J. O.* No. 975, p. 2390-91. General Billot, speaking for the commission, stated
that it was impossible to train a competent soldier in less than four years. *AAN*,
May 29, 1872, pp. 51-52. Another official spokesman for this group, M. Sarrette,
stressed that he and his friends, believing that the solidity of the army was of prime
importance, felt that only a long term of service would guarantee such a result.
Ibid., June 6, 1872, pp. 163-64.

[52] This was a favorite argument of Thiers, who added that Prussia possessed a
strong and enlightened aristocracy which could furnish the necessary leadership.
Ibid., June 8, 1872, pp. 207-08. General Ducrot, in giving the official reply to
Trochu, took great pains to point out that the Prussian conscript arrived in camp

Nevertheless, although the parliamentary majority favored long-term service, it was obvious that the French military budget could not support an army in which every young man would have to spend four or five years of his life; the cost would have been ruinous. Nor did the existing state of German armaments warrant a French army of excessive size. The government actually believed that it would be sufficient to have an army of 450,000 men (including 120,000 career soldiers) under the colors at all times and planned, at the outbreak of war, to expand it to approximately 1,250,000 by recalling reservists. But since several hundred thousand men were available for induction each year, the literal application of any four- or five-year conscription system was clearly impossible.

Under these circumstances it was therefore necessary to devise a formula which would reconcile the desire for long-term service with budgetary realities and actual security needs. The device eventually chosen was the familiar lottery. The annual contingent was to be divided by lot into two portions; a "good number" meant six months to a year of army duty, but a "bad number" led to five full years of military service. The division of the contingent into two portions serving unequal lengths of time made it possible to have a five-year service, to preserve the semblance of compulsory military service for all, and yet at the same time to keep the total size of the army within bounds. But this juggling could not conceal the fact that the obligation for all to serve in the army was to be unequally apportioned. And, although the deputies who devised this system could argue that they had based it upon realities and not sentimental, egalitarian fallacies, they had in fact established a method of con-

---

with a well-developed sense of discipline and a congenital willingness to obey orders. *Ibid.*, June 7, p. 187. There were of course many other arguments in justification of a five-year service; the commission report maintained that unless the term of service was sufficiently long to get men habituated to the military way of life, they would have no desire to re-enlist and, consequently, there would be a shortage of non-commissioned officers. Further, without a stable body of noncoms, the army itself would be lacking in solidity. *J. O.* No. 975, pp. 2390 ff.

scription which could not long withstand the charge that universal service had been sabotaged in the interest of an army of "old soldiers." [53]

At all stages in the elaboration of the 1872 law—and particularly in the provisions for the split contingent and the length of service—the influence of Thiers, the venerable founding father of the Third Republic, was strongly in evidence. Like Poincaré a half century later, Thiers was a chief executive who took military affairs as seriously as any graduate of St. Cyr, and he was sublimely certain that his opinions were correct. [54] Thiers, however, saw few advantages in universal service. Intellectually still a man of the July Monarchy, he preferred the military institutions of that era and believed that the length of service should never be less than eight years. To those who pointed to the German success with universal military service, Thiers retorted that Frenchmen were all too prone to heedless imitation of policies which, though successful abroad, were unsuited to their own nation. The concept of the nation in arms particularly aroused his anger; at one time he defined it as "putting a gun on the shoulder of every Socialist," and on another occasion he maintained that "only barbarian peoples have the

[53] The legislative process by which the five-year service was made law was in fact both complicated and frequently obscure. It involved not only the juggling of the factors already mentioned but also a certain amount of deception. Its proponents knew that they could be accused of sabotaging universal service. Hence their language was guarded, and some arguments were stressed out of proportion to their value or importance. It is quite obvious, for instance, that the budgetary issue served a very useful purpose to legislators who wanted a five-year service. They could always argue that the requirements of the military budget forced the Assembly to accept their solution. But it is doubtful if finances were as all-important as the conservatives maintained. Good discussions of the entire question are to be found in the latter pages of the commission report (pp. 2393-95) and the speeches of Billot and Sarrette to the assembly. *AAN* May 28, 1872, pp. 51-53 and June 6, 1872, pp. 162-67.

[54] Jules Simon noted in his history of Thiers' administration that the chief executive rarely missed a session of the army commission discussions and went out of his way to discuss the conscription bill with any and all interested deputies. Simon, *Gouvernement*, II, 64.

nation in arms." [55]   And although in 1872 he finally accepted the principle of universal service, his influence on policy was such that he could write in his memoirs, with no little pride, that

> . . . to win the reality of things we had to sacrifice words. M. de Chasseloup-Laubat advised me to this effect, and I did not hesitate to follow his advice. It was agreed then that the words "compulsory service" should be set at the head of the law but that the principle should be applied in the following way. . . .[56]

There were more than a few instances in which, to use his own formula, Thiers helped to apply the principle "in the following way." He was, for instance, particularly influential in preventing the National Assembly from deciding that the members of the second portion of the contingent would have to serve a full year. Thiers insisted that the expense of maintaining the second portion for more than six months would be so great that it would impair the efficiency of the regulars and five-year soldiers. He claimed that the government had accepted the proposed law only on the condition that the second portion of the contingent could be discharged after six months of service, and he freely prophesied that if the minimum tour of duty was raised to one year, then it would be impossible to maintain an army of any military worth whatsoever.[57]

[55] See Thiers' speech of June 8, 1872 (*AAN*, pp. 199-215) in which he entertained the deputies with a discourse lasting for several hours and in which he maintained that professional soldiers were far more reliable than a horde of half-trained conscripts.

[56] *Memoirs of M. Thiers (1870-73)*, trans. F. M. Atkinson (London: Allen and Unwin, 1915), p. 233.

[57] The entire issue was debated in the session of June 17, 1872. See *AAN*, pp. 371-85. An amendment proposed by Lt. Colonel Chadois (p. 372) was based on the idea that the soldier with but six months of training was worthless in the event of war. The commission view that it was impossible to keep every member of the second portion for a full year was contained in the speeches of de Bastard, Ducrot and Thiers, pp. 375-76, 378-80 and 383-85, respectively. At the conclusion of his speech Thiers insisted that he had accepted the reform only because of the six-month provisions, and his view was immediately confirmed by Jules de Lasteyrie, the president of the army commission.

The French president likewise helped to inspire two other features of the 1872 conscription law, both of which were to produce years of controversy. One was the importation from Germany of the system of one-year volunteers, an aspect of the law which was in fact one of the few provisions copied almost directly from Prussian experience. Young men who possessed certain educational degrees and who could pay the state approximately 1,500 francs for board and equipment were permitted to enlist for a single year, receive special officer training, and thus fulfill all their military obligations. The other controversial provision of the conscription legislation was one which granted total exemptions from military service to those who intended to follow so-called "liberal careers" in education and the Church.

The articles establishing these exemptions and privileges produced more argument in the assembly than any other issue. Nothing offended French republicans more than such provisions, which ran counter to all their egalitarian principles and which, they claimed, would benefit only the privileged classes. The French Left felt so strongly that republican deputies abandoned their attitude of moderation and entered vigorous protests in the style of 1868.[58] But these were to no avail. The parliamentary majority of 1872 was not egalitarian-minded; the deputies believed that to compel future priests and teachers to serve in the army would injure the spiritual and intellectual life of the nation, and they were convinced that to force a young man of talent to interrupt his studies for military service would deprive him of a professional career of benefit not only to himself but to his country.[59] Nevertheless, however tiresome the

[58] *AAN*, June 12, 1872, p. 292-94. Gambetta claimed that these privileges mutilated the principle of obligatory service beyond recognition. A good example of impassioned republican oratory against this system "of special privilege" was a speech by M. Beaussire, *ibid.*, June 21, 1872, pp. 396-99.

[59] *J. O.* No. 975, p. 2388-89 for the commission view and, in particular, speeches by Paul Bethmont, Octave de Bastard and the Bishop of Orleans, M. Dupanloup. *AAN*, June 12, 1872, pp. 283-84, June 18, pp. 399-400, and May 29, pp. 44 ff. Dupan-

incessant moralizing of French republicans, there was at least a kernel of truth in their charge that the real purpose of the assembly of 1872 was to protect the sons of the middle class from the full rigors of a five-year service. Money and education were, after all, the means for escaping a full term of service, and hence the conscription law of 1872 did tend to draw class lines within the nation.

These, then, were the main aspects of the military reform of 1872. Though principle was modified in practice, the law was based upon the idea of personal and obligatory service for all and was therefore a definite step towards the achievement of the nation in arms. It was also obviously not a law which could forever withstand the challenge of egalitarian-minded republicans. But at the same time it did not break so completely with established French custom and tradition that, once the moral enthusiasm generated by the disaster of military defeat had passed, the principle of compulsory service would be swept into the discard. As General Victor Pelissier advised the assembly when republican moralists were pressing for the abolition of exemptions and one-year volunteers,

We cannot hide from you the fact that, in the present condition of our people, the law will certainly disturb some habits and some interests. It is a precious plant which we must cultivate with care, and above all one which we must guarantee against the attacks of parasitic plants which have been the masters of our soil for a long time and which we have not yet had the time to uproot.[60]

loup, a cleric who treated his colleagues to long harrangues upon the necessity of protecting the spiritual welfare of conscripts, claimed to be no opponent of conscription but feared that unless there were many safeguards for the "liberal" careers French culture would be harmed. "A society in which every man is a soldier will soon become a barbarous society." It is pointless to examine in detail the long and tedious discussions about these exemption and one-year volunteer provisions. They were debated on 18, 19, 20, and 21 June, 1872, (*ibid.,* pp. 396-468) and immediately became bogged down in technicalities. A great deal of oratory was devoted to attempts to expand the lists of schools whose degrees carried military privileges and exemptions with them.

[60] *Ibid.,* June 1, 1872, p. 111.

Reform of the French recruitment system was not, of course, the only important aspect of the post-1871 military regeneration of the nation. During the decade of the seventies the French established a system of military academies to provide advanced education for the officer corps, rewrote their outdated field regulations, and, at long last, revamped their inefficient staff system. Likewise, the Assembly enacted a series of laws which put flesh and blood on the bare skeleton of the recruitment act; between 1873 and 1875, for instance, laws were passed dealing with such matters as the organization of the army, the recruitment of noncommissioned officers, and the organization of the cadres and effectives of the army.[61]

Much of this legislation designed to implement the system of compulsory service was concerned with narrowly military and technical considerations, and, as such, it lies beyond the scope of this book. However, it should be noted that these laws provided further indications of the prevailing military conservatism of these years and of the reluctance with which the French military leaders embraced the concept of the nation in arms. When the question of recruiting noncommissioned officers was debated, for instance, War Minister Du Barail loudly lamented the fact that the 1872 law prohibited the payment of re-enlistment bounties to *sous-officiers*. He insisted that without bounties it would be impossible to attract a sufficient number of professional noncoms and that, without these old soldiers, an army of conscripts would be valueless. Similarly, when it was necessary to decide how many companies and battalions would comprise a regiment of the regular army, the military leaders demanded the maximum number that was considered possible.

---

[61] Any standard military history, (such as Revol, *Histoire de l'armée*, pp. 203-14) contains convenient summaries of this legislation. The impetus for many of these reforms, incidentally, came not from the Assembly but from the ranks of the professional army men. Likewise, the rewriting of field regulations, the creation of a staff system, and other such measures did involve more borrowing from the German army than was the case with the recruitment law. A particularly good source is General François-Charles Du Barail, *Mes Souvenirs* (3 vols., Paris: Plon, 1894-96), III, 459-90.

Their insistence on a large number of companies and battalions was based on their desire to keep the number of professional officers and noncommissioned officers at the highest possible level and to have positions available for these men.[62]   Both of these examples—though in part motivated by the human desire to provide fatter promotion lists—furnished considerable proof that the military hierarchy still thought in terms of the "old soldiers" of the pre-1870 period.

Moreover, although the 1872 law had provided for a system of reserve and territorial formations, the military hierarchy continued to set but little stock in such units.   The debate on the army organization bill of 1875 showed that the French military leaders expected that in the event of a future war the active army, composed of five-year conscripts and a large body of professionals, would do the fighting, while the reserves, particularly the territorials (or second-line reserves), would perform noncombat duties in the supply corps or as interior guards.[63]   One officer testified that when he attempted to establish programs to bring reserve officers into closer contact with regular army officers, the War Minister warned him, "I will never tolerate the introduction of a civil element into the army." [64]   Although this particular story may be apocryphal, there is abundant evidence that the military leaders of the seventies still hoped to preserve much of the old army.

However, despite these tendencies, it was already apparent that if and when political control of France passed into republican hands, the concept of the nation would have a more liberal interpretation.   On the very day the 1872 law was enacted Gambetta's newspaper, *La République française*, announced that it must be revised immediately, and by early April of 1873

---

[62] *J.O.*, August 3, 1874, No. 2672, p. 7519; Du Barail, *Souvenirs*, III, 485-87.

[63] *J.O.*, August 24, 1874, No. 2677, pp. 7589-90.

[64] Colonel Nathanael Fix, *Souvenirs d'un officier d'etat-major (1870-94)* (Paris: Juven, n.d.), p. 123.

Gambetta was declaring in his political speeches that the Republic would eventually establish a military system in which neither wealth nor privilege would receive special benefits.[65] Already republicans were becoming restive, and the history of French military thought for the next thirty years was to be in large part the history of the many and varied republican attempts to fulfill Gambetta's prophecy.

[65] Katzenbach, *Charles-Louis de Freycinet,* p. 181; Robert Dreyfus, "Les Premières Armes de Gambetta," *Revue de France,* XII (Dec. 15, 1932), 138-39.

II

The Politics of Conscription
1872-1914

THE LAW OF 1872, whatever its merits or failings, was soon challenged by other concepts of the nation in arms. Persistent republican attempts to modify that law and bring it into harmony with their own military theories characterized the years after 1872. The result was that no conscription law was able to endure for more than seventeen years. And on three separate occasions—1889, 1905, and 1913—the French drastically revised the legislation upon which their entire military edifice rested. As early as 1881 there were more than 277 candidates for the Chamber who were pledged to reform the five-year service, and this issue was considered second in importance only to the problem of constitutional revision; as late as the summer of 1914 the Viviani ministry was able to assume office only because it promised to give careful study to the question of rewriting the conscription law that had been passed only the preceding year. Fluidity and change were thus characteristic of the legislation which governed French military institutions prior to 1914.

Nevertheless in the years after the founding of the Third Republic, the principle of the nation in arms continued to make steady advances on two distinct if not always related planes. In the first place, if the nation in arms is defined only in terms of the number of men under arms or subject to mobilization, then there was no small "progress." The size of the army in peace and in war steadily increased. Under the 1872 law the number of men on active duty in peacetime was approximately a half million. By 1900 the French maintained nearly 600,000 soldiers, and the 1913 law raised the total to over 800,000. The legislation of the seventies assigned a total of twenty annual classes to either active, reserve, or territorial formations but decreed that only nine of these would be designated as part of the active, or front-line army, in time of war. The law of 1905 raised the total number of classes to be mobilized to twenty-five and assigned thirteen to the actives. By 1914 twenty-eight classes were subject to wartime service, and fourteen of these were considered to be an integral part of the front-line army. In 1872 the total number of Frenchmen to be mobilized at the outbreak of hostilities amounted to 1,250,000; by 1914 the figure was over 3,500,000. In little more than forty years France, in terms of military statistics, had become a nation in arms.[1]

Secondly, during the years of the armed peace after 1871 French military policies were steadily brought in line with republican military theories. The length of service was both shortened and equalized; after 1889 no one was conscripted for more than three years, and after 1905 every young man, regardless of family, status, or future career, served for the same length of time. As republicans desired, more emphasis was placed upon the role of the reserves, the conditions of military life were democratized, and the army was frequently considered not simply as a fighting force but as a school in which French youth acquired basic principles of citizenship. By 1905 there were indeed but few republicans still unsatisfied with the evolution of French military institutions. There was, to be sure, a mild reaction from republican military theories in the years immediately preceding the First World War, but the over-all

---

[1] These statistics are available in tabular form in Colonel Joseph Revol, *Histoire de l'armée française* (Paris: Larousse, 1929), pp. 203-04. It has also been pointed out that by 1911 the French inducted almost 83 per cent of each annual contingent whereas the Germans at that time found it necessary to draft only 53 per cent of theirs. Alfred Vagts, *Militarism: Romance and Realities of a Profession* (New York: Norton, 1937), p. 233.

tendency of the period 1872-1914 was the achievement of the republican military program.[2]

Back of this dual achievement stood a multitude of theoretical and practical considerations. The years after 1870 saw in Europe the beginnings of a competitive militarism which affected all nations. The breakdown of the pre-Crimean Concert and the disruptive wars of the sixties produced in their wake an unstable state system in which even a victorious Bismarck suffered nightmares. Save for Britain, all the powers remodeled their armies along lines roughly paralleling the German system of compulsory military service—and even the peace-loving Gladstone sponsored a reform of Her Majesty's forces. Throughout the Continent the strident voices of the first generation of Social Darwinists loudly proclaimed that war was a test of national fitness for survival. In such years, with their heightened nationalism, frequent war scares, and competitive alliances, it was not strange that France became a nation in arms.

At least three special forces had a particular role in the evolution of French military institutions and the development of French military thought. The military power of Germany, the emergence of new theories of warfare, and, perhaps the most important, the steadily increasing political power of the republican groups were the factors which most notably affected the course of French military history in the late nineteenth century.

Of primary concern to any French military theorist or politician was the army on the other side of the Rhine, a force whose power no Frenchman could overlook. What particularly impressed French observers was the success and viability of the

[2] Most useful in tracing the progressive achievement of republican policies is the partisan history of Joseph Monteilhet, *Des Armées permanentes à la nation armée* (Paris: Giard and Brière, 1903), a detailed treatment of thirty years of military legislation. Useful guides to the legislative record are Arpad Kovacs, "French Military Legislation in the Third Republic, 1871-1940," *Military Affairs*, XIII (Spring, 1949), 1-13 and a semi-official French government publication, *Historique des diverses lois sur le recrutement depuis la Révolution jusqu'à nos jours* (Paris: Imprimerie nationale, 1902).

German system. As one text used in French military academies flatly stated, the Prussian military organization had made such an impact upon the rest of Europe that every nation now realized that its independence was in jeopardy unless it possessed an army comparable to Germany's in size and ability.[3] Although not a few publicists opposed any "Prussification" of the French army, and in 1872 the French had successfully resisted the temptation to make their organization a carbon copy of Moltke's system, at the same time the Prussian example was not and could not be ignored.[4] When in the nineties Germany lowered the term of service from three to two years, it was a powerful argument in the hands of Frenchmen who had similar aims. When on the eve of 1914 the Germans increased the size of their army, it was likewise a challenge to which the French felt they could not fail to respond. Throughout the years after 1870, then, the German organization served as a standard against which the French could check their own achievements and acted as a spur to further changes.

Developments in military theory were a second and equally important aspect of the history of post-1870 French military institutions. French military theorists, inspired by the writings of German army officers, came to believe that European industrial growth, the expansion of railways, and the technological development of weapons had ushered in the age of the mass army. They began to anticipate a future war between the great powers in which huge masses of men—the total available man-

[3] General Ildephonse Favé, *Cours d'art militaire professé à l'École Polytechnique* (Paris: Dumaine, 1877), pp. 15-16. Moreover, a republican like Gambetta was so impressed by German military achievements that, after a trip to Germany in 1876, he advised his countrymen that they must remain aloof from European quarrels simply because their army could not hope to defeat the German military machine. See Émile Pillias and Daniel Halévy, eds., *Lettres de Gambetta* (Paris: Grasset, 1938), No. 287 of September 20, 1876.

[4] After 1870 there was a prevailing belief among many Frenchmen of the Left that the institutions of monarchical Prussia were antidemocratic and hence unsuited for imitation by republican France. See, for instance, Urbain Gohier, *L'Armée nouvelle* (Paris: Stock, 1897) for a collection of such arguments.

power of the belligerents—would be hurled against each other in combats of herculean proportions. As this feeling grew, military men came to appreciate the nation in arms—as a quantitative if not as a democratic concept.

The railroad occupied the forefront of the new military theory. The steam engine had not only speeded the timetable of war but had also vastly increased the numbers of men and supplies which could be moved into any operational area. To the generation of military theorists after 1870 universal conscription now seemed feasible because the railroad permitted effective employment of tremendous numbers of soldiers.[5]

At the same time, through study of such German writers as von der Goltz, French military men rediscovered the ideas of Clausewitz and their own Napoleon Bonaparte. The result was that the Napoleonic concept of mass warfare, so much in disfavor before 1870, won converts from a new generation of officers.[6] And the logical corollary was that in French military doctrine the idea that the quality of the individual soldier was the primary consideration became of considerably less importance. The quantity of troops available became a matter as important as their quality. After 1886 the doctrines of Clausewitz became dominant at the *École de Guerre,* and the principal French military writers of the era—Foch, Colin, Gilbert—accepted the premise of mass warfare as a basic axiom. These men taught that henceforth all war would be unlimited national war in which the entire male population would fight. It would be "total war," and the single objective of battle would be the annihilation of the enemy in the field. Ferdinand Foch,

---

[5] General Henri Berthaut, *Principes de stratégie* (Paris: Dumaine, 1881), pp. 31-32, made the point that the railroad made it essential to develop a mass army. For a general discussion of the impact of the railway upon warfare, the best and most important study is General J. F. C. Fuller, *Armament and History* (New York: Scribners, 1945), pp. 104 ff.

[6] See Dallas D. Irvine, "The French Discovery of Clausewitz and Napoleon," *Journal of the American Military Institute,* IV (Summer, 1940), 143-61, for a complete discussion of this development.

for example, wrote that France had been defeated in 1870 because she had forgotten the Napoleonic example of *"la guerre absolue"* and because Prussia had, by contrast, established a military system which made warfare truly national. "It is because all Europe has returned to the era of national theses and as a consequence of nations in arms that we today are obliged to take up again the *absolute* concept of war." [7]

As a result French military theorists became supporters of broadened and more inclusive conscription laws; universal service, obviously, was the only method for obtaining the hordes of men needed for mass warfare. There was, likewise, an increased interest in the reserves. To be sure, many officers long refused to consider that the reservists had any military value. But as early as the eighties there were such men as General Miribel, then Chief of Staff, who felt that French security depended upon equaling German manpower potentials and who, as a result, believed that it was necessary to enlarge the role of the reserves in the French military structure.[8] The very fact that high ranking officers were beginning to consider the reservist was in itself a further step in the fulfillment of republican military theory. The citizen recalled to active duty at the outbreak

[7] Ferdinand Foch, *Des Principes de guerre* (Paris: Berger-Levrault, ed. of 1917), p. 24. An impressive number of the citations in this book are drawn from such German writers as Clausewitz and von der Goltz, an indication not only of German influence upon Foch's thinking but also of his acceptance of the theory of mass war. For a thorough critique of Foch see the article by Stefan Possony and Etienne Mantoux, "Du Picq and Foch: The French School," in E. M. Earle, ed., *Makers of Modern Strategy* (Princeton: Princeton University Press, 1943), Chap. IX. Jean Colin, a theorist widely read in both France and abroad, noted that modern weapons had altered the very nature of warfare, praised Clausewitz for driving formalism out of military theory, insisted that war had become national in scope and required the utilization of the total manpower of belligerents, and stressed the importance of number in modern battle. See his *France and the Next War*, trans. Major L. H. R. Pope-Hennessey (London: Hodder and Stoughton, 1914), pp. 167, 253-54, 287-89, and 299 ff.

[8] See General Arthur Boucher, *Les Doctrines dans la préparation de la grande guerre* (Paris: Berger-Levrault, 1925), pp. 70-73. Important also in this connection was the work of Freycinet as War Minister, as recounted in his *Souvenirs, 1878-93* (Paris: Delagrave, 1914), pp. 409, 469, 506-07.

of war was being placed on a par with the soldier who served in the regular army. The emphasis in the French military structure was thus beginning to shift from the soldier on active duty to the civilian returned to uniform at the hour of mobilization.

The political rise of the loosely formed group of deputies known, whatever their individual differences and the intensity of their radicalism, as republicans was most important in the evolution of both French military thought and institutions. From 1873, when Gambetta indicated that military reform was a cardinal article of republican faith, until 1905, when a new conscription law achieved most of their goals, the republicans conducted a long and ultimately successful offensive against the theories and practices of the National Assembly of 1872.

As before the Franco-Prussian War, the ultimate objective of the French Left was the "republicanization" of the army. In such an army the citizen in uniform would be more important than the professional soldier, the term of service would be short so that the conscript would not be militarized, and every man would serve the same length of time. Likewise, as before, this republican program served a broad political interest.

Now, however, the enemy was not the regime but the army hierarchy and its monarchist, clerical allies who were thought by all good republicans to desire the overthrow of the Third Republic. During the Second Empire republicans had advocated their program as a means of weakening the existing political order, but after 1870 the same policy was designed to create an army which would be loyal to the Republic and which, above all, would not be the pliable tool of the officer caste. Since the officer corps was in fact largely antirepublican, and since the gravest political crises of the young Republic—the Sixteenth of May, Boulanger, and Dreyfus—did involve the question of whether the military hierarchy was loyal to the state, the drive to republicanize the army, if sometimes pushed to extremes, was at least understandable.

In the last analysis, then, the attempt to build a military structure in harmony with republican concepts was a means of breaking the political power of men believed hostile to the Republic and of establishing the Republic on more solid grounds. The case for reform and the political impetus behind it were never more clearly expressed than by the deputy who wrote, "It is with such a system of military training (the long-term system of semiprofessionals) that we end up by creating armies capable of any sort of crime at any given moment. The law of 1832 permitted the Second of December to occur. Who would dare to swear that without the modifications—however insufficient they may be—that have been introduced into our organization, a comparable crime wouldn't have been committed in 1877?" Or as General Théodore Iung, one of the exceedingly rare French officers with republican sympathies, observed, "Under a republic the military forms cannot be the same as under a monarchy. The army will be republican or it will no longer exist." [9]

In moments of extreme zeal republican politicians worked with a missionary spirit which made it exceedingly difficult to determine where military policy ended and purely party politics began. During the anticlerical campaigns of the eighties the Left incessantly demanded the abolition of military exemptions for the clergy. The attempt to put a knapsack on the back of the priest—*le sac au dos*—was justified as the logical consequence of egalitarian principles, but it was in reality little more than another aspect of the political anticlericalism which was in

[9] General Théodore Iung, *La République et l'armée* (Paris: Bibliothèque Charpentier, 1892), p. 357. The previous quotation is from *Historique des diverses lois de recrutement*, p. 69. The familiar objective of "republicanizing" the army was frequently set forth in parliamentary reports; see especially the report of the Chamber army commission which approved the two-year bill, *J. O. C. Doc.*, March 3, 1904, No. 1553, p. 142. An earlier example is the report of the reform-minded deputy Laisant in 1880, *J. O.*, May 23, 1880, No. 2581, p. 5582 ff. Laisant, for instance, informed his fellow deputies that the time had come to establish democratic military institutions so that the voters would have concrete evidence that "the acts of republican legislators are in accord with the principles they proclaim."

those years paying rich electoral dividends to its radical sponsors.[10] General Louis André, the War Minister whose administration of the Rue Saint Dominique terminated with the disclosure that he employed junior officers and Masonic leaders to determine the religious and political views of the top-ranking commanders, was easily the most extreme representative of this type of overzealous republicanism. Pointing with pride to the concrete achievements of his policy for republicanizing the army, André observed in his memoirs,

Let any one note these two dates: 1900-1904. Let him remember that under my ministry four annual contingents, after receiving this education, have returned to political life. Then let him ask himself what influence these classes may have had upon the elections of 1906 which were so admirably republican.[11]

Yet despite the logical symmetry of their program, the republicans were not able to achieve their minimum goal of a conscription law in which the term of service was short in length and equal for all until the opening years of the twentieth century.

There was, in the first place, a persistent budgetary problem. Throughout the eighties when the republican objective was a three-year service with no exemptions for any members of French society, such a system would have inflated the army far beyond the resources of the military budget which was geared for a military establishment of approximately a half million men. Although the French birth rate had become stationary and demographers were already pointing out that Germany's population would soon be far superior to that of France, there were still too many young men available for induction each year for a three-year system to be established without upsetting the

---

[10] The best description of the military aspects of French anticlericalism is Evelyn Acomb, *The French Laic Laws* (New York: Columbia University Press, 1941), pp. 183-93.

[11] General Louis André, *Cinq Ans de ministère* (Paris: Louis-Michaud, 1907), p. 108.

budget. Furthermore, it should be noted, the size of the German army at this time did not appear to warrant any great peacetime expansion of French forces. Consequently, however much the republicans praised their egalitarian nation in arms and desired its establishment, in practice they were forced to compromise. A considerable portion of every military debate concerned various attempts to solve the problem of an excess number of conscripts and to establish some system of exemptions which would do the least violence to egalitarian principles. Gambetta, for instance, as a good republican opposed the use of educational tests or the lottery, and would have created special Departmental councils to exempt men from service on the basis of personal need.[12]

In any event, the difficulty of reconciling short-term service with budgetary realities continuously hampered the enactment of the republican program of military reform and remained a factor until the beginning of the twentieth century. Indeed, at that time the problem was "solved" only because the French adopted a two-year system at a time when the size of each annual contingent was itself decreasing, an arrangement which put an end to the period of excessive numbers of conscripts. Thereafter, as European tensions mounted and the Germans began to conscript more men from their larger population, the French problem became not a surplus but a deficiency of potential soldiers.

Another factor which slowed the progress of republican military reform was the intense patriotism of the majority of republicans. Their leaders were men like Gambetta who taught that while Frenchmen must never speak openly of *revanche,* they must always think of it. Boulangism, with its promise to

---

[12] *J.O.,* March 25, 1882, No. 659, pp. 770-71. As in 1872 the budgetary problem was fantastically complicated, as reference to almost any parliamentary debate on military affairs will show. The republicans always charged that their conservative opponents used the budget question as an excuse to prevent reductions in the length of service. This charge is true but not exhaustive since the republicans themselves had to consider the financial consequences of any military reform.

restore French military prestige in Europe, attracted many a convert in republican ranks until its seamier aspects became embarrassingly obvious. Hence, since republicans were interested in national defense and a strong military edifice, they were frequently led to modify their abstract principles in concrete legislative practice.[13] The republican chieftain, Gambetta, was for long unwilling to advocate a flat three-year service because he feared that such a reform would make it impossible to recruit a sufficient number of trained noncommissioned officers and would thereby reduce the effectiveness of the army as a whole. Even when Gambetta did approve the change, he categorically insisted that three years was the absolute minimum length of time required to form a reliable soldier.[14] His reforming instincts, in short, were frequently subordinated to his desire to maintain the French army as a reliable instrument of national defense.

A third and final reason why the republican program was not achieved until after 1900 was the fact that for many years after the establishment of the Republic the so-called "opportunists" were politically supreme. These were men willing to accept a few crumbs rather than to insist upon the entire republican cake. To be sure, the broader ideological issues were always

[13] Jules Ferry, for instance, justified conscription in a speech which concluded on this patriotic note: "In a military race and on this frontier, this obligation is accepted without murmurs. It can be spoken about in front of the mothers of Lorraine. Yes, ladies, if the charge seems heavy to you, if your maternal tenderness trembles before it and worries about it, raise your eyes toward the sky, in the direction of the east, look at the blue line of the Vosges." Paul Robiquet, ed., *Discours et opinions de Jules Ferry* (7 vols., Paris: Colin, 1893-98), VII, 256. The *revanche* spirit was so strong in some republican circles that the *Nouvelle Revue*, for many years the magazine of the republican patroness, Juliette Adam, maintained as its military columnist a writer, Captain Georges Gilbert, who opposed any tampering with French military institutions because of the German peril.

[14] *J.O.* March 25, 1882, No. 659, p. 770. For Gambetta's earlier arguments, in which he insisted that "the recruitment and organization of noncommissioned officers . . . is the true question" and that three-year service was impossible until this problem was solved, see *ibid.*, June 12, 1876, pp. 4126-27 and November 30, 1876, No. 542, p. 8832. When at a later date this same argument was utilized by conservatives, the republicans called it a red herring.

raised, and the Chamber itself was highly susceptible to demands for radical military reform, but at the same time most republicans were usually willing to settle for limited victories. Until the Dreyfus case brought every phase of civil-military relations into the sharpest focus, the issues of military reform were not fought to their ultimate conclusion.

In view of the unchanging nature of French military debates it would be both pointless and tedious to trace the long, complicated, and lugubrious history of the many legislative attempts to refashion the French nation in arms. There were, for instance, more than a dozen such projects in the years between 1876 and 1889, and as early as 1885 the Chamber of Deputies had approved a three-year conscription bill only to find that the Senate flatly refused to enact the legislation—a setback which led to four years of controversy, confusion, and stalemate. As in the past every debate upon conscription policies produced heated arguments upon such issues as the relationship between state and army, the ideal form of a military establishment, or the special attributes of an army serving within a republic. These, to be sure, were fundamental problems, but they were not always germane when the debate was actually over the more prosaic question of just how long a soldier should be kept under arms. Debate on the length of service rarely centered on the question of just how long it took to train a conscript and make him a resolute, effective soldier; perhaps more often the deputies ranged far and wide over ideological terrain and reversed the question at issue to speculate upon how the length of service affected the character of the army. Most arguments returned to the military concepts of the Revolution for their starting point, and most deputies believed it necessary, figuratively and literally, to base their theories upon the military events of the Year I. And, though emphasis might vary, the content of both debates and projected laws was markedly repetitious. As an example of the nature of the republican approach and the character of their arguments one can cite no passage more typical than the opening of the Chamber of Deputies report on the two-year law of 1905:

It is from the lofty ideas born of the French Revolution that the military legislation of a great republican democracy . . . must be inspired; and when, after more than a century, the legislator can ask all citizens—without distinction of wealth, instruction, or education—to consent to give an equal part of their time to their country without any exceptions or privileges of any sort, the proof is there that the democratic spirit has once again bound up the chain of time.

The principal aspect of the long political fight which culminated in the law of 1889 was the desire of republican reformers to make the length of service equal for all. Republicans insisted that the fundamental principle of the nation in arms was that no specially privileged groups in French society should enjoy exemptions or abbreviated terms of service because of wealth, education, or career. In the words of a Chamber document of 1889:

The French nation has a passion for equality. Whether people are pleased by this as we are, or whether they regret it, as certain of our opponents do, it matters little. It is a fact which we cannot ignore when we have to pass judgment upon the recruitment law.[15]

To the ardent egalitarian Charles de Freycinet it was an axiom that on "the day when the conception of a national army, or the nation in arms, was born, the idea of absolute equality imposed itself as a natural consequence." [16] All too often the republican approach was on purely moral grounds and took no account of the varying needs of the army or of individuals for more or less military training. Equal service for all was a "cause," and republican leaders firmly believed that they would achieve great victories for their principles if they could accomplish nothing more than the equalization of service.[17] Indeed, the other as-

---

[15] *J.O.*, February 21, 1889, No. 3050, p. 348.

[16] Freycinet, *Souvenirs, 1878*, p. 411.

[17] See Monteilhet, *Des Armées*, pp. 137 ff., for criticism of the overemphasis upon egalitarianism.

pects of the military reform movement—the desire to reduce the length of conscription and the hope of ending the split contingent, the special exemptions for teachers and priests, and the system of one-year volunteers—were all considered as but subordinate corollaries of the main egalitarian theme.

In the late eighties a long, impassioned dispute developed between the Chamber and the Senate over egalitarianism and delayed enactment of military reform for over four years. The dispute was not resolved until the deputies, aware of the approach of national elections, decided for purely political reasons to accept the views of the upper legislative house.[18] The Senate, expressing opinions similar to those of the 1872 Assembly, held firm to the principle that the burdens of military service should be apportioned on a basis of social utility and insisted that it was contrary to the national interest for young men about to enter "liberal careers" to have to spend three full years in service.[19] That schoolteachers and priests should be beneficiaries of the senatorial concern for French culture was particularly galling to the deputies. But despite republican pleas that the teacher must provide an example by spending a full three years with the colors and that the priest must not avoid duties incumbent upon all other citizens, the flood of oratory in the Chamber produced no effect upon senatorial ears.[20]

[18] Freycinet made the decisive speech in which he pointed out that the Senate absolutely refused to change its stand and that if the deputies desired to go before the electors with the claim that they had lowered the length of service, then they had no choice but to follow the wishes of the upper house. Freycinet, *Souvenirs, 1878*, pp. 229-30.

[19] *J.O.S. Doc.*, March 21, 1888, No. 204, pp. 134-47. General Deffis, the bill's *rapporteur*, wrote, "The grandeur of a people does not depend solely upon the number of its soldiers or the force of its military institutions, but also upon its degree of civilization and on the development of agriculture, industry, commerce, sciences, and arts. The more a country develops its power and its intellectual forces during peacetime, the more it is suited for the labors and combinations of war" (p. 135). On the Chamber dissatisfaction, see *J.O.*, February 21, 1889, No. 3050, p. 348.

[20] Republican concern for the schoolteacher was of long standing. In the early eighties Paul Bert, an enthusiastic sponsor of laic legislation, was also sponsoring bills to force the teachers into military service. "The teacher," according to Bert, "must

Yet in spite of republican dissatisfaction the law of 1889 was a further step towards the goals which French military reformers so ardently desired. The length of service was lowered to three years, and this provision alone meant that, in time of war, the citizen-reservists would inevitably play a larger role in the national defense. Moreover, many of the inequalities of 1872 disappeared. Even the young men whose careers were so highly regarded by the Senate did not wholly escape the draft but were compelled to spend a full year learning, in addition to their other knowledge, the *métier* of the soldier. And in statistical terms the reform was impressive: under the 1872 law thirty per cent of the annual contingent had been completely exempted, twenty per cent served a maximum of a year, and only half the class remained in the army for the full legal term of duty; but under the provisions of the new legislation none were completely exempted, thirty per cent spent a year with the colors, and seventy per cent served the complete three-year term.[21]

The recruitment law of 1889 enjoyed a history no less checkered than that of its predecessor. Within a decade there were strong demands for its replacement by more "liberal" legislation, and by 1899 no less than two hundred deputies were on record as advocates of a flat two-year term of service.[22] Finally, in 1905, after many long debates, the republicans achieved their goal: a two-year service from which no physically qualified young man could be exempted or partially deferred.

be an instructor of patriotism. And how can he do this, if he himself has not provided the example? With what authority will he speak of the love of the *patrie*, of the supreme duty, if he sees in the eyes of the child who is listening to him an expression of doubt and defiance; if he reads there the thought that he has perhaps fled to this chair to escape the fatigues and perils of the battlefield?" *J.O.C. Deb.*, April 6, 1881, p. 772. On the republicans' desire to put the priests in uniform, see Acomb, *Laic Laws*, pp. 183 ff.

21 *Historique des diverses lois*, p. 105.

22 Louis Boudenoot, "L'Armée en 1899," *Revue politique et parlementaire*, XXII (Nov., 1899), 282-83.

The most striking feature of the discussions which led to the two-year law was not the content of the debates, which, as might be expected, remained invariable, but the tone. The angry emotions of the years of Dreyfusard agitation produced an atmosphere of republican intransigence. Like the radicals of the Second Empire, the deputies who wrote the 1905 law were dogmatic, overconfident, and, in the broad sense of the word, antimilitarist. Convinced that a clique of monarchists, anti-Semites, clerics, and high ranking military officers threatened the existence of the Republic, republicans united in a common endeavor to safeguard the state by gathering the controls of church and army into their own hands. The 1905 law was the work of the famous *Délégation des gauches,* a genuine working coalition of the political Left which openly sought to bring church and army under firm republican control.[23] Thus, while the stated purpose of military reform was to reduce the length of service and make it equal for all, the two-year law was in fact an integral part of republican efforts to smash the political power of the men who had condemned Captain Dreyfus.[24]

Republicans in these debates advanced a concept of the nation in arms in which the citizen-soldier formed the heart and soul of the national defense.[25] They maintained that the standing army should be regarded primarily as a vast training school in which the young conscripts learned the fundamentals of soldiering. Consequently, they tended to minimize the army's role as a body of troops already prepared to defend the nation. In the eighties the deputies had believed that it was necessary to maintain three annual contingents, plus professionals, under

---

[23] R. A. Winnacker, "The Influence of the Dreyfus Affair on the Political Development of France," *Papers of the Michigan Academy of Science, Arts, and Letters, 1935,* XXI (Ann Arbor: University of Michigan Press, 1936), 476.

[24] It is not without significance that during these years domestic issues were primary and little attention was paid in the Chamber debates to problems of foreign affairs. See Bertha R. Leaman, "The Influence of Domestic Policy on Foreign Affairs in France, 1898-1905," *Journal of Modern History,* XIV (Dec., 1942), 449-51.

[25] For the objectives of Chamber and Senate, see *J.O.C. Doc.,* No. 1553, March 3, 1904, pp. 141 ff. and *J.O.S. Doc.,* December 23, 1901, No. 475, pp. 510 ff.

arms at all times. In those years republicans had considered
that a three-year period was necessary to train reliable soldiers
and had also believed that national security required an ever-
present force of at least three classes. But republicans of the
Dreyfus era—while never willing to decrease the size of the
permanent military establishment—desired to minimize the role
of the active army and insisted, rather, that the mass of trained
reserves should provide the principal instrument of national defense. Consequently they maintained that French youth should
be conscripted merely for the length of time necessary to provide basic military training, argued that soldiers should be released from the army as soon as their period of instruction was
completed, and insisted that under no circumstance should conscripts be kept on active duty once their basic training was over.
Under such a conception the role of the active army was simply
to train conscripts and provide a body of skilled reservists; its
function, in short, was to be that of a school.

The contrast between civilian and professional military values
was a recurrent theme of the Dreyfusard reformers. The nation in arms, they said, was a democratic concept; the idea of a
professional army attracted only those who did not prize liberty.[26] When their opponents argued that a two-year service
would provide an insufficient number of men under arms and
that it would therefore be necessary to recruit an increased
number of career soldiers, republicans countered with lengthy
statements on the ways in which professional soldiers harmed
the moral fibre of a national army.[27] When General André,
the ordinarily tractable War Minister and advocate of reform,
spoke of the need for additional professionals, the sponsor of the
two-year bill, Senator Rolland, brushed off his protests with the
words, "To tell the truth we are infinitely more preoccupied
with the question of principle than with the practical conse-

[26] *J.O.C. Doc.*, No. 1553, March 3, 1904, p. 142.
[27] *Ibid.*, July 6, 1901, No. 2650, p. 1550.

quences of the solution proposed by M. le Ministre." [28] On the last day of debate an enthusiastic partisan summed up the attitude of the men who wrote the new law when he exclaimed, "This law, gentleman, evidently opens for the army an era which I will dare to call . . . the era of civilianism." [29] To be sure, in practice the republicans still accepted some compromise —the recruitment of additional career soldiers was ultimately sanctioned—but the spirit which motivated the reform of 1905 was no less clear.

The two-year law was enacted by deputies who were fully aware of the fact that the French population was falling behind that of Germany and that the number of men in each annual class was steadily decreasing.[30] But in the atmosphere of 1905 these considerations produced few worries. In the first place the decline in the size of the annual contingent could be used as a powerful argument in favor of the goal of equal service for all. As Premier Waldeck-Rousseau pointed out, in the coming years of smaller annual contingents the army would be almost 100,000 below its authorized strength unless all the young men who had heretofore escaped with but a year in the ranks were now compelled to serve the full two-year period.[31] More important than such tactical considerations, however, was republican faith in the reserves. If the reservist was to be considered the key to national defense, then it mattered little if annual contingents slowly decreased in size. The mobilized mass of the nation, not the size of the peacetime army, would be the deci-

[28] *J.O.S. Doc.*, December 23, 1901, No. 475, p. 520.

[29] *J.O.C. Deb.*, March 16, 1905, p. 925.

[30] See, for instance, Émile Levasseur, *La Population française* (3 vols., Paris: Rousseau, 1892), III, 258. For evidence that the bill's authors were aware of the population problem, see *J.O.S. Doc.*, December 23, 1901, No. 475, pp. 511, 519-20.

[31] See Waldeck-Rousseau's speech, *J.O.C. Deb.*, February 21, 1902, pp. 869-70. This was also the thesis of Senator Charles Dupuy and a standard argument in the ultimate debates. Charles Dupuy, "Le Service de deux ans et les dispenses," *Revue politique et parlementaire*, XXXIV (Feb., 1903), 236 ff. André, *Cinq Ans*, pp. 172 ff. made the supression of exemptions one of the conditions on which he accepted a two-year service.

sive factor in any conflict. Furthermore, the republicans were convinced that a military establishment founded upon their concept of the nation in arms reduced the danger of war—certainly, of aggressive, unjustified war. A citizen-army, it was alleged, was "inappropriate for conquest" and "the only war it can wage . . . is a war of national defense." [32] Thus, since such ideas dominated the debate over the two-year law, the decrease in the size of the annual contingents and the declining birth rate were items of secondary concern.

Finally, and perhaps most characteristic of the republican military ideology of these years, there was a striking evolution of the idea that the army was a school and that, as such, it could perform an important social role in French life. French military reformers had always been prone to moralize about conscription, but in post-Dreyfus years they drew a seemingly endless series of consequences from the fact that every citizen served in the ranks and that the army was now the image of the nation. Republicans insisted that since the nation in arms was now a reality and the citizen-soldier the principal defender of the *patrie,* it was necessary to transform the army itself into an institution which fully recognized that the conscript entering its ranks was a citizen first and a soldier second. In their view a thorough revision of the entire military establishment was a logical corollary of the fact that the recruits now came from all strata of society and not merely from the ranks of the poor and the dispossessed. The disciplinary system, the relationship between officers and men, and, ultimately, the scope of military education were in need of reform. Moreover, the republicans concluded, if the army underwent such reform, then it could become not merely a school in which the raw recruit learned the basic military arts but also an educational establishment in which he could discover the way to become a better citizen. More ardent republicans—realizing the possibilities for indoctrination and education which were latent in an institution which

[32] *J.O.C. Doc.,* No. 1863, July 10, 1900, p. 2097.

encompassed the totality of French youth—spoke and wrote as
if they believed that the primary function of the army was to
serve not as a fighting force but as an instrument for the self-
improvement of the citizen.[33]

Republicans were no less insistent that, with the achievement
of the nation in arms, the traditional role of the officer corps
must be modified.[34]   In the first place, the officer of the new
army must adapt himself to the political and social values of the
times and must realize that the evolution of French military institutions had been in full harmony with the needs and demands
of French democracy.[35]   As early as 1898, for instance, the
noted historian Ernest Lavisse was giving lectures to the Saint
Cyr cadets in which he not only justified all the military reforms which the republicans had made since 1872 but also
reached the conclusion that "our military regime is in accord
and harmony with our institutions; it is that of a democratic
regime; the *patrie* for all, all for the *patrie*." [36]   Once indoctri-

[33] The best single source for a full-length discussion of this concept is André,
Cinq Ans, pp. 70 ff.   But see also such bits of fugitive military literature as Captain
Émile Potez, *Le Moral de nos soldats* (Paris: Charles-Lavauzelle, 1904) and Captain
Charles Condamy, *La Loi de deux ans et la conflit Franco-Allemand à propos du
Maroc* (Paris: Charles-Lavauzelle, 1905), neither of which devote much attention to
purely military considerations.   For excellent examples of the opinions of republican
deputies on the "army-school" concept, see *J.O.C. Doc.*, July 6, 1901, No. 2650,
pp. 1492 ff. and *J.O.C. Deb.*, March 16, 1905, p. 925.

[34] The originator of the idea that the officer's role had vastly changed was not a
simon-pure republican but the future Marshal Lyautey.   See his article, "Du Rôle
social de l'officier," *Revue des deux mondes*, CIV (Mar. 15, 1891), 443-58.   Though
it was published anonymously, the article was immediately credited to Lyautey,
and all of the men who later wrote on this subject regarded Lyautey as the first to
understand that the officer's functions must be modified.

[35] *J.O.C. Doc.*, July 6, 1901, No. 2650.

[36] Ernest Lavisse, ed., *L'Armée à travers les âges* (Paris: Chapelot, 1899), Introduction.   Shortly thereafter André initiated courses of instruction in the leading
French military academies to explain the new social role of officers.   See such representative texts for these courses as George Duruy, *L'Officier éducateur* (Paris:
Chapelot, 1904) and Lt. Colonel Charles Ebener, *Conférences sur le rôle social de
l'officier* (Paris: Charles-Lavauzelle, 1901), both of which elaborate the full program.
Both texts, for instance, were ardently republican and written to "prove" that the
changes in French military institutions were a necessary evolution caused by the

nated with republican values, the officer must also realize that the military evolution of France had altered his role as an officer and demanded a new relationship between his men and himself. In the words of War Minister André,

The officer must be to the soldier what the soul is to the body. He must know him as he knows himself, not only to command him, to instruct him in his temporary profession and his military obligations, but even to counsel him in everything—even in what concerns his normal profession and his social existence.[37]

The officer, then, was not to be a disciplinarian but a sort of older brother; he was to be as much a teacher and educator as a commander; he was, in short, to become an agent of republican ideas.

After 1910, particularly after Joffre came to head the army, these ideas tended more and more to fall into the background.[38] Nonetheless, the idea that the army should be the school of the citizen and the officer his teacher was one of the high points of pre-1914 republican thought on the nation in arms. In origin it was obviously political and aimed, at least in part, at restricting the power of the army hierarchy by converting young officers to republican purposes. But the scheme was nevertheless the work of men who were attracted by the vision of a republi-

---

establishment of the Third Republic. Ebener argued, to cite but one example, that unless an army adapted itself to the institutions of a country, it ran the risk of perishing (p. 29). For a shorter version of the same arguments see also École Polytechnique, *Rôle de l'officier dans la nation armée* (1911-12), a text prepared for and used in a course at this school.

[37] André, *Cinq Ans*, p. 70. For similar statements see also Duruy, *Officier*, pp. 110 ff. and Ebener, *Conférences*, pp. 30 ff.

[38] A recent historian of the French army has maintained that one of the reasons the army leaders of 1913 so eagerly adopted a three-year service was because they were disgusted with the tendency to look upon the army as anything but a fighting machine. Revol, *Histoire*, p. 224. For some sharp criticism of the "army-school" idea, see in particular General Jules Bourelly, "L'Armée française au commencement de 1904," *Correspondant*, CLXXVIII (Feb. 10, 1904), 402 ff. and General Henri Bonnal, *La Première Bataille* (Paris: Chapelot, 1908), pp. 157 ff. Bourelly regarded the republican program as nothing more than a scheme to "glorify the regime of the moment", while Bonnal was convinced that it was part of a standing plot by the enemies of the army to demilitarize the country.

can army which would bring about a complete fusion between the nation and the army. Back of the idea that the army should be a school was the belief that the achievement of universal short-term service made it necessary for the functions and responsibilities of the army and its officer corps to be re-evaluated. The reformers hoped to establish rapport between army and nation and, by so doing, to strengthen the national defense. The concept of the army as a school and the officer as a teacher was thus a logical and not unworthy outcome of the republican theory of the nation in arms.

Although republican military theories enjoyed singular successes in the years after 1872, they were far from being the only concepts of military organization which were advanced as a solution to the ever-present problem of national defense. There was thunder on the right as on the left; neither conservatives nor Socialists ever fully accepted the theories or the practices which the dominant republican-radical-opportunist bloc had written into law in 1889 and 1905. Indeed, by the outbreak of the First World War the orthodox republican views were encountering considerable opposition. Certainly theirs was no longer the most "advanced" theory—French Socialists, guided by Jean Jaurès, were gaining an increasing audience for their skillfully contrived concepts of a national militia. Certainly theirs was not the only popular theory—French conservatives, led by Raymond Poincaré and assisted by "renegade" Socialists and republicans, were able in 1913 to enact a recruitment law which both in spirit and in content challenged many of the basic premises upon which earlier legislation had been based.

The principal ideas of the Rightists, like those of the republicans, changed but little between 1870 and 1914. In debate after debate conservatives presented theories as stereotyped as those of the republicans; a few basic arguments formed the perpetual ammunition in the controversies about French military policy. Yet at the same time the attitude of the Right towards conscription and the concept of the nation in arms was modified in the years after 1872. At the earlier date there were many conservatives who were dubious about the merits of compulsory service and who believed that even a five-year term of service would be insufficient; by 1913 men of the same political stamp would consider it a great victory when the length of service was extended from two to three years. Similarly, the popularity of Rightist military theories likewise shifted markedly with the times. During the parliamentary debates on the two-year bill of 1905, a moment when conservative indignation was at its peak and their influence at its nadir, the Right tacitly confessed the unpopularity of its military theories by offering to approve a twelve-month service in return for legislation authorizing a strong force of professional soldiers. Yet within a decade opinion in France had shifted to such an extent that conservative criticisms of republican military theory were widely accepted and many of their own ideas were included in a law which passed both legislative houses by wide margins.

The history of Socialist thought on the nation in arms was parallel yet dissimilar. The influence of the extreme Left was negligible until the beginning of the twentieth century, and the Socialist military program—summed up by the catch phrase, "suppression of permanent armies, general arming of the people"—remained a stereotype until the era of Jean Jaurès. Yet even Jaurès, the foremost military thinker of the Left, did not present ideas that were wholly original: he owed much to Engels and earlier Socialist writers; his inspiration came from the French Revolution; his theories of a militia had been tested by the nineteenth-century Swiss; and he adapted many of the concepts first proclaimed by French republicans. But Jaurès did combine these ideas into a unified program and sustained them with a logic which was distinctive. As a result, by 1914 French Socialism possessed a coherent and consistent body of military

doctrine.   Perhaps even more noteworthy was the fact that Socialists had changed from a dissident group of Marxist thinkers
who maintained that conscription was just another tool of the
bourgeois state to a more disciplined political party which
eagerly advanced its own theories of universal military service.

For Socialists to develop any positive military theory or to
accept any form of the nation in arms was a difficult task.   To
the first followers of Marx war was the great evil, and French
Socialists as early as the period of the Second Empire had called
for the general disarmament of all peoples and the outlawing of
war.[39]   In the Marxist interpretation of history the army was
not only an agent of overseas imperialism but also the instrument, *par excellence,* by which the dominant bourgeoisie kept
the toiling masses in permanent subjection.   As late as 1898 Socialists in the Chamber of Deputies defined the army as "a
brutal, disciplined force, composed of a fraction of the proletariat supplied with arms and directed by its economic and political masters to keep the entire proletariat under the capitalist
yoke and under the tyranny of the reactionary state." [40]   And
there were, in addition, other intellectual difficulties to resolve.
Any Socialist concept of the nation in arms had to be adapted
to their own ideas of social justice; it was, for instance, incon-
ceivable for the Socialists to approve any military system which
kept young men away from their jobs and their families for
long years.   Even more important was the fact that for years
the French Left was antipatriotic; in the thought-world of
Marxism, patriotism, like religion, was an opiate with which the
masses were deluded.[41]

[39] Albert Thomas, *Histoire du Second Empire* (*Histoire socialiste de la nation
française,* ed. Jean Jaurès, 12 vols., Paris: Rouff, 1901-08), Part II, Vol. VIII, 265-
70, 297, 314.
[40] *J.O.C. Doc.,* June 27, 1898, No. 112, p. 1257.   See also Jules Guesde,
État, politique et morale de classe (Paris: Giard and Brière, 1901), pp. 376-77, a
re-editing of newspaper articles Guesde wrote in the eighties.   "The army doesn't
look toward the frontier but toward the factory . . . Its sole objective . . . is the defense of the capitalist and the directing bourgeoisie."
[41] See Harold Weinstein, *Jean Jaurès: A Study of Patriotism in the French So-*

Consequently, even though Engels had approved the *levée en masse* of the Franco-Prussian War and although many Socialists, attracted by the Swiss militia system, had included the general arming of the people in post-1870 party platforms, Socialist military thinking remained essentially negative throughout the nineteenth century.[42]   The extreme Left, for instance, totally denied that the republican reforms of the eighties possessed any merit.   Jules Guesde described the debates which led to the 1889 law as no more than a long, meaningless fight to put priests in uniform and commented at length upon the care with which the bourgeoisie protected its sons from the full rigors of conscription.[43]   What military legislation the Socialists sponsored in the Chamber placed almost exclusive emphasis upon the evils which a militia would prevent: imperialistic adventures, aggressive wars, and military intervention in domestic industrial disputes.   They were not much interested in whether or not a militia would actually improve national defense.[44] Moreover, the concept of the general arming of the people had another and more ominous implication: Socialist writers observed with some satisfaction that, on the day of class revolution, the workers would possess the weapons with which the capitalist state could be overthrown.[45]

There could be no real development of Socialist theories of the nation in arms until the era of reformism, that is, until the

---

cialist Movement (New York: Columbia University Press, 1936), *passim*, but particularly his introductory remarks, pp. 3-6.

[42] Friedrich Engels, *Notes on the War*, ed. Friedrich Adler (Vienna: Wiener Volksbuchhandlung, 1923), pp. 51-54, 64. For some of the early French Leftist programs, see Alexandre Zévaès, *Histoire du socialisme et du communisme en France de 1871 à 1947* (Paris: Éditions France-Empire, 1947), pp. 43, 108-09, 163-64.

[43] Guesde, *État*, pp. 393 ff.

[44] *J.O.C. Doc.*, June 27, 1898, No. 112, pp. 1255-57.

[45] See, for instance, Guesde, *État*, p. 380. But even at a later date Jaurès was still aware of the possibilities. "In great and tragic upheavals, would not the proletariat be better prepared to use every chance, being already lodged in such masses in the very heart of the capitalist citadel?" Jean Jaurès, *L'Armée nouvelle* (Paris: *L'Humanité*, ed. of 1915), p. 357.

day when Socialists, abandoning the theory of violent revolution, adopted the tactic of limited cooperation with the bourgeois state and began to think of the gradual evolution of a collectivist regime.   Once the vision of an international class solidarity began to dim, Socialists could distinguish between nations
and realize that, through his associations with the Third Republic, the French worker obtained tangible benefits—benefits
which he would lose if, for instance, the German army invaded
his country.   In short, the logic of reformism slowly drove Socialists to give serious thought to the problem of defending the
nation they had newly discovered.[46]

The man whose name was most closely associated with this
development was Jean Jaurès, the most brilliant star in the
galaxy of French Socialism and, in addition to his many other
achievements, an outstanding military theorist.   Jaurès brought
to his work, if not originality, at least the firm conviction that
the French worker had a *patrie*.   He taught patriotism, the need
for arms to protect the nation, and the danger of the German
army to France.   Above all, he insisted that the national defense must be organized by and for the proletariat.   And his
military writings attracted attention because, unlike the vast
majority of his colleagues in the Chamber, he was a painstaking
student of military affairs.[47]

[46] In addition to Weinstein, *Jaurès*, the theme of which is the change in Socialist
military theories with the coming of reformism and the era of Jaurès, see also
Alexandre Zévaès, *Histoire du socialisme*, Chapter X, which discusses Socialist military thought in the decade prior to the war of 1914.

[47] His great book was *L'Armée nouvelle*, originally intended to form part of a
larger work, *L'Organisation socialiste de la France*, a series designed to show how
France was to be transformed into a collectivist society.   *L'Armée nouvelle* alone appeared in print.   It was published in 1910, but there are numerous editions, including an English abbreviation, *Democracy and Military Service*, ed., G. G. Coulton
(London: Simpkin, 1916).   Citations in this paper are from the edition published
by the Paris newspaper *L'Humanité* in 1915.   On his indebtedness to Engels, see
Sigmund Neumann, "Engels and Marx: Military Concepts of the Social Revolu-
tionaries," in Earle, *Modern Strategy*, pp. 170-71.   For his recognition that the Swiss
had first worked out a viable militia, see *L'Armée nouvelle*, pp. 149, 215 ff.   For the
text of his proposed law, see pp. 549-57.

The result of his studies was *L'Armée nouvelle,* then and since the military bible of French Socialists, a book which has influenced the development of Leftist military thought until the present. The purpose of *L'Armée nouvelle* was to create a national defense organization based upon a militia system which, Jaurès believed, would be the ultimate expression of the nation in arms. He carried the republican idea that the army was a school to its logical conclusion, for his "new army" would exist solely to provide military training, and, after a conscript had completed six months of service, he was to be discharged. Jaurès was completely confident that national security needed no permanent units under arms; he was even willing to entrust the defense of the Franco-German frontier to militiamen living in the region. Reservists, given special instruction and assigned their defensive positions in advance, would keep arms and equipment in their homes. When the alarm tocsin sounded, an aroused citizenry would form their battalions in the tradition of 1793.[48]

Jaurès was firmly convinced that a genuine militia system would provide a sure means of national defense. He was equally positive that such an organization would serve to check any aggressive French foreign policies and would prevent French involvement in unjust wars. Professional armies were, *per se,* the instruments of aggressive wars, but a citizen army, largely composed of married men with families, could fight only in a just cause. And, since the men would be defending their homes, they would fight more resolutely than any professional force. Moreover, Jaurès argued that if a nation created a militia organization, the very fact of its establishment would be an indication of the peaceful intentions of the country: "A nation in arms is necessarily a nation actuated by justice and up-

---

[48] Jaurès, *Armée,* pp. 221-27. He conceded that it might be necessary to retreat from the frontier and yield these regions to the enemy, but argued that his militia army, fighting on native soil, would soon establish unbreakable defenses and ultimately drive the invader from France.

rightness. Governments which shrink from the immediate use of their reserve forces confess by their hesitation the existence of elements of aggression and injustice in *their* policy." [49]

There was, indeed, much that was fanciful and utopian in the Jaurès program. It was also strongly reminiscent of many previous republican and Leftist plans, themselves based more on legend than on fact, more on hope than reality. His system was too closely Marxist in phraseology and too rigidly based upon class concepts. But it had the merit of recognizing that, in the face of a declining birth rate, France could never hope to match the German army man for man, whatever the length of service, and that, in any future war, the security of the nation would depend upon the military virtues of the reserves. Furthermore, unlike previous advocates of a militia, Jaurès recognized the dangers of hasty improvisation. Adopting an idea which many republicans had previously advanced, Jaurès in all his plans stressed the need for premilitary training. Under his system, although recruits would serve only six months in the active army, every French boy would begin premilitary training at the age of thirteen, such instruction to include drill, marching, and rifle marksmanship.[50] To Jaurès the concept of the nation in arms meant that French youth should begin to prepare for their ultimate military obligations at the age of thirteen; indeed, in

---

[49] *Ibid.,* p. 48.

[50] *Ibid.,* pp. 215-18. Premilitary training was a favorite idea of many republicans. As early as 1872 there had been a few deputies who had desired to establish such training programs, and both the laws of 1889 and 1905 had contained clauses which anticipated the inauguration of premilitary instruction. In addition, there were a number of voluntary societies which gave such training to young men who were interested in learning something about the army before their induction. The voluntary program became quite extensive, and young men who had attended such training programs were given preferential treatment when they were inducted into the army. But prior to 1914 it was always politically impossible to establish any compulsory system of premilitary training which would have affected all the youth of France. On this whole question, an important though subordinate aspect of the nation in arms, see *J.O.C. Doc.,* November 13, 1908, No. 2102, pp. 60 ff. (reprinted as No. 300 of July 11, 1910). Also valuable are Commandant Félix Chapuis, *Manuel de la préparation militaire* (Paris: Berger-Levrault, 1910), pp. 5 ff. and Louis Vuillemin, *Les S.A.G. dans la nation* (2 vols., Paris: Charles-Lavauzelle, 1914), I, Introduction.

his system the establishment of compulsory premilitary training was a basic prerequisite for the six-month term of service. The nation in arms of Jaurès might be a militia, but it would not lack organization or training, for, as the Socialist leader wrote, "It would be a crime against the *patrie* to let any one believe that the sudden inspiration of courage, of enthusiasm, or of talent can compensate for patient, methodical, and strong organization.[51]

At the other pole of French military thought were the opinions of the conservatives. They were a diverse group of politicians, aristocrats, army officers, clergy, and writers who tended, in the years after 1872, to oppose republican and Socialist military theories and who desired to prevent change in French military institutions. Not a few held extreme opinions. At the time of the 1872 debates it was by no means unusual to find conservatives who believed that no conscript army could ever secure the national defenses: in the words of General Joseph Vinoy, "The nation in arms is a horde of barbarians, the permanent army is the substitution of skill for number and brute force."[52] To integral nationalists like Charles Maurras and Maurice Barrès, who dreamed of revenge against Germany, the army was an "untouchable," and republican attempts to modify the conditions of recruitment could only weaken French military power. Both maintained that the concept of the nation in arms rested upon a grave historical error and that a professional army, based upon the logical principle of the division of labor, was the only viable instrument for *revanche*.[53] Likewise, those political conservatives who hated and distrusted the Republic were also opposed to republican military theories. Their oppo-

[51] Jaurès, *Armée*, p. 149.
[52] General Joseph Vinoy, *L'Armée française en 1873* (Paris: Plon, 1873), p. 184.
[53] Charles Maurras, *Enquête sur la monarchie* (Paris: Nouvelle Librairie Nationale, ed. of 1925), pp. 47 ff., 459; Maurice Barrès, *Scènes et doctrines du nationalisme* (Paris: Émile-Paul, n.d.), pp. 268-69. See also discussion in William Buthman, *The Rise of Integral Nationalism in France* (New York: Columbia University Press, 1939) pp. 286, 294, 321 ff.

sition was not merely a matter of principle but arose also from their firm conviction that the state would disintegrate without a strong and reliable army. To an "Ultra" like the Academician Étienne Lamy the republican reform legislation of the eighties threatened the one remaining institutional bulwark which held French society together.[54]

Yet despite the frequency with which such opinions occur in the post-1870 military literature and in the parliamentary debates of these years, it would be wrong to consider conservative military thought as the complete antithesis of any and all republican concepts of the nation in arms. In the last analysis there were but few Frenchmen who hoped to turn back the clock and return to a purely professional army. Rather, the majority of French conservatives recognized the need for conscription, a mass army, and trained reserves. What the French Right hoped to accomplish was to limit the application of republican thories, to prevent reductions in the length of service and the trend toward reliance upon the reserves, and, in short, to preserve as much of the 1872 settlement as possible.

Many and varied were the lines of argument put forth by conservatives in their attempt to preserve the military *status quo.* Perhaps the most telling—and the one with the most validity—was the charge that republican plans to reduce the length of service were political in character and designed to win votes from the unsuspecting masses.

In a word, the promise to reduce the length of service has become a compulsory electoral springboard—to such an extent that an aspirant for public office cannot free himself from it without running the risk . . . of positive failure.[55]

---

54 Étienne Lamy, "L'Armée et la démocratie," *Revue des deux mondes,* LXIX (Jun. 15, 1885), 835 ff., an article which contains just about every possible argument then and since advanced by the extreme Right.

55 Colonel Frédéric-Léopold Bidault, *L'Armée française et le service de deux ans* (Paris: Charles-Lavauzelle, 1898), p. 9. See also General Jules Bourelly, "L'Armée est-elle et doit-elle être la nation?", *Correspondant,* CLXXI (Apr. 25, 1902), 198.

In later years the conservatives looked back with nostalgia to the debates of 1872; at that time, it was said, no deputies had played politics with conscription, and every legislator had thought only of the national interest.[56]

More important than this petty wrangling was the line of reasoning which found expression in a series of "catch words"—cohesion, solidity, military education—that studded most conservative military arguments. The thought behind these words indicated that the military opinions of the Right rested upon different assumptions and different beliefs than those of the dominant republican bloc.

No military force, said conservative spokesmen, was of value unless it possessed cohesion. Units of the regular army possessed this quality by virtue of the long association of officers and men. But even a regular army unit lost its cohesion when a group of unassimilated reserves was added to it at the hour of mobilization, for the new men did not know one another, and commanders were unfamiliar with their duties. The result was that any military unit was a more effective fighting force before the arrival of its reserve components than afterwards, since the increase in its numerical strength was more than offset by its lessened cohesion. Thus General François de Négrier, an officer of pronounced conservative temperament, insisted that the public was wrong in assuming that the maintenance of large numbers of trained reserves was a guarantee of French security. In his opinion the reserves were a detriment, for they lacked cohesion and could not operate as a team in effective combination with the regulars.[57]

Conservative military writers also insisted that another of the basic soldierly traits possessed only by the men on active duty was what they called solidity. This quality could be attained

[56] See, for instance, the speech delivered to the Senate in 1902 by General Jean-Baptiste Billot, one of the few participants in the 1872 debates who was still active in political affairs. *J.O.S. Deb.*, June 27, 1902, p. 899.

[57] General François de Négrier, "Le Moral des troupes," *Revue des deux mondes*, XXV (Feb. 1, 1905), 481 ff.

only by long months of service in the ranks and was something which even the trained soldier quickly lost as soon as he returned to civilian life. It followed from this, then, that reductions in the length of military service destroyed the solidity of the army—an opinion, the conservative spokesmen always insisted, which was shared by all officers who had ever commanded troops under fire.[58]

Unlike their republican opponents, the theorists of the Right drew a sharp distinction between military training and military education. A conscript could indeed obtain his basic military training within a short period of time; he might quickly learn how to handle a rifle or to march many miles; but he was still not a soldier. The recruit, on the contrary, did not become a soldier until the time when his own personal interests meant nothing to him, and he felt that his own personality was dominated by "the spirit of the collective being." [59] Military education was the all-important process which produced this change in the mental and spiritual outlook of the conscript. Moreover, it was a process which required at least several years of active service over and beyond the period of basic training, and it could be accomplished only within the ranks of the regiment on active duty. Conservative military theorists never tired of claiming that the republicans were unaware of the distinction between military training and military education and that, as a result, they established the total length of service upon the time needed for military training and without thought of the more

[58] See, among others, the long discussion on this point in Captain Georges Gilbert, *Lois et institutions militaires* (Paris: Librairie de la *Nouvelle Revue*, 1895), pp. 22 ff. and in his "Le Service de deux ans," *Nouvelle Revue*, CXIII (Jul.-Aug., 1898), 385 ff.

[59] André G., "L'Armée: les formes et les forces," *Nouvelle Revue*, CXV (Nov., 1898), 239. For further discussions of the difference between military training and military education, see General Charles Kessler, *La Guerre* (Paris: Berger-Levrault, 1909), p. 27 and the same author's "La Loi du service de deux ans," *Correspondant*, CLXXVII (Nov. 10, 1903), 483-87; General Jean-Joseph Farre, *Observations sur les réformes militaires à l'étude* (Paris: Baudoin, 1882), p. 11.

extensive period required for military education.[60]   Consequently, it was said, the short-service army of the republicans would be unsound because its soldiers, provided with nothing more than basic training, would lack all those virtues and qualities that only years of military education could bring.

This stress upon solidity, cohesion, and military education led conservatives to the logical conclusion that it was a dangerous practice to lower the length of service and an unsound policy to rely upon the mass of reserves to defend the nation in time of war.   On the other hand, they concluded, France must maintain not only a large standing army in which conscripts served more than a minimum length of time but also a sizable corps of professional soldiers around whom both conscripts and reservists might rally and from whom they could learn the attributes of the soldier.   As the Count de Mun warned, if the French paid no attention to these arguments and followed the erroneous republican doctrines, France might well have "a nation in arms, but she would no longer have an army."

Conservative indignation at the nature and tenor of the republicans' military reforms of course reached its peak in the early years of the twentieth century.   At that time a general like Henri Bonnal was so angered that he could only splutter helplessly that such changes as the two-year law were but the last phase of a plan long elaborated by French Freemasons to reduce the army to a helpless militia.   To the former War Minister Gallifet, this same law was proof that "The French people no longer want an army . . . nor religion." [61]   However, in the

[60] Captain Henri Choppin, *L'Armée française, 1870-90* (Paris: Savene, 1890), pp. 7-14, 291.

[61] Bonnal, *Première Bataille,* p. 158; André Brisson, *Deux Ministres de la guerre,* an otherwise unidentified pamphlet—now in the possession of the New York Public Library—which appears to have been translated from an article originally appearing in the *Nouvelle Presse libre de Vienne,* Apr. 26, 1903.   This pamphlet compares the work of André and Gallifet at the War Ministry, and what makes it particularly interesting is the fact that the Public Library copy has Gallifet's personal comments, of which the above quotation is a typical sample, scribbled in the margins.   Of the many bitter articles of these years, perhaps the best is General Jules Bourelly,

years which immediately preceded the First World War, the influence of Rightist military concepts began to grow. The culmination of this development was the legislation of 1913, an act which raised the length of service from two to three years and which, even if it did not completely repudiate the past, was certainly founded upon assumptions that differed considerably from those which had prevailed a decade earlier.

One of the factors most responsible for this change was the obvious fact that tensions were steadily mounting between the members of the two competing European alliance systems. War scares increased with the outbreak of the Balkan Wars, and all the European nations, feeling their security threatened, began to look to their armaments and to increase the size of their armies. The French were no exception. The political groups which represented the nationalist, conservative point of view took a new lease on life and by 1912 had succeeded in electing Raymond Poincaré to the French Presidency. In such an atmosphere of heightened nationalism and international tension the military theories of the Right secured a wider audience.

No less important in its effect upon military thought in these years was the declining French birth rate and the fears produced by the decrease in the size of the annual contingents. In 1905 it had been possible to discount this phenomenon, but as international friction increased and, particularly, as the Germans began to conscript more men from their larger population, many a Frenchman began to wonder if the optimism of 1905 had not been misplaced. Population experts presented elaborate statistical proofs to show that Germany could soon put into the field an army double the size of the French.[62] Alarmed deputies

---

"L'Armée française au commencement de 1904," *Correspondant*, CLXXVIII (Feb. 10 and 25, 1904), 402-26, 686-713.

[62] Jacques Bertillon, *La Dépopulation de la France* (Paris: Alcan, 1911), pp. 15-16; Paul Leroy-Beaulieu, *La Question de la population* (Paris: Alcan, 1913), p. 343. The best discussion of the whole birth rate question, with particular attention to the military implications drawn by the French, is Joseph Spengler, *France Faces Depopulation* (Durham, N. C.: Duke University Press, 1938), Chapters VI and X.

argued that the decline in the birth rate had already made it necessary to raise the percentage of inductions from forty-three per cent of the total annual contingent in 1900 to almost fifty-three per cent in 1909 and that this, in turn, meant that the ranks of the army were being filled with the physically deficient and weak.[63]

Parenthetically, it should be noted, the first concrete result of these fears was the attempt made to extend conscription to the natives of French colonial possessions and to create what General Charles Mangin named *la force noire*. Advocates of overseas conscription claimed that such a policy was the only way to escape the consequences of reduced contingents and that it would also be a logical extension of the principle of the nation in arms upon which all French military institutions were based.[64] But although many of the proponents of overseas conscription were good republicans, the concept to be exported differed sharply from the one that was in domestic circulation. The idea of colonial conscription contained no egalitarianism, and almost the entire emphasis was upon the possibility of obtaining more soldiers. Republicans, in fact, specifically argued that the black soldier was not to be considered a citizen and that there was no necessity to grant civic rights to natives simply because they might be compelled to serve in the ranks of the French army.[65] Thus, the familiar republican theory that citizenship and conscription were inextricably bound together formed no part of the case for compulsory service in French colonies.

[63] *J.O.C. Doc.*, July 11, 1907, No. 1233, pp. 1441 ff. See also Colonel Charles Mangin, *La Force noire* (Paris: Hachette, 1911), pp. 82-90 and Bertillon, *Dépopulation*, p. 20.

[64] *J.O.C. Doc.*, July 11, 1907, No. 1233, pp. 1441-42. The objectives of the program were ably put forth by Mangin, *Force noire*, pp. 97-101, 283, 312. A useful summary is Achille Sébe, *La Conscription des indigènes d'Algérie* (Paris: Larose, 1912), pp. 22-43.

[65] *J.O.C. Doc.*, July 13, 1908, No. 2037, p. 753; Mangin, *Force noire*, pp. 239 ff. But despite this pressure, little was accomplished prior to 1914, though a decree of 1912 did establish conscription in Algeria. Many feared a possible uprising of "janissaries" or objected on the grounds that colonial conscription would be harmful to economic development.

However, the principal result of the widespread fear that a declining birth rate would seriously affect the army was that conservative military critics obtained a better hearing for their views. Now they could argue with considerable effect that if France was to have as many men on active duty as Germany, if units were to be kept at their authorized strength, and if the ranks were to be filled only with men who were physically fit, then the only remedy for the decreasing size of the annual contingents was to lengthen the term of service. To meet this argument the republicans and their allies could only resubmit their familiar thesis that French security depended upon making the fullest possible use of the reserves.

Particularly helpful to the conservative cause was a significant development of French military theory in the years immediately prior to 1914. A new school of theorists within the army began to insist that only the offensive could produce victory in war, that all tactics must be offensive tactics, and that every improvement in weapons worked to the advantage of the army on the attack. The motto of Colonel Grandmaison and the other "Young Turks" who developed the credo of the *offensive à outrance* was that "the French army, returning to its traditions, no longer knows any law other than the offensive." As Marshal Foch later wrote:

There had been deduced from our autumn maneuvers and colonial wars a single formula for success, a single combat doctrine, namely, the decisive power of offensive action undertaken with the resolute determination to march on the enemy, reach and destroy him. . . . Nothing had been so persistently preached to generals and regimental officers as well as to private soldiers as the power of morale, and above all, of the will to conquer; and this had been done with a total absence of either qualification or discernment.[66]

---

[66] Ferdinand Foch, *The Memoirs of Marshal Foch*, trans. Colonel T. Bentley Mott (New York: Doubleday, Doran, 1931), p. lvii. For critical accounts of the ideas of Grandmaison and the "Young Turks", see Hoffman Nickerson, *The Armed Horde, 1793-1939* (New York: Putman, 1940), p. 224, Boucher, *Les Doctrines*, pp. 132-37, and General de Trentinian, *The General Staff in 1914* (Paris: Fournier,

Moreover, many of the leaders of French political life were influenced by the "Young Turks" and subscribed to the doctrine of the unlimited, unqualified offensive which had become the *mot du jour* in military circles.[67]

This revival of interest in offensive warfare inevitably undercut much of the logic upon which the republicans had based their concept of the nation in arms. In the first place, the republican army was, by the admission of republicans themselves, primarily designed for defensive warfare. But now it appeared that, if victory was to be achieved, France must have an army geared for the offensive and for immediate attacks upon the enemy. Military theorists could argue with some plausibility that if an army was to succeed in the offensive, its troops must be skilled in the art of maneuver, especially competent in the handling of weapons, and particularly trained to work together. From this line of reasoning it was but a simple step to the conclusion that the reserves were unsuited for the offensive and that the existing system of two-year service did not provide sufficient training for French conscripts. Thus, like the arguments deduced from the declining birth rate, theories of the offensive led directly to demands for an additional year of military service on the grounds that such a change would make conscripts into better soldiers and, by providing an additional class of men on active duty, would make it unnecessary to rely upon untrustworthy reservists. To be sure, none of the theorists of the *offensive à outrance* denied the need for a mass army, but they did insist on a longer term of service, the maintenance of a full cadre of professional soldiers, and a minimum employment of reserves in battle.

1927; unpublished English translation by G. de Lagerberg for the U. S. Army War College), pp. 26 ff. For evidence that Foch at least partially subscribed to the doctrine he later condemned, see Stefan T. Possony and Etienne Mantoux, "DuPicq and Foch: The French School," in Earle, *Modern Strategy*, pp. 226 ff.

[67] See the statement of President Fallières that the offensive alone was suited to the French temperament, cited in *Mémoires du Maréchal Joffre* (2 vols., Paris: Plon, 1932), I, 34. A similar admission was made by Adolphe Messimy, the French War Minister in 1914, in his *Mes Souvenirs* (Paris: Plon, 1937), pp. 114-15.

To buttress their case, military writers incessantly tried to convince the French people that the German army intended to place no trust in its own reserves. The first blow of a new war would be struck by units of the German regular army, secretly assembled on the frontier, and, because few if any reserves would be employed, capable of launching an immediate offense into the very heart of France. This was the famous *attaque brusque*—an attack which, it was claimed, could never be repelled by an army of reservists. Obviously, in creating the fear of such an onslaught, military writers possessed another powerful argument to turn against the republican concepts, for the only solution which they envisaged to the *attaque brusque* always involved an increase in the size of the active army and an extension of the length of service.[68]

As early as 1910-11 both the questions of offense versus defense and of the employment of the reserves had produced a crisis within the top echelon of the French command itself. General Michel, then Commander-in-Chief designate of all French forces, began to fear that, if war came, the Germans would launch their principal attack on France through neutral Belgium. He also reached the conclusion that the French army was not large enough to withstand such an offensive. He therefore proposed to scrap the existing plans for the concentration of the army and to substitute for them a purely defensive plan of operations in which the number of reservists employed as front-line troops would be twice as great as in any preceding system. His proposal was simplicity itself: each regiment of the active army would be assigned a corresponding regiment of re-

---

[68] As early as 1905, at the time of the first Moroccan crisis, fear of an *attaque brusque* was manifest in the French cabinet. When Delcassé attempted to argue that the British might provide military aid in the event of war, the Council President answered by reading a report of General Négrier which stated that French frontier defenses were incapable of withstanding a German *attaque brusque*. See Ministère des Affaires Étrangères, *Documents diplomatiques français (1871-1914)* (32 vols., Paris: Imprimerie nationale, 1929 ——), 2nd series (1901-11), VI, 601-07. For extended discussions of the *attaque brusque*, see, in particular, the various writings of Captain Gilbert that have previously been cited.

serves, and at the hour of mobilization the two regiments would be amalgamated into a single brigade. In support of his plan of fusion Michel argued, "The radical separation between active and reserve units was once justifiable when we had a five-year service; but with a two-year service, it no longer has any reason for existing." [69] But at a stormy meeting of the *Conseil Supérieur de la Guerre* not a single one of Michel's colleagues voted to accept his scheme. Michel himself shortly resigned. Joffre, who replaced him as head of the French army, developed a plan of concentration and operations based upon ideas almost diametrically opposed to those of Michel. Under Joffre's direction the French staff produced the famous Plan 17 which not only committed all French units to the offensive in August of 1914 but which also made less use of the reserves than earlier war plans. [70]

The crisis within the French High Command was in itself an indication that the theories of offensive warfare, the increased international tensions, and the concern for the French birth rate were all combining to give new life to the conservative interpretation of the nation in arms. There were significant foreshadowings of a changed parliamentary attitude as early as 1912, but it was the debate over the three-year conscription bill,

---

[69] Ministère de la Guerre, État-major de l'armée, *Les Armées françaises dans la grande guerre* (10 vols. in 66, Paris: Imprimerie nationale, 1922-36), Vol. I, Part I, (Annexe), 13. The documents reproduced here give the details of the Michel scheme of February, 1911 as well as the minutes of the meeting of the *Conseil Supérieur de la Guerre* that rejected the plan.

[70] For further details, see the account of Messimy, the War Minister at the time of the Michel crisis, in his *Souvenirs*, pp. 72-76 and Joffre's own version of the incident in his *Mémoires*, I, 7-11. The issue took on a new importance after the French defeats of August, 1914, and since then the French Left has insisted that if Michel had remained in command, the reserves would have been given more prominence, the German invasion through Belgium would have been checked, and, indeed, there would have been no need for the "miracle" of the Marne. See, among others, General Alexandre Percin, *1914—Les Erreurs du haut commandment* (Paris: Michel, 1920), pp. 7-20, 42 ff. and General Émile Taufflieb, *Souvenirs d'un enfant d'Alsace* (Strasbourg: Imprimerie Alsacienne, 1934), pp. 267-69. It would be beyond the compass of this book to point out the many details that show this view to be an oversimplification of the facts. Michel did not trust the reserves as far as Socialists have claimed, nor did Joffre misuse them to the extent that the Left has insisted.

introduced early in 1913 as a government measure, which clearly indicated that the atmosphere in French military debates was far different from what it had been barely a decade earlier.[71]

One of the principal differences between the ideas expressed in 1913 and those of previous years was that, while the advocates of preceding laws had stressed the social and political aspects of conscription, the men who framed the three-year project concentrated upon the argument that the international situation and the proven need for a larger number of men on active duty made it mandatory to raise the term of service. To the Minister of War, Étienne, it seemed obvious that the present danger was such that no past formula of the nation in arms could be considered either sacred or untouchable.[72] Drawing on the fund of ideas so frequently expressed by conservatives in recent years, he went on to insist that the decline in the size of the annual contingents made it impossible to obtain more soldiers as long as the two-year law remained in force and that it was highly dangerous to place too much faith in the reserves. The government's objective was clearly to increase the number of effectives and to have three classes under arms at all times. So strong was this desire that the original bill was withdrawn in favor of a measure, proposed by Joseph Reinach, which established tables of minimum strength for all units and decreed that none should drop below this level.[73]

[71] There are many competent accounts of the political struggle around the three-year law. Most of the argument centers around issues secondary to the purposes of this book, such as whether it was the German law of 1913 which provoked the French response or whether, as the French Left has claimed, the three-year bill was long nurtured in "reactionary" bosoms. For the former view, see Joffre, *Mémoires,* I, 85 ff. and Raymond Poincaré, *Au service de la France* (10 vols., Paris: Plon, 1926-33), III, 144 ff. For the views of the orthodox republicans and Socialists, see Georges Michon, *La Préparation à la guerre: la loi de trois ans* (Paris: Rivière, 1935), pp. 93 ff. By far the best study of the role of Poincaré, the key figure in these affairs, is Gordon Wright, *Raymond Poincaré and the French Presidency* (Stanford: Stanford University Press, 1942), pp. 77 ff.

[72] *J.O.C. Doc.*, March 6, 1913, No. 2587, p. 170. See also report of Chamber army commission, *ibid.*, May 14, 1913, No. 2716, p. 321.

[73] For the Reinach counter-project, see Joseph Reinach, *Mes Comptes rendus* (4 vols., Paris: Alcan, 1911-18), IV, 174 ff.

What lay behind these demands was a fear that the German army, enlarged by recent legislation, was more than a match for the French forces. The arguments designed to prove French inferiority were drawn from the current storehouse of conservative military theories. Much was made of the possibility of an *attaque brusque*—President Poincaré was, in these months, apparently hypnotized by reports from the French military attachés in Berlin, dispatches which indicated that the Germans were prepared to launch an immediate, all-out attack with their regular army.[74] The bill's proponents also consistently argued that the Germans would make a minimum use of their reserves and, consequently, would have an army far superior to that of the French.[75]

Moreover, despite their interest in increasing the size of the active army, the proponents of the three-year bill attached even greater importance to the idea that an additional year of training was essential if French soldiers were to be the equals of the Germans in fighting qualities and if France was to avoid having an army in which unreliable reserves were the dominant element. In other words, it was not simply a question of increasing the number of men under arms; the advocates of a three-year service, influenced by the theorists of the *offensive à outrance*, believed with the *Conseil Supérieur de la Guerre* that soldiers with only two years of training were inadequately prepared to fight a modern war and that an extra twelve months would increase the quality of the army.[76] And they felt, too, that their scheme provided a way to minimize the role of the reserves.

[74] See, for instance, the dispatches No. 494 of March 1, 1913 and No. 551 of March 11, both reprinted in *Documents diplomatiques*, 3rd series, (1911-14), V, 598 and 668 ff. Much information on Poincaré's fear of an *attaque brusque* is to be found in Maurice Paléologue, "Comment le service de trois ans fut rétabli en 1913," *Revue des deux mondes*, XXVII (May 1, 1935), 76 ff.

[75] The Chamber *rapporteur* was particularly insistent on the subject of this danger, *J.O.C. Doc.*, May 14, 1913, No. 2716, p. 322. See also Reinach, *Mes Comptes*, IV, 208-13.

[76] Joffre, *Mémoires*, I, 100; Reinach, *Mes Comptes*, IV, 234-36.

Nevertheless, the doctrine of the nation in arms was so widely accepted that the "reaction" of 1913 went no further. There was never any question of rejecting conscription, nor was it argued that a soldier could not acquire a good basic training in two years—rather, it was claimed that men needed an extra year of service in order to acquire the skills needed for offensive warfare. Likewise, the advocates of the three-year law vehemently insisted that they had no desire to attack the "sacred" principle of 1905: an equal length of service for all regardless of social position or status.[77] And even the warmest adherents of the reform claimed that they were not repudiating the reserves—their point was that the reserves, though admittedly an important part of the national defense organization, were not competent to meet the first shock of an enemy attack.[78]

The counterarguments developed by republicans and Socialists require little discussion. These men, in essence, claimed that the three-year service would not add a single soldier to the total number of men available at mobilization but that, on the contrary, it would put an intolerable burden on the public. As far as they were concerned the solution to the French military problem was to make a greater utilization of the reserves within the traditional framework of a short-term service. Jaurès, reintroducing his scheme for a national militia, insisted that a better organization of the reserves was the only viable means of securing French defenses.[79] Many republicans, too, took the same line and, under the leadership of Joseph Caillaux, remained true to the old formula: "Follow the organization of the nation in arms which has been undertaken but which remains unachieved and incomplete." [80] As one Radical Socialist put it, there was no need for any new conscription law, since the problem "is a simple matter of organization which it is easy

---

[77] *J.O.C. Doc.,* May 14, 1913, No. 2716, p. 322.
[78] Joffre, *Mémoires,* I, 96; Reinach, *Mes Comptes,* IV, 234.
[79] Weinstein, *Jaurès,* pp. 138 ff.
[80] Joseph Caillaux, *Mes Mémoires* (3 vols., Paris: Plon, 1942-47), III, 63.

to resolve if the military authorities and the government really want to take the trouble." [81]

Yet despite the familiar ring and appeal of such words, not a few of the deputies of the Left abandoned their traditional views and supported the three-year bill. For the first time since 1872 republican "unity" was broken in debates and voting on a conscription bill. Moreover, although the principal backing for the measure came from center and right-of-center parties, it was the disaffection of numerous republican and quondam Socialists which made the differences and which resulted in passage of the legislation. [82]

Whether or not the French people accepted the new interpretation of the nation in arms was then—and remains today—a matter of conjecture. Though the law easily passed the legislature, political passions were raised to fever heat, and Caillaux and Poincaré engaged in a long political battle centering around the three-year law. [83] It was a principal issue in the elections of the spring of 1914, elections in which the Left won significant victories. But so many other factors affected the vote that it is extremely doubtful if the Leftist parties achieved their successes simply because the French people did not approve the changes in the military laws. [84] However, the outcome of the election

[81] Jean-Louis de Lanessan, *Nos Forces militaires* (Paris: Alcan, 1913), p. 343, one of the bitterest accounts of the struggle over this law. See also Édouard Herriot, *In Those Days*, trans. Adolphe de Milly (New York: Old and New World Publishing Corp., 1952), p. 268.

[82] In the elections of 1910, more than two hundred new deputies had been elected on the radical and republican tickets, but their objective at the time appears to have been to put an end to anticlerical and labor agitation and to avoid further reform legislation. Despite their election under the radical banner, they were men of moderate tastes, and many of them provided the necessary votes for the three-year law. François Goguel, *La Politique des partis sous la IIIe République* (Paris: Éditions du Seuil, 1946), pp. 181-82, 186.

[83] Wright, *Poincaré*, pp. 82 ff.; Caillaux, *Mémoires*, III, 61 ff.

[84] Goguel, *Politique des partis*, p. 188. The views of Colonel Mott, the American military attaché, are of some interest though obviously inspired by "sources" of more than questionable accuracy. Mott believed that the law had been motivated by nothing more than the German threat and insisted that the French public strongly supported it. He cabled to Washington, "In connection with the above

did produce a first-rate political crisis which made it very doubtful if the new law could long survive.

The crisis was not resolved until mid-June of 1914 when
René Viviani succeeded in establishing a ministry which adopted
a compromise position on the three-year law. The legislation
was to remain in force until such time as international conditions permitted change. And the thankless task of Adolphe
Messimy, the new Minister of War, was to find a formula which
all parties could accept.[85]

Thus the long fight between partisans of two different types
of armies and two different concepts of the nation in arms was
still far from over. What the outcome would have been if
there had been no war no one can say. The French had carried
their long, domestic political battle down to the last minute of
the last hour, and only the outbreak of war proved to be a
solvent for their dispute. When overnight party politics
changed to the *union sacrée,* when active, reservist, and territorial soldiers were fighting for their lives and the life of France,
then, and then only, did theoretical arguments over the form
and composition of the army cease to matter.

There was, of course, always a genuine issue involved and, on
these matters, there was always room for honest differences of
opinion. Nor can it be denied that in the years from 1872-1914
the French, amid the oratory and bickering, did in fact do
much to reform an army which, due to its aristocratic leanings,
was out of touch with the republican institutions of the state.
Yet at the same time the suspicion remains that in these long and
arduous debates the French demonstrated their pecular facility

---

measure is to be noted an outburst of patriotic approval all over the country in approval of the government's action" (Dispatch 1906, 9 April 1913, File 7019 Second
Section, General Staff, War Department, National Archives, Washington, D. C.).
In September of 1913 he was willing to admit that "It is true that there was opposition from labor unions of anarchistic tendencies and from the red socialistic
groups, but their clamor was silenced by the patriotic enthusiasm of the people at
large and the firm attitude of all the more conservative elements of parliament"
(Dispatch 2014).

[85] Messimy, *Souvenirs,* p. 124.

for "historical thinking" and for refighting old battles long after the immediate issues had evaporated and that, by so doing, they had hindered as much as helped their military evolution.

III

1914: The Economic Consequences of a Military Theory

IT IS A COMMONPLACE of the contemporary world that 1914 marked the opening of the era of total warfare. Since that date war has involved, provided the belligerents so choose, not just armies but entire populations, not just military weapons but industrial systems, not defeat but near annihilation. The waging of the First World War made it necessary, for the first time in history, for the belligerents to harness their total productive forces in the interest of their armies. And the only real victor in that four-year struggle was the machine: the output of factories was as important as the size and quality of armies; the productivity and the potential of a nation's economic system became critical elements on military balance sheets; and the war of attrition against the home front produced victories denied military commanders in the field. During the years 1914-1918 war had passed, in the words of the historian James Shotwell, from its military into its industrial phase. And, since then, the concept of the nation in arms has implied the mobilization of industrial and economic resources as well as the mobilization of armies.

The generation which felt the full impact of the influence of industrialism upon the conduct of war was the generation which lived and died in the years 1914 to 1918. But perhaps no generation was ever less prepared for a long and costly war of attrition. The proof of this lack of both intellectual and physical preparation for total war is abundant and overwhelming.

On that August day when the mobilization placards went up throughout France, the very wheels of society seemed to cease turning. Factories and shops closed; a moratorium on all debts was declared; railroads stopped carrying civilian goods and civilian passengers. Chamber and Senate turned over the powers of government to the Viviani ministry, authorized the cabinet to rule by decree, and closed their doors without bothering to set a date for future meetings. Believing that war was the business of the generals, France settled back to give them full freedom to conduct the campaign. In brief, the commercial and business world shut down, political life came to an abrupt termination, and—in a very real sense—France herself adjourned, *sine die*, to await the news from the battlefront.

But once decisive victory had failed to emerge from the first great battles, the awakening was rude. General Joffre became suddenly aware that a month of fighting had consumed over half of the total stockpile of artillery ammunition and that replacement was impossible. He was forced to telegraph his field commanders in late September: "Rear at present exhausted. If consumption continues same rate, impossible to continue war failing ammunition in fifteen days. Cannot draw your attention too much to capital importance of this condition on which depends the fate of the country." [1] The Minister of War, Millerand, was just as suddenly informed that the army needed a production of 80,000-100,000 shells per day and that the current output was just over 12,000. He was forced to call an urgent meeting of all industrialists, whether metallurgists or not, whose factories had any sort of precision machinery that could be adapted to the feeding of the voracious appetite of the guns. [2]

---

[1] Lt. Colonel Charles Menu, *Applications de l'industrie* (2 vols., École Supérieure de Guerre, 1928-31), I, 8-9. This is a text used in Menu's course at the war school on the importance of industry in modern warfare. For an abbreviated summary of his discussion of the critical munitions shortages of the early autumn of 1914, see *The Influence of Industrial Production on Military Operations* (Washington, 1934), pp. 1-3, a translation prepared for the U. S. War Department of a speech that Menu delivered at the Centre des Hautes Études Militaires.

[2] General Louis Henry Baquet, *Souvenirs d'un directeur d'artillerie* (Paris: Charles-Lavauzelle, 1921), pp. 69-70.

Yet at the time of these desperate appeals for munitions much French industrial capacity was lying idle, and hundreds of thousands of men were unemployed pending the outcome of the war. Throughout France the mobilization of the army had closed fifty-two per cent of the industrial establishments and left unemployed some forty-two per cent of the industrial workers who were exempt from military call.[3] A total of but 52,000 workers had been assigned to the armament factories, such plants as Schneider and Creusot lost many of their skilled operatives to the army, and the majority of the officers of the *Direction d'artillerie,* the military agency which supervised the manufacture of armaments, had gone to join the ranks of combat units.[4] By mid-October the manpower situation alone was so critical that the generals in command of military regions were ordered to return any and all soldiers possessing certain skills as machinists to a central depot in Paris, and shortly afterwards many industrialists were authorized to go to the collecting points and select any of the returned men who could be employed in their factories.[5]

[3] André Créhange, *Chômage et placement* (Paris: Presses universitaires de France, 1927), p. 2; Arthur Fontaine, *L'Industrie française pendant la guerre* (Paris: Presses universitaires de France, 1924), pp. 53-61, 367 ff. (both in the series sponsored by the Carnegie Endowment for International Peace under the general heading, *Histoire économique et sociale de la guerre mondiale, série française.* Hereafter indicated as HESGM). Unemployment statistics were made on the basis of a prior allowance for the twenty-four per cent of the French male population which was mobilized.

[4] Menu, *Applications,* I, 351-54; Baquet, *Souvenirs,* pp. 38-45. Robert Pinot, *Le Comité des Forges de France au service de la nation* (Paris: Colin, 1919), p. 75, pointed out that the effect of mobilization on French metallurgical industries was particularly disastrous since many of the directors, engineers, and department heads of these firms were graduates of either the École Polytechnique or the École des Mines and hence held reserve commissions in either the artillery or engineers.

[5] At a later date industrialists were provided blank forms on which to write the names of workers needed for their operations, and such persons were released from the army. William Oualid and Charles Picquemard, *Salaires et tarifs* (HESGM) (Paris: Presses universitaires de France, 1928), pp. 48-49. See also Roger Picard, *Le Mouvement syndical durant la guerre* (HESGM) (Paris: Presses universitaires, 1927), pp. 64-65 and Pinot, *Comité des Forges,* p. 184 for further information on the allocations of personnel. An interesting though abbreviated account of this and other aspects of the French war effort is an otherwise unidentified document entitled

Lack of preparation for industrial and siege warfare was not uniquely confined to the manufacture of munitions. It was duplicated again and again—in the arrangements made to finance the war, to feed and employ the civilian population, or to assure continuity of essential production of all types. To chronicle this lugubrious history would be unnecessary; what needs to be said is that, as in 1870, the French had to resort to improvisation. Muddling through—or what the French call "Système D"—produced at high cost and with considerable waste the vast organization by which the French economy was brought to the service of the French armies.[6]

So far this book has discussed how and why the French succeeded in the years before 1914 in erecting a vast nation in arms formed by the conscription of the total male population into the national army and its reserve components. It has also indicated that when the French considered the problems of national defense, they focused their attention almost exclusively upon the issues arising out of compulsory military service and, further, that they were primarily concerned with the social and political aspects of conscription. But, at this point, some further questions must be posed. Why, in view of their awareness of the need to organize their military manpower, were the French not equally aware of the need to organize their economy for war? Why did the concept of the nation in arms have nothing more than military conscription as its frame of reference, and why did it have no economic implications? Why did it not imply, as it does today, the mobilization of economic resources and the endless array of controls, regulations, and decrees which gear a national economy for the purposes of war? Why, in short, did the French stop short on the road to total war?

The French Economic Effort in the World War, a paper translated for the Military Intelligence Division, U. S. Army, during the war and now in the National War College Library.

[6] For an over-all survey see Shepard B. Clough, *France: A History of National Economics* (New York: Scribners, 1939), Chap. Eight, and Pierre Renouvin, *The Forms of War Government in France* (HESGM) (New Haven: Yale University Press, 1927).

Or, to ask a final question, is it possible that the prevailing theory of the nation in arms itself led the French to anticipate a type of war which failed to materialize and, moreover, served to keep them unaware of the role of industrial production and economic resources in modern war?

The French themselves asked these same questions not only during the war but after its conclusion. In 1919 a parliamentary investigating committee sat for long months collecting evidence from a wide variety of persons who had been important in planning national defense policies or in executing these plans at the outbreak of war. The whole scope of French war planning was not under study, but the commission, nominally empowered only to investigate "the role and situation of metallurgy," operated over a large area. In particular, the parliamentary commission set out to learn why the region in Eastern France known as the Briey Basin had been captured, almost without fighting, in the opening week of August, 1914, and, of greater significance, how the loss of this area with its mines and factories had hampered the French war effort. The answers that were produced, while confined to a relatively restricted field, throw a revealing light upon the lack of awareness in pre-1914 France of the relationship between economics and military planning and also upon the French failure to incorporate economic factors into their theories of the nation in arms.[7]

7 *J.O.C. Doc.*, 1919, No. 6026 (Annexe to the session of April 16, 1919). This report was separately published as *Procès-verbal de la commission d'enquête sur le rôle et la situation de la métallurgie en France* (Paris: Imprimerie de la Chambre des Députés, 1919). The commission report was over a thousand pages in length, and it covered a wide range of topics, from economic policies to military strategy and diplomatic dealings. Former premier Viviani testified on the origin and purpose of the famous ten-kilometer withdrawal of 1914; an embittered General Michel reported how his rejected mobilization and concentration plan of 1911 would have spared France the loss of her territories and forestalled the Belgian invasion; "Papa" Joffre was called upon to explain his strategies and the 1914 failures. There were charges that the Comité des Forges, through agents with low military rank but high political influence, prevented the aerial bombardment of its properties—and this, in turn, has frequently provided ammunition for those who wished to "expose" the nefarious practices of that villain of the 1930's—the "munitions maker." See, for instance, Clarence Streit's *"Where Iron Is, There is the Fatherland!"* (New York: Huebsch, 1920), a typical exposé which makes great use of the Briey findings.

In 1914 the Briey basin was located on the frontier between France and German-controlled Lorraine. Ever since the end of the Franco-Prussian War the strategy-conscious Germans had realized that Briey occupied a point of land which would be of great military value in any future war. Here, actually within range of the German guns situated in and around the fortress city of Metz, there grew up after 1885—particularly between 1910 and 1914—a complex of mines and factories which comprised an important percentage of the total French iron production. All of France, for instance, produced twenty-one million tons of iron ore in 1913, of which nineteen million came from the department of Meurthe and Moselle; the Briey area, within that department, produced fifteen million tons—that is, approximately seventy-five per cent of the total French tonnage. Some seventy per cent of France's production of pig iron came from the eighty-five blast furnaces located in this department, and fifty of these furnaces were in the Briey basin. This concentration had been a recent development. As late as 1897, Briey produced only four million tons of ore, and by 1909 the total was only two million tons greater. The tremendous expansion from six to fifteen million tons of ore had actually taken place within the three years from 1909 to 1912.[8]

One would imagine that such an industrial concentration, occurring on the German frontier and at a time when international tensions were increasing, would have drawn the attention of military planners or of officials of government. But, although in the thirties the French were to construct the Maginot Line to stand guard over the area, prior to 1914 Briey and its environs received no special attention. In fact, as the invading

---

[8] For the over-all development of Briey and an account of the industrial concentration in the region, see Lucien Brocade, "Le Développement économique de la Lorraine française," *La Réforme sociale* (Jun., 1913), 727-45. Statistics are taken from testimony presented to the investigating commission, *J.O.C. Doc.,* No. 6026, Part I, pp. 1-5, 24-25, 73 ff., and 222 ff. Despite many veiled hints that the industrial concentration was due to the sinister collaboration of Franco-German "big business," it appears that the rapid build-up was actually the result of locational competitive advantages.

German army swept through Belgium to the gates of Paris, Briey was overrun in the opening campaign of 1914. There was in truth no defense of Briey—the *couverture,* units placed on the frontier to guard against the dreaded *attaque brusque,* took up its main defensive positions on the heights of the Meuse and was assigned the mission of protecting the assembly and concentration of the French Third Army. That army, in accordance with the terms of Plan 17 and its variants, undertook an offensive through the Ardennes to smash what Joffre and his advisers thought would be a limited German operation in Belgium.[9] After the true character of the German wheel through Belgium became apparent and the great battle of Charleroi had been fought and lost, then orders came through to break off the engagements in the East and rush for the defense of Paris. Thus, after the Marne, when the western front was at length stabilized, the line of trenches which stretched from the North Sea to the Swiss border passed near Verdun and left the Briey area well in the rear of the German positions. It was not recaptured until the closing weeks of the war.

As the war dragged on and the demands for increased war production mounted, the French began to realize what the occupation of their eastern industrial regions was costing them in terms of armaments. Fifty-five per cent of the French coal resources lay behind the German lines, and another twenty per cent was in areas too close to the battlefront for regular mining operations to be feasible. In addition, the French had lost eighty per cent of their iron ore, eighty per cent of their iron production, and seventy per cent of their facilities for manufacturing regular-grade steel.[10] Under such circumstances many people began to wonder just why and how Briey had been lost virtually without a fight. There was agitation in the chambers and in

[9] Based on scattered testimony by French military leaders, particularly Joffre in *ibid.,* Part II, pp. 135 ff. See also General Charles Lanrezac, *Le Plan de campagne français et le premier mois de la guerre* (Paris: Payot, 1921), an account of these operations written by the commander of the Fifth Army who was ousted by Joffre.

[10] Statistics from Menu, *Applications,* I, 355.

some sections of the press for a limited offensive to recover the area from which, it was claimed, the Germans obtained the production which enabled them to remain in the war.[11] After the Armistice a routine interpellation on the government's metallurgical policy led to a speech by a deputy from Calvados, Fernand Engerand, in which he charged that all the troubles of the French mining and metals industries could be traced back to the capture of Briey in 1914.[12] This, in turn, led after a stormy session to the establishment of the previously mentioned investigating commission whose task it was to discover why the region had been lost and what the significance of that loss had been.

In the course of a prolonged investigation, one conclusion became apparent: no responsible member of the High Command or of the government had truly foreseen that a region producing great quantities of ore and finished iron goods would be of any value to France in the prosecution of a war. The evidence was essentially negative but no less significant. Given the publicity attendant upon the inquiry and the general interest in the subject, any witness would have been acclaimed a great prophet had he been able to present convincing evidence that he had not only realized the importance of Briey but had also

[11] A typical example of the rabble-rousing popularized literature on Briey is a series of three anonymous articles, "La Guerre et le bassin de Briey," *Nouvelle Revue*, XXVII-VIII (Feb. 1, May 15,, and Jun. 1, 1917), 139-62, 268-74 and 193-214. These articles maintained that Briey was of incalculable value to the Germans and implied that anyone who disagreed was guilty of a deliberate lie. See also the report of Senator Bérenger in *J.O.C. Doc.*, No. 6026, Part I, pp. 222 ff. These arguments rested in large part on the numerous demands for the annexation of Briey that were made during the war by German industrialists who claimed that the region was vital to the German war effort. French officials accepted these claims at face value, but the commission investigation tended to show that the Germans had, in fact, not depended on Briey and that the petitions were more than likely just an aspect of Pan-German propaganda. See *ibid.*, Part II, pp. 62-63, 83 ff. and Pinot, *Comité des Forges*, p. viii. This latter book, indeed, seems to have been written in large part to offset the unfavorable publicity attending the parliamentary investigation.

[12] Engerand also wrote a number of books on the subject, the principal of which was *La Bataille de la frontière* (Paris: Éditions Brossard, 1920), another book filled with the conventional charges about Briey and how it was neglected.

taken concrete actions upon the basis of that assumption. But none could do so.

The arguments and testimony of Marshal Joffre, though based upon sound reasoning, were essentially those of a military man and were established almost exclusively upon strategic and tactical considerations. Briey, he maintained, had been indefensible because of its location under the guns of German-held Metz, and neither a strong *couverture* nor a series of fortifications could have made any difference. He claimed, in addition, that if the investiture of Metz—a part of the initial plan—had been a success, then there would never have been any "Briey question," but that these operations had failed because of the incompetence of the local commanders.[13] Yet in neither instance did his argument reveal any preoccupation with Briey and its industry by and for itself, nor did he indicate that Metz should have been made a special target because it menaced the industrial area on the French side of the frontier.[14]

Several prewar directors of French mines, themselves officials of the Ministry of Public Works, testified that while they had been personally worried about the concentration of industry upon an exposed frontier, none of them had ever called the attention of the Ministry of War or the High Command to this dangerous situation.[15] Adolphe Messimy, the former War Minister, stated that, after examining all the pertinent documents on file, he could find no evidence that either his ministry or the General Staff had ever studied the economic or industrial importance of Briey in connection with military plans.[16] Guy

13 *J.O.C. Doc.*, No. 6026, Part II, pp. 135 ff. His entire statement was reprinted in book form as *1914-1915—La Préparation de la guerre et la conduite des opérations* (Paris: Chiron, 1920).

14 Likewise, the account in his memoirs of the origins of Plan XVII are essentially strategical in content. Joffre, *Mémoires*, I, 141 ff.

15 *J.O.C. Doc.*, No. 6026, Part I, pp. 5-6, 13, 24-25 (Testimony of M. Weiss, Director of Mines, 1911-16, and M. Charguérand, the director from 1905 to 1910).

16 *Ibid.*, pp. 262-63. And he indicated that Briey had itself never appeared in any *couverture* plan.

de Wendel, president of the Comité des Forges, described how, at the outbreak of war, he had ordered a complete shutdown of all the blast furnaces he operated in Briey because the workers were leaving for the army and raw materials were ceasing to arrive. Asked by the commission's presiding officer if men of his acquaintance in the iron and steel business had ever discussed or thought about the possibility that the French metallurgical industry would play an important part in a future war, de Wendel responded, "In all sincerity, no." [17]

Evidence could be added to evidence, but the main features of the story would be no different. Frenchmen simply did not think that an area such as Briey would be essential to national defense until after it had been lost. In 1914 mobilization was an event which concerned only the armies, and the nation in arms was a concept which referred solely to the utilization of manpower in the military services.

Yet despite the validity of the findings of the Briey commission, the report of that group was not exhaustive. And to state that the French were not prepared for a war of attrition and had no plans to gear their economy to serve their armies is merely to state the obvious. The fact of the matter is that the relationship between war and the national economy, as envisaged by the men of 1914, was considerably more complex than the evidence so far presented would seem to indicate. In the first place, French military leaders—whose views were fully shared by public officials and responsible economists—had apparently sound reasons to expect that any general European war would be fought in such a way that the long-range economic potential of the country would not be a factor. Their reasoning and their anticipations were actually the logical consequence of the prevailing military theories of the prewar years. Hence, to understand why the concept of the nation in arms did not include a full consideration of economic and industrial matters, it is first

[17] *Ibid.*, pp. 50-51.

necessary to consider some of those theories and their consequences.

The military doctrine which prevailed in the French staff, a credo which differed but slightly from the accepted theories of the other Continental armies, was that henceforth all warfare would be unlimited, national warfare and that the goal of all military operations was the annihilation of the enemy forces on the field of battle. As the preceding chapter pointed out, two of the principal aspects of this doctrine were the need for a mass, conscript army and the belief that the offensive was the sole means to military victory. There was a third and even more important corollary: the conviction that future European wars would be of short duration. These three military axioms affected both plans and preparations for the war of 1914, and their net effect was to prevent the concept of the nation in arms from including within its scope any of the factors which might influence the conduct of a war except manpower.

Consider, for example, the faith in the mass army. To be sure, at the time of the enactment of the 1913 law French military leaders laid great stress upon the quality of the individual soldier, but these same officers continued to demand an army as large as that of Germany and insisted that the totality of French youth must be drafted. They were, in short, convinced that the conscript army, whatever its failings, was the only instrument which could achieve the total destruction of the enemy in battle. Hence, if for no other reason, the French officer corps accepted the idea of the nation in arms because it provided them, through conscription, with the masses of trained men that were necessary to put their theories of war into operation.

But the consequence was an emphasis upon manpower for the army—and upon manpower almost exclusively. The military leaders demanded more and more soldiers for their armies and, consequently, left less and less men available for industry and agriculture. This unending insistence upon an ever-increasing number of soldiers meant, in turn, that it was almost impossible to consider that there might be other uses for French manpower. In fact, the military pressure for a larger army was so strong in 1913 that the effect of the three-year law was to produce a drastic reduction in the number of deferments heretofore granted to men who performed vital, nonmilitary jobs of all sorts. Thus the military demand for a mass army, arising out of current theories of warfare, stood as a powerful block against the development of other ideas for the employment of manpower; it meant that French officers thought only of using men in the army and rarely considered that a man might be more valuable to the nation if he remained at his civilian job instead of joining his unit at the outbreak of war.

Similarly, the prevailing faith in the offensive not only affected French war preparations but also restricted their thinking about the nature of warfare within limited channels. The credo of the offense assumed that armies would be highly maneuverable, able to make rapid changes of position, and capable of a high degree of tactical flexibility. Accordingly, a large number of officers were convinced that heavy artillery had no place in offensive operations and in a war of movement. They were confident that the lightweight '75, with its ease of maneuver and flexibility, was the only fieldpiece that could be employed in the kind of operations they anticipated, and they were equally certain that heavy artillery would be a clumsy burden to an army on the offense. Moreover, these same officers were sure that a well-trained infantry could take its objectives with a minimum of assistance from other arms. The French command therefore assigned a secondary role to the artillery; it was regarded as a support weapon, and its role was to perform a series of rapid-fire operations on a multitude of numerous, fugitive targets— rather than, as actually happened in the First World War, to crush all enemy resistance by a saturation of high explosives. Thus, the credo of the *offensive à outrance* together with its corollary, the war of movement, led the French military leaders to develop but a modest artillery program based upon the '75 and left them unprepared for a war of material in which thousands of men and scores of factories were needed to build and supply artillery pieces of all calibers.[18]

The third principal element of French military thought prior to 1914 was the belief that any European war would be a conflict of short duration. Itself the logical consequence of confidence in the abilities of the mass army and of faith in the offensive, this belief in a short war was of the greatest significance because it limited the outlook of all those individuals who adhered to it. It led to the assumption that a war could be fought with existing stocks and prevented both military and political leaders from considering economic and industrial matters until it was obvious to all that the peril point had been reached and passed. Consequently, because the belief in a short war so restricted the outlook of the men who planned the French mobilization in 1914, it was perhaps the most significant reason why the concept of the nation in arms had a limited scope prior to the First World War.

The belief that any war between European great powers would be short was not only widely held but venerable and respected. In the first place, the wars which had attracted the

[18] On the artillery question the best summary of pre-1914 theories is General Frédéric Herr, *L'Artillerie* (Paris: Berger-Levrault, 1924), pp. 1-24, a work considered so authoritative that it was translated and published both in Germany and the United States. For representative opinions of a military writer who believed that using heavy fieldpieces was "like taking a club to kill a fly," see General Hippolyte Langlois, *Lessons from Two Recent Wars*, trans. for the British General Staff (London: H. M. Stationery Office, 1909), pp. 35, 119-22. It should, however, be noted that prior to 1914 French Socialists and Radical Socialists did demand a heavy-artillery program as an alternative to the three-year service bill. Likewise, shortly before the outbreak of war the army did initiate a heavy-artillery program, but because of delays and hesitations by various technical committees it never reached the production stage. There is a wide literature on this, particularly, Joffre, *Mémoires*, I, 60 ff., Baquet, *Souvenirs*, pp. 27-41, Georges Michon, *La Préparation à la guerre: la loi de trois ans* (Paris: Rivière, 1935), pp. 211-25, and General Frédéric Culmann, *Tactique d'artillerie* (Paris: Charles-Lavauzelle, 1937), pp. 27-30. During the war there were many one-sided articles in French periodicals which criticized the High Command for blindness in drawing up artillery programs, a typical example of which is the anonymous piece "L'Artillerie lourde avant la guerre," *Nouvelle Revue*, XXVIII (Apr. 15, 1917), 289-301.

attention of military theorists—and with which the French were most familiar—were the mid-nineteenth century campaigns of Prussia, and no one could deny that they had been carried out with neatness and dispatch. Since the Continent had witnessed no major war between any of its five great powers since 1870, the example of these quick and decisive victories possessed continuing authority. As Europeans were proud of their own military traditions and prowess, there was always a pronounced tendency to regard any war fought on other continents or by other peoples as a sort of biologic sport which, if it broke the pattern of short wars that had been established by Prussia, was of little or no consequence to Europeans. Moltke's reported comment that the American Civil War was not worth study since it had involved little more than the spectacle of two armed mobs chasing each other around the countryside was matched by the opinions of numerous French officers around the turn of the century who regarded the protracted length of the Boer War as the result of certain peculiarities and ineptitudes in the British ways of war.[19]

Added to the devotion to European precedent was the knowledge that the railroad had greatly speeded the tempo of military operations, for it had reduced the time necessary to mobilize and concentrate armies for the first blows. Hence the ability of

---

[19] Not, of course, that these wars were not studied and "lessons" derived therefrom. But writers were inclined to see what they wanted to see. General Langlois, for instance, in an attempt to show that the Boer War had not increased the strength of the defensive, argued that the length of that conflict arose from the fact that the armies were not comparable to European armies, that the military conditions did not approximate 1870, and that English lack of success arose from poor tactical preparation and faulty combat doctrine. See his *Tactical Changes Resulting from Improvement in Armament* (Paris: Charles-Lavauzelle, 1903; unpublished English translation by W. G. Penfield for the U. S. Army War College), pp. 4-13. Similarly, Captain Charles Condamy, a resolute foe of the militia, proved to his own satisfaction that the Boer War showed the insufficiency of English training methods and not the value of improvised armies. Captain Charles Condamy, *La Loi de deux ans et la leçon du conflit Franco-Allemand à propos du Maroc* (Paris: Charles-Lavauzelle, 1905), p. 36. The pronounced tendency of European military writers to regard non-European wars as exceptions to their own ideas is discussed at some length in Hoffman Nickerson, *The Armed Horde, 1793-1939* (New York: Putnam, 1940), pp. 201-03, 220.

armies to transport great numbers of men in a short time made it appear that decisive results could be expected at an early date.[20] And, finally, because the military leaders were convinced that the offensive would achieve immediate and smashing victories, they had yet another reason to anticipate an early, complete triumph.

The fact that European armies were huge conscript armies, formed on the principle of universal service, was in itself an argument for a short war. A sceptic like General Bonnal, one of the few theorists who still distrusted the mass army and its horde of reserves, believed that the first great battle fought between such armies would be decisive. He reasoned that the very magnitude and shock effect of such battles would make early and final victory [or defeat] a certainty. In fact, after the shock of an initial reverse, he said, the very size of a conscript army would cause its early collapse because panic and disorganization would spread through the entire military structure. Futile resistance by improvised troops might prolong the outcome, but the eventual victor would be decided less than a month after the opening of hostilities.[21] Other military writers, less hostile than Bonnal to the principle of the nation in arms, observed that in any war involving mass conscript armies there would be a tremendous increase in the loss of life. After a short period of hostilities, it was said, the belligerents would realize that they had suffered more casualties than they could

[20] As early as the seventies both Generals Vinoy and Favé had noted the ways in which the railroad had speeded the conduct of warfare. General Joseph Vinoy, *L'Armée française en 1873* (Paris: Plon, 1873), pp. 163-64, 304 ff. and General Ildephonse Favé, *Cours d'art militaire professé à l'École Polytechnique* (Paris: Dumaine, 1877), pp. 18-20.

[21] General Henri Bonnal, *La Prochaine Guerre* (Paris: Chapelot, 1906), pp. 47-48. He believed, in contrast, that a smaller professional army could fight a longer war because there was no danger it would collapse at the first battlefield reverse. Similar were the views expressed in General François de Négrier's article, "Le Moral des troupes," *Revue des dux mondes*, XXV (Feb. 1, 1905), 481-506, in which the argument advanced was that reservists would easily panic. These, it should be emphasized, were minority views, for, as indicated earlier, by 1900 the vast majority of French officers had come to accept the mass army.

endure, and, as a result, they would be forced to bring the conflict to an early halt.[22] One typical observer pointed out that the nation in arms meant that all the able-bodied men would be mobilized at the outbreak of war and employed in the struggle. Thus, if one army was defeated, unlike 1870, there would be no additional elements left in the country to prolong the war.[23] In short, a war involving mass conscript armies could not drag on over a period of years.

An equally important aspect of the short-war thesis was the belief that mobilization would produce such a shock to the life of the nation and to its economy that it was impossible to visualize a conflict of long duration. All the able-bodied men over twenty would leave their jobs in the factories and on the farms, and, under such circumstances, all normal business activities would cease. Those remaining at home would find commercial or business life impossible because, in addition to the sudden departure of millions of men, all transportation facilities would be reserved for the sole use of the armed forces. A society deprived of the normal flow of civilian goods and services could not withstand such intolerable conditions over an extended period of time—hence, war must be short. The French manual of 1913 which prescribed the authorized tactics in the handling of large units especially urged commanders to seek an immediate military decision on the grounds that the interruption of the nation's social and economic life made it mandatory to bring a war to a quick termination.[24] Other writers warned that even if a country could withstand the hardships imposed by the mobilization, it was impossible for the financial resources of any nation to be sufficient to pay the cost of modern war or to avert total economic collapse. Thus, even without a

[22] Lt. A. Froment, *La Mobilisation et la préparation à la guerre* (Paris: Librairie illustrée, 1887), p. 4.
[23] Colonel de la Panousse, "L'Organisation militaire," *Revue des deux mondes,* XXI (May 15, 1904), 335.
[24] Cited in Nickerson, *Armed Horde*, p. 244.

military decision, financial pressures would soon force one or all of the belligerents to sue for peace.[25]

The very logic of the nation in arms, with its mobilization of all men of military age, thus imposed a short war. If by some mischance the armies themselves should fail to achieve a speedy decision by force of arms, then economic and social dislocations would bring an early peace. As the future Allied Commander-in-Chief Foch explained in his famous book on strategy, any war simply had to be short because:

> These armies which we are putting into action are not professional armies, they are armies composed of civilians who come from all different careers, from all ranks of society, and have been completely taken away from the families, careers, and society which they cannot do without. War necessitates suffering, everywhere civilian life ceases when it begins. From all this it comes as a consequence that war cannot last a long time.... [26]

Likewise concurring in this logic was a young captain named Bernard Serrigny, an officer who published shortly before 1914 several books explaining the effect of war upon the French economy and who, in post-1918 France, was to be the principal military authority on economic mobilization. Serrigny, after studying the economic consequences of wars involving mass armies, reached the gloomy conclusion that unless future conflicts were of short duration, complete and total ruin would

---

[25] In addition to the writings of Captain Bernard Serrigny—shortly to be separately discussed—this paragraph is essentially based upon such sources as General Cosseron de Villenoisy, "La Nation armée, à propos de l'ouvrage du Baron von der Goltz," *Revue des deux mondes*, LXIV (Aug. 1, 1884), 545. de Villenoisy sharply rebuked the German theorist for imagining that a long war was possible since a condition "which absorbs all the force of a nation, to make them unproductive, cannot prolong itself." See also Froment, *Mobilisation*, pp. 5, 206-08, for arguments that the financial cost of war would make it short. The best discussion of the whole question is Lt. Colonel Henri Mordacq, *La Guerre au vingtième siècle* (Paris: Berger-Levrault, 1914), in which an entire chapter is devoted to the subject of the probable length of the next war and in which the opinions of many writers are cited (pp. 255-300).

[26] Ferdinand Foch, *Des Principes de la guerre* (Paris: Berger-Levrault, ed. of 1917), p. 37.

overtake the nations involved. And he prophesied without hesitation that the length of a war could be calculated with precision since each day that it lasted would add measurably to the intolerable costs and social disorganization. He thought that the side which lost the first battle might prolong its death agonies for another six months but that peace would come within ten to twelve months under any circumstances—though public opinion might well force it to come much earlier.[27]

Thus for a multitude of reasons the belief in a short war was dominant in pre-1914 military theory. General Bonnal—himself qualified to judge because of his official position and his own adherence to the credo—confessed in the midst of the First World War that neither France nor her opponents had visualized a war of attrition since almost all officers, unaware of the defensive powers of current armaments, had put their faith in the offensive and had expected a short war.[28]

There were of course dissenters, but, in many respects, they were men whose counterarguments amounted to a form of special pleading. General Mangin, the advocate of African conscription, maintained that it was folly to believe that early defeat would result from the loss of the first battles—but he wanted Frenchmen to believe that with time the hordes of his *force noire* could be brought into the struggle and right the balance.[29]

---

[27] Captain Bernard Serrigny, *Les Consequénces économiques et sociales de la prochaine guerre* (Paris: Giard and Brière, 1909), pp. 30-35. But at the same time he was making these gloomy prophecies Serrigny possessed many insights into the characteristics of modern war. He argued, for instance, that metallurgical industries could not be closed down in wartime and called for an increased number of deferments for men of military age who worked in such fields as mining, railroad operation, and credit and banking. Wartime France, he felt, would need the services of such men who, by staying on the job, would "fulfill their civic duty as well as on the most glorious of battlefields" (pp. 275-83). This latter principle was to be a fundamental aspect of the postwar concept of the nation in arms. See also Serrigny's earlier work, *La Guerre et le mouvement économique* (Paris: Charles-Lavauzelle, 1905), pp. 129-30, 151-62, 203-05.

[28] General Henri Bonnal, *Les Conditions de la guerre mondiale* (Paris: Boccard, 1916), pp. 168-71.

[29] "As long as we can keep a port and mastery of the sea, we must not despair of

Ardent admirers of the reservists, like Jaurès, claimed an initial reverse was not necessarily fatal—but they hoped to convince Frenchmen that the intervention of hundreds of thousands of citizen-soldiers could and would stem the German tide. Jaurès, for instance, charged that the military hierarchy insisted that a European war would be short because the officers distrusted the citizen-soldier and falsely imagined that a nation was irretrievably lost when its active army had sustained a defeat.[30] Others, aware that German strategy dictated a rapid campaign to crush France in a matter of weeks before the sluggish masses of Russia could be brought into operation, warned that to believe in the decisive character of the first battle was to play the enemy's game and might, if French armies did suffer initial reverses, lead to an unwarranted surrender.[31]

One of the more resolute opponents of the short-war thesis was Lt. Colonel Henri Mordacq, later a general officer who became Clemenceau's *chef du cabinet* during the war and who was regarded in the twenties as one of the more influential French military writers. In his *La Guerre au vingtième siècle,* a book published in 1914, Mordacq took sharp issue with those who believed in a short war. He scouted the idea that governments might run out of funds; he thought that the presence of huge numbers of reserves made a quick decision unlikely; and he believed that all governments were sufficiently aware of the need for supplies and equipment that there was little likelihood any

---

success. In the present state of Europe, the *force noire* will make the most formidable of adversaries." Charles Mangin, *La Force noire* (Paris: Hachette, 1911), p. 313.

[30] "Even after a serious and cruel defeat, even after the defeat of its best army, a nation which does not want to die is not lost." Within any country there were still a "multitude of resources" available for prolonging the defense until an invader's armies were spread so thin that his power was weakened. Jean Jaurès, *L'Armée nouvelle* (Paris: L'Humanité, ed. of 1915), p. 43. For the views of an earlier and militantly republican theorist who believed that the reserves of the nation could never be eliminated at a single stroke and that therefore a long war was feasible, see General Théodore Iung, *La République et l'armée* (Paris: Charpentier, 1892), pp. 86-7.

[31] As, for instance, General Langlois, cited in note appended to Mordacq, *Guerre au vingtième siècle,* pp. 299-300.

army would run short of material. Hence he argued that the accepted beliefs were wrong and that it was more probable that the next war would be one of long duration. But Mordacq was not essentially arguing from an economic viewpoint; rather, he utilized a few economic arguments to bolster his central thesis which was, simply, that it was psychologically dangerous to believe that a war could be won or lost in a matter of weeks. He wanted his compatriots to steel their nerves so that, in the event they were victims of a German onslaught, they would fight on until the weight of Russian numbers could make itself felt. Furthermore, though he so strongly argued against the short war, Mordacq reached interesting conclusions. "After a few months there will have been such a stoppage in industrial, economic, agricultural, and commercial life . . . that the governments will feel they have reached the very limits of exhaustion." He refused to predict whether this would occur after three, four, or five months, but he concluded that, if all the economic and social factors were taken into consideration, "a future war cannot last as long as certain wars of the past and cannot last more than a year." [32]

French economists, it would seem, not only did not challenge the theory of a short war but also wrote little which anticipated the ultimate military-economic relationships which came to pass between 1914 and 1918. They were of course aware that economic power was an important factor in war—as early as the Franco-Prussian War, Paul Leroy-Beaulieu wrote in the *Revue des deux mondes* that, despite the grave losses suffered in the opening battles of the war, France's thriving railroad network, superior financial resources, and more advanced economy gave her a long-run advantage over Prussia. [33] Nevertheless, the traditional liberal economists, schooled in the values of peace, prosperity, and free trade, tended to approach war from a stand-

[32] *Ibid.,* pp. 297-98.

[33] Paul Leroy-Beaulieu, "Les Ressources de la France et de la Prusse dans la guerre," *Revue des deux mondes,* LXXXIX (Sept. 1, 1870), 135-55.

point which frequently made their opinions mere platitudes. War, the liberal economist believed, was an evil which all right-thinking men should strive to avoid. To Émile Levasseur it was self-evident that "the soldier, who is unproductive, lives on the taxpayers' money and lives so dearly [that] he contributes in two ways to the impoverishment of his country since he not only does not produce wealth but also consumes it." [34] Hence when the liberal economist had to discuss the problem of war, he usually chose either to ignore it entirely or to dwell at length upon the harmful effects of war upon the political economy of nations.

The school of national economists, whose founding father was List and whose principal French theorist was Paul Cauwès, did not share the same opinions and did not ignore questions of national defense. These men argued that only a nation with a diversified economy could preserve its independence since industries capable of manufacturing war materials were absolutely essential to the prosecution of any successful war.[35] Hence a part of their argument for protective tariffs was founded upon the assumption that French national defense required protection for such basic industries as iron and steel. Cauwès, for instance,

[34] Émile Levasseur, *La Population française* (3 vols., Paris: Rousseau, 1889-92), II, 255. Another liberal economist, Léon Colson, confined the discussion of military affairs in his six-volume text to a condemnation of the economic effects of conscription. Léon Colson, *Cours d'économie politique* (6 vols., Paris: Gauthier-Villars, 1907-09), V, 144-49. See Edmund Silberner, *The Problem of War in Nineteenth Century Economic Thought* (Princeton: Princeton University Press, 1946) for an extended discussion of the reaction of liberal economists to military affairs. Silberner sums up the liberal attitude with these words: "For the liberals war is a phenomenon economically and socially harmful. In their view it is one of the greatest misfortunes that can befall a nation. . . . War is not only immoral but also stupid; it is in effect merely the natural state of man ignorant of the laws of political economy . . . it is an element purely destructive of national wealth and prosperity" (p. 280). Though most of his examples were drawn from the era of the "juste milieu" (Jean-Baptiste Say, Frédéric Bastiat, and Michel Chevalier), Silberner shows that the traditional antimilitarism of the liberals remained until the end of the century. See, for instance, his discussion of Frédéric Passy and Gustave de Molinari (pp. 105, 114-16).

[35] Silberner, *Problem of War*, pp. 284-87.

wrote that free trade enabled a few favored nations to obtain overwhelming industrial and military supremacy but that a system of tariff protection assured the independence of even those states which did not possess natural economic advantages.[36] But, although men like Cauwès were aware of the fact that economic strength produced military strength, they did not carry the discussion any further—probably because their essential interest was in tariffs and tariff legislation.

All economists, regardless of their particular outlook, were of course conscious that sound finances and solid credit were necessary in wartime. In 1870 Leroy-Beaulieu could write that the phrase, "Money is the nerve of war," was not of recent origin, and his confidence that France would ultimately defeat Prussia was in part based upon his belief that French financial resources were superior to those of the enemy.[37]

But the writers of texts in economics usually stopped at this point in their arguments. Even among the nationalist school of economists there was no discussion of the ways of gearing an economy to military purposes in time of war or of the nature of wartime economic relationships. "The economics of war," in short, was a branch of economics which did not develop until after the First World War had shown the need for it.

On the other hand, many an economist tended to agree with the military theorist that the outbreak of war meant dire injury to the French economic system and that, as a result, the conflict must be of short duration. Paul Leroy-Beaulieu, by 1914 a member of the Institute and editor of *l'Économiste français,*

---

[36] Paul Cauwès, *Cours d'économie politique* (4 vols., Paris: Larose, 1893), II, 501-02. The influence of Cauwès upon other national economists who believed tariffs necessary to maintain national defense is discussed in Rodolphe de Planta de Wildenberg, *Cauwès et l'économie nationale* (Dijon: Belvet, 1938), pp. 137 ff. Likewise, many of the arguments advanced in behalf of protective tariffs for French agriculture rested on the assumption that such duties would serve French military interests. See Eugene Golob, *The Méline Tariff: French Agriculture and Nationalist Economic Policy* (New York: Columbia University Press, 1944), pp. 137, 151.

[37] Paul Leroy-Beaulieu, "Les Ressources de la France et de la Prusse dans la guerre," *Revue des deux mondes,* LXXXIX (Sep. 1, 1870), 146.

was one who held this belief. Earlier, when he wrote his *Traité théorique et pratique d'économie politique*, he had restricted his account of wartime economics to a discussion of the reasons why armed conflict produced economic crises.[38] When August of 1914 arrived, Leroy-Beaulieu wrote in the columns of his review that, while it might be sanguine to expect a decision in less than three months, he thought it quite possible the war would end within six or seven. Even as late as the beginning of 1915 Leroy-Beaulieu was still of the opinion that the total duration of the war could not exceed a year. Similarly, he voiced the confident judgment that France would be the victor because the German economy would be unable to withstand the crisis provoked by mobilization and war for any long period of time. In October, 1914—when the munitions shortage was already forcing the country to resort to a wide variety of improvised manufacturing techniques—the noted economist held to the view that it was more important to find jobs for the men made unemployed by mobilization than it was to fill the vacancies in industries where workers had left to join the army.[39]

[38] Paul Leroy-Beaulieu, *Traité théorique et pratique d'économie politique* (4 vols., Paris: Guillaumin, 1896), III, 446-49.

[39] See Leroy-Beaulieu's articles for the week August 1-7 and October 2-8, 1914, reprinted from *l'Économiste français*, in *La Guerre de 1914, vue en son cours chaque semaine* (Paris: Delagrave, 1915), pp. 6-7, 78, 83-84. See also the citations in Michel Augé-Laribé, *L'Agriculture pendant la guerre* (HESGM) (Paris: Presses universitaires de France, 1925), p. 54. Augé-Laribé chose Leroy-Beaulieu's articles as representative of the views of French economists in 1914 and pointed out that the belief in a short war was prevalent everywhere. Although it is irrelevant to the French story, there was one individual who as early as the beginning of the twentieth century predicted that any general European war would be a stalemate. This man was a Polish-Jewish banker named Ivan de Bloch whose views were put forth in a multi-volume work on the nature of war—translated into English as *The Future of War* (Boston: Ginn and Co., 1899). Because he correctly anticipated the trench warfare of 1914-1918, de Bloch has frequently been acclaimed a minor military prophet (for instance, Nickerson, *Armed Horde*, pp. 231-32). But de Bloch's economic views were more "orthodox"—that is, he devoted his attention to showing the economic dislocations which would result from war, and he envisaged the actual economic mobilization of 1914-1918 so little that he believed that Russia, due to her lack of industrialization, was better suited than any other European power to wage a long war. (*The Future of War,* pp. xlii ff.).

That nearly all Frenchmen subscribed to the belief in a short war can be demonstrated though it would be of little value to do so. The fact that the Chamber of Deputies so readily adjourned *sine die* and had no plans to exercise a wartime function is sufficient evidence of the confidence of the legislators that the war would not be long; likewise, the fact that the principal financial step taken by the government was to decree a moratorium on all debts reveals the same assumption.[40]   The example of the French economists, which has just been discussed, points to the conclusion that specialists in other fields, instead of challenging the opinions of the military theorists on the character and duration of a major European war, actually confirmed the prevailing views.

Yet, in fairness to the French military and political leaders, it should be pointed out that these men were not as naive as many postwar writers have maintained.   None of the belligerents of 1914, for instance, was any more prepared for industrial warfare than the French.   When Rathenau attempted to organize the German economy for war, he encountered a situation as chaotic as that which existed in France.   Nor were the theories held by the French High Command on the nature and duration of warfare essentially different from those held by all Continental military authorities.   Moreover, it is not illogical to claim that the First World War could well have been as short as the theorists anticipated—the younger Moltke's modifications of Schlieffen's original conception of a sweep through Belgium may well have been the factor which deprived Germany of an early and overwhelming triumph.   Likewise, the series of books

40 See Renouvin, *Forms of War Government*, pp. 18-26. As early as 1912 Millerand had insisted, as spokesman for the government, that there were in readiness a whole series of decrees which assured the legal organization of the national defense at the outbreak of war. While he refused to discuss details, Millerand indicated that the sole objective of these decrees was to achieve victory and that the government believed the best policy was "to leave to the military authorities, charged with and responsible for the operations of war, full and entire liberty of action." Alexandre Millerand, *Pour la défense nationale* (Paris: Charpentier, 1913), pp. 139-41, reprint of a Senate speech of June 7, 1912.

published by the Carnegie Endowment for International Peace concerning the economic and social history of the war have furnished multi-volume proof that the dislocations and damages produced by the conflict were far more serious than even the most pessimistic of pre-1914 writers had anticipated.

In the last analysis, then, the failure of the French leaders reduces itself simply to the fact that, in drawing up their plans and estimates, they did not provide for a margin of error. That is, they did not envisage alternatives in the event the war was not speedily decided. And, more important, they did not realize the power inherent in the modern state to avert collapse by mobilizing both its peoples and its resources for the conduct of warfare.

The significance of the ideas which have been discussed in this chapter—the confidence in the mass army, the faith in the offensive, and, above all, the belief in a short war—was that they served not only to limit the scope of French war plans in 1914 but also to retard the evolution of the concept of the nation in arms. The effect of these prevailing beliefs can be seen in all those aspects of war planning in which there was an important relationship between economic and military factors. For, although the early months of the war would appear to deny it, ever since 1870 the men who drew up French war plans had been increasingly aware of the importance of industrial and economic factors in their planning. By 1914 there were in fact many and elaborate plans, and they involved a surprisingly large sector of the national economy. But they lacked scope and depth; they were oriented for short-run and not long-run needs. Because of the prevailing military theories, for instance, French railroads were exclusively valued for the speed with which they could transport millions of men to the battlefront. Factors of production, even industries producing war goods, were prized almost entirely for the assistance which they could provide prior to and at the time of mobilization. And, above all, it was believed that, with a minimum of help from private industry, a war could be waged with the materials on hand, that is, from existing stockpiles. Hence, while plans were precise and complex, they were exceedingly limited in scope. Hence, too, none of these plans constituted an economic or industrial mobilization.

That the French were not completely unaware of the military value of their national resources was indicated as early as 1877 when comprehensive legislation for wartime requisition was enacted. As part of the general military reform movement of the seventies, army commanders were authorized in time of war to requisition virtually any article which they considered essential for the supply, feeding, billeting, or clothing of their troops. They could, in addition, requisition the services of personnel needed to make these demands effective.[41] In the passage of such a law there was nothing essentially unique; the armies of the *ancien régime* had lived off the land, the French Revolution had found it necessary to rely upon requisition to feed and supply its forces, and the armies of Gambetta had been succored in similar fashion.[42] The sponsors of the 1877 law, therefore, encountered no difficulties in establishing precedents for their actions, or, for that matter, in pointing out that since the Germans possessed efficient requisitory legislation, it was advisable for the French to codify their own jumbled and insufficient laws on the subject.[43]

The significance of the 1877 law lay in its extended and sweeping scope. The legislators were not satisfied merely to em-

[41] The best study of this and subsequent French requisition laws is Maurice K. Wise, *Requisition in France and Italy* (New York: Columbia University Press, 1944). For details on the 1877 law, see pp. 9-13.

[42] *J.O.C. Doc.*, July 27, 1876, No. 380, pp. 6477-78.

[43] For the argument of the war minister, de Cissey, that German legislation was superior and that French laws were inadequate, see the original *exposé des motifs. Ibid.*, March 21, 1876, No. 21, p. 2735. It appears that from 1815 to 1870 the practice of requisition had fallen into abeyance because of excesses during the Napoleonic era and that, as a result, the Government of National Defense had had to resort to improvised decrees designed to solve specific emergencies. General Jules Lewal, *Études de guerre* (2 vols., Paris: Baudoin, 1889), I, 6.

power the military authorities to requisition a wide variety of enumerated goods and services; they added a blanket clause which permitted the requisition "of all the other objects and services the furnishing of which the military interest may require." Realizing the importance of communications, the deputies devoted an entire section of the law to the requisition of railroads and their personnel, both of which were to come under the complete control of the military command. An elaborate mechanism was set up to provide for the wartime requisition of privately owned horses, mules, and animal-drawn carts—according to the provisions of the law, military and civil officials were to make an annual census of animals and vehicles, to carry out frequent inspections, and to prepare lists of animals and equipment that were considered suitable for military use. The lawmakers also recognized that factories might be useful in a future war. They empowered the War Minister, as well as the commanding officers of armies and army corps, to requisition industrial establishments and to convert them, no matter what their normal manufactures might be, to the production of articles needed by the army.

The provisions of the law indicated that as early as 1877 the French War Ministry and military command realized that in time of war they might be forced to draw upon the resources of the national economy. Moreover, in the years between 1877 and 1914 the scope of this legislation was continually expanded —indeed, by the latter date the coverage was so complete that, aside from a few changes of detail, it was possible to wage a four-year war without enacting any further requisitory laws.[44] In 1900 requisition of merchant vessels and boats of all kinds was specifically authorized, and six years later the military authorities were given the power to commandeer the services of the inland waterways. In 1911 it was thought necessary to expand the terms under which industrial plants could be taken

[44] Wise, *Requisition*, p. 12.

over in the military interest; a decree in that year stated that the owners of such establishments might be compelled at the time of mobilization to furnish the military authorities with

all the resources of their operation in personnel, equipment, raw materials, and finished products, and to effectuate the production, manufacture, and repairs required for the service of the armies and the fleets, the establishments of war and navy, and the provisioning of fortified areas.[45]

When the automobile began to become an important means of transportation, this fact was likewise noted by the military authorities.   Procedures were established in 1909 by which automobiles could be requisitioned for military purposes, and, as in the case of four-footed means of transportation, there was an attendant paraphernalia of censuses, inspections, and classifications.

Yet however broad the concept of requisition in pre-1914 France might have been, these laws and decrees were not true parents of industrial or economic mobilization.[46]   In the first place, the Chamber seemed unaware of the implications of the requisition laws—as indicated by the fact that both in 1877, when the original law was passed, and in 1911, when the requisition of private industrial establishments was being considered, there was an almost complete absence of debate and discussion by the deputies.   To the legislators, requisition was a sort of insurance policy against the day when the needs of war might require many goods and services for which there had been no chance to make an adequate preparation.   The discussion of the original 1877 law, for instance, clearly indicated that the legislative interpretation of requisition was that it was something abnormal, something to be permitted only when the customary supplies and services were temporarily and unexpectedly in-

---

[45] *Ibid.*, p. 32.

[46] Though one writer could claim in 1905 that the powers of requisition were based upon the knowledge that modern war, "as it is conceived today comprises the utilization of all the forces of a nation,"—a point which, however, was not elaborated.   Charles Pont, *Les Réquisitions militaires* (Paris: Berger-Levrault, 1905), p. v.

sufficient. Indeed, one of the principal motives for enactment of the law was not simply to provide for the needs of the army but to make it legally possible, in the event of war, for property owners to obtain reasonable indemnities for any of their possessions which might be appropriated by the military forces. Moreover, the fact that the power to requisition was granted to army officers in the field rather than to agents of the civil government was an indication that requisition was a procedure designed to meet the immediate, pressing needs of the army and not a genuine forerunner of economic mobilization.[47]

French railroads early attracted the attention of the military authorities, and their utilization in wartime was long considered vital to the success of any mobilization plan. The Prussian victories in 1866 and 1870—campaigns in which Moltke achieved striking success through the movement of troops by rail—had made the military value of the railroad self-evident. The employment of the steam engine made it possible to plan every phase of troop movements and army concentrations with the greatest precision and accuracy. It thus became mandatory for every European war ministry to formulate detailed mobilization plans. Moreover, the need to coordinate plans for the military use of railroads had, in turn, much to do with the development of the general staff system.[48]

Even before the Franco-Prussian War there had been French officers who recognized the potential military value of the railroad. In 1859 the government and rail companies agreed that, if it was ever necessary to dispatch troops by train, the companies involved would put all their facilities at the disposal of the government at half of the normal rates.[49] After the Austro-Prussian War had again demonstrated the military value of the steam

[47] Wise, *Requisition*, pp. 10-11.

[48] Dallas D. Irvine, "The Origin of Capital Staffs," *Journal of Modern History*, X (Jun., 1938), 177-78.

[49] Gabriel Lafon, *Les Chemins de fer français pendant la guerre* (Paris: Rousseau, 1922), p. 37.

engine, Marshal Niel, then serving as War Minister, had appointed a commission to coordinate and systematize existing arrangements for wartime use of the French rail network. But Niel died before the work was completed, his successor was not interested in these matters, and France in 1870 went to war without a viable system to use her railroads to move troops and supplies. The results—one aspect of the controversial debacle of 1870 on which there is unanimity of opinion—were disastrous.[50]

After the 1870 defeat the French began an intensive campaign to make their railroad system an integral part of the national defense structure. Specially constructed strategic railroads, designed for the quick and efficient transfer of troops to threatened points, were built in the area of the Paris fortifications and in the direction of the German frontier. At the same time the government concluded agreements with the operating companies under the terms of which no branch or secondary lines which contributed either directly or indirectly to national defense could be discontinued, even if they lost money, without the express approval of the Minister of War.[51] A vast administrative and legal apparatus was set in motion to correct the errors of the past and to provide for the efficient use of the rail system in time of war. The War Ministry itself established a

[50] On the Niel projects and their subsequent neglect, see General Hugues-Louis Jarras, *Souvenirs du Général Jarras* (Paris: Plon, 1892), pp. 15 ff. On the role of railroads in the defeat of 1870, see Lafon, *Chemins de fer*, pp. 22-30 and, especially, Edwin A. Pratt, *The Rise of Rail Power in War and Conquest, 1833-1914* (London: King, 1915), pp. 138 ff.

[51] "After the debacle they [the deputies] were resolved to perfect and consolidate their rail networks and never to allow even secondary lines to abandon service; once proved to be indispensable to the efficient management of France's communications as a whole, these roads were to be maintained and operated at any cost." Kimon Doukas, *The French Railroads and the State* (New York: Columbia University Press, 1945), pp. 52-55. On the building of strategic railroads, see Eugène Ténot, *Les Nouvelles Défenses de la France* (2 vols., Paris: Ballière, 1880), I, 166 ff., and General Joseph Le Hénaff and Captain Henri Bornecque, *Les Chemins de fer français et la guerre* (Paris: Chapelot, 1922), p. 22. The French mobilization plan of 1888, Plan IX, called for building independent and parallel lines leading eastward so that troop trains could have unhampered movement.

special Fourth Bureau, an organization intended to plan the minutiae of troop and supply movements. The army organization law of 1873, the cadres and effectives law of 1875, and the requisition law of 1877, all contained provisions dealing with the wartime employment of the railroads.

The most important feature of the new system was a joint commission composed of military officials and civilian technicians employed by the roads. This commission, first established in 1872, was designed to bring about proper coordination in drawing up war plans between the army and the private companies. The sponsors of these arrangements hoped that a close collaboration in peacetime between military agents, representing the General Staff, and civilian officials, representing the railroad companies, would lead to efficient coordination of effort at the outbreak of hostilities.[52] With the creation of this system the French thus recognized not only the importance of rail communications in military planning but also the need for advance consultation with civilian experts in the task of drawing up plans.

But the use to which this elaborate mechanism was to be placed at the outbreak of war was sharply limited by the prevailing French military theories. Its *raison d'être* was solely to fulfill the needs of the armed forces, and all plans, drawn on the assumption of a war of limited length, were designed to accomplish such short-run purposes as the mobilization and concentration of troops for the initial battles. Moreover, when the important railroad law of 1888 was enacted, its sponsor indicated that the only reason for such a law was to make it certain that no one could challenge the absolute authority of the Minister of War to direct every phase of rail operations at the moment of mobilization.[53] Thus, even though civilian experts assisted military authorities, all wartime plans were designed solely to

[52] Lafon, *Chemins de fer*, pp. 41 ff. and Pratt, *Rise of Rail Power*, pp. 149 ff.
[53] Charles de Freycinet, *Souvenirs, 1878-1893* (Paris: Delagrave, 1914), pp. 446-47; Lafon, *Chemins de fer*, pp. 45-46.

meet military demands. It was assumed long before 1914 that when war broke out and the army took over control, all normal commercial and passenger traffic would immediately cease.[54] As General Joseph Le Hénaff, the officer who came to control French railroads in the First World War, pointed out, the military railway service was under the direction of a command which believed in a short war and which directed all of its efforts to solving the problems of initial troop concentrations.[55]

All of the railroad plans were based on the assumption that there would be little for the railroads to do once the French mobilization was accomplished. To be sure, some plans were made to supply the armies by rail, but since the French command expected a war of movement in which material would not be all-important, it arranged to dispatch only one train a day to each army corps and to send a variable number of munitions trains at the moment of battle. It was in fact only with great difficulty that these arrangements were revised when the era of trench warfare began.[56] Likewise, during the period of mobilization there were to be extensive deferments for key operating personnel, but once the initial troop movements were accomplished, the army insisted that the principal job of the railroads would be finished and that deferred employees should immediately join their assigned military units.[57]

[54] The much-heralded civil-military collaboration in planning amounted in practice to a subordination of the civilian technicians to the wishes of the military representatives. Jacques Razouls, *La Responsabilité des chemins de fer en temps de guerre* (Paris: Sirey, 1942), pp. 69-70.

[55] General Joseph Le Hénaff, *Le Rôle militaire des chemins de fer* (Paris: Berger-Levrault, 1923), pp. 2-3. The wartime director of French railroads also claimed that in prewar years if any officer had advocated the organization of commercial rail traffic, his colleagues would have considered him deficient in "military spirit" (p. 50).

[56] General Joseph Le Hénaff, *Conférence sur les chemins de fer* (Centre des Hautes Études Militaires, 1919), p. 27, a paper designed to show postwar staff officers the deficiences of the earlier rail organization.

[57] Marcel Peschaud, *Politique et fonctionnement des transports par chemin de fer* (HESGM) (Paris: Presses universitaires de France, 1926), pp. 136-37. It might also be noted that the arrangements made for wartime utilization of French naviga-

The structure of the army supply services offers another example of how pre-1914 plans and preparations were affected by the belief in a short war in which the offensive and maneuver would predominate.[58] Unlike the present tables of organization in both the French and the American armies, the prewar staff sections of the French army were formed on a triangular basis, and a separate Fourth Bureau, charged with responsibility for problems of supply and maintenance, was not created until the needs of the war clearly showed that supply was a military function important enough to warrant a separate section of its own. Before 1914, though separate staff sections handled the problems of intelligence and operations (Second and Third Bureaus), all questions of supply, organization, and personnel were the responsibility of a single First Bureau. This triangular structure was founded upon the assumption that supply services—classified, in fact, as impedimenta—must be pared to a minimum in order to prevent them from hampering the mobility of armies engaged in a war of maneuver. It was also based upon the belief that in a war of short duration supply would not be a critical factor.[59]

---

ble waterways were similar to those made for the railroads. The officials who drew up the plans for the use of the waterways were aware of their importance, but all plans were for the period of mobilization and concentration, and, at the outbreak of hostilities, all commercial operations were to cease. Long before 1914 an elaborate administrative organization had been established to operate the waterways, and an annual census of personnel was conducted so that the military authorities could make definite plans to transport men and supplies during the mobilization. But all arrangements were made on a sixty-day basis. Deferments for civilian employees expired after that period, and it was believed that the role of the waterways would cease with the concentration of the armies and the initial movement of supplies. Georges de Kerviler, *La Navigation intérieure en France pendant la guerre* (HESGM), (Paris: Presses universitaires de France, 1926), pp. 16-23.

[58] See Major S. Raoult, "The Fourth Bureau of the French General Staff," (*Revue militaire générale*, Oct.-Nov., 1924; an unpublished translation by Capt. E. M. Benitez for the U. S. Army War College). Also James D. Hittle, *The Military Staff—Its History and Development* (Harrisburg, Pa.: The Telegraph Press, 1949), pp. 108-13, an account based upon Raoult's article.

[59] Raoult, "Fourth Bureau," pp. 13-15.

The feeding of mass armies created a problem which the military authorities had long recognized would have to be solved well in advance of the outbreak of war. But prewar plans, based upon the familiar assumptions about the character of a European conflict, had deficiencies similar to those which have already been discussed. It was felt, for instance, that all of the foodstuffs that the French army would need to fight a war could be obtained from the yield of a single harvest. Nor did the French government or its military officials make any arrangements to feed the civilian population except for those who lived in fortified areas. Nothing was done to defer enough men to keep agricultural production at normal yields.[60] However, counterbalancing this, the French had established a complicated civil-military apparatus which functioned in time of peace to procure the foodstuffs necessary to wage a war and to insure the army's wartime food supply. Though these administrative arrangements operated upon the postulates of traditional, liberal economic thought, they were an indication that, within the framework of a short war, pre-1914 military planners were beginning to become aware of some of the long-range problems created by the nation in arms.

It was realized at an early date that in time of war a huge conscript army could not be fed from stocks on hand. Between the years 1885 and 1890 General Ducuing, chief of the mobilization section of the French Intendance, worked out a detailed system to insure the daily troop rations.[61] First of all,

[60] See Augé-Laribé, *L'Agriculture*, pp. 53-54 for a critical account of the prewar arrangements. The government and the army, however, were aware that even during a short war certain areas in France might run short of food, and some steps had been taken to remedy the situation. The military command had made arrangements to send a few food trains to parts of the Midi and, when war broke out, the General Staff intended to notify businessmen that the trains were ready. Intendant General Ferdinand Laporte, *Mobilisation économique et intendance militaire* (Paris: Charles-Lavauzelle, 1931), p. 148.

[61] *Ibid.*, pp. 139 ff., a description of the prewar arrangements and their evolution. Laporte's book was written for a course given about 1930 in the École Supérieure de Guerre and the Centre des Hautes Études Militaires.

agricultural statistics, itemizing not only the normal annual harvest but also patterns of variation, were collected in peacetime for each of the French departments. Then these statistics were assembled by specially created departmental *Comités de ravitaillement,* commissions headed by the prefect of each department but which included local agricultural experts as well as military representatives. The War Ministry, to which the committee reports were forwarded, studied these documents and, after determining the minimum quantities of agricultural products needed to feed the civilian population of each area, assigned definite quotas for each region to supply to the army in time of war. The departmental commissions then reassigned their quotas to smaller local subdivisions—groups of communes—and established subcommittees in each of them to obtain the necessary foodstuffs. The collection of statistics and the assignment of military quotas was carried out every year. In addition, the army from time to time conducted actual mobilization exercises in selected departments as a means of testing the efficiency of the system, familiarizing military personnel with their wartime duties, and acquainting French peasants with the techniques by which the army would obtain its food supplies in a real war.[62]

The military authorities also realized that in the event of war supplies of certain foods, notably breads and canned meats, would not be available in sufficient quantities on the open market. To secure the supply of these products they established procurement techniques which, in effect, amounted to a small-scale economic mobilization. The army made detailed arrangements with certain selected producers of these foods and agreed to furnish them with the equipment and food supplies which would enable them, at the hour of mobilization, to change over

[62] A military textbook which gives an account of the operation of this system and which lists French agricultural resources for the benefit of officers who might become associated with the Intendancy is Eugène Delapierriere, *La France économique et l'armée* (Paris: Charles-Lavauzelle, 1893), pp. 279 ff. For a description of a typical experimental exercise, see *J.O.C. Doc.,* July 6, 1901, No. 2650, p. 1514.

from their normal output to the production of foodstuffs that were suitable for army rations. In addition, workers in these establishments received deferment from military service.[63] Thus, because the problem of feeding conscript armies was so immense, pre-1914 military authorities had realized that a war could not be fought on the basis of existing stocks and had also made specific plans to supplement the production of certain necessary foodstuffs during and after mobilization.

But the procurement policies by which the army was to obtain its food were formulated in keeping with traditional, liberal economic principles and were, in addition, established on the assumption that the French peasant might not respond to the demands made upon him. General Ducuing believed that war did not increase the number of consumers but only displaced them. Hence he built his food procurement system on the supposition that French metropolitan sources were more than adequate to satisfy all wartime demands. And, as a result, he came to believe that the principal problem was not to maintain or increase agricultural production but rather to devise means of procuring the necessary food products from reluctant peasants. The subcommittee of the department (known as the *commission de réception*) therefore became the most important link in the entire chain, and, in addition, the most important member of each *commission de réception* was considered to be not its military representative but a local resident known and respected by the peasantry of the region. This local dignitary, rather than a military officer, was especially selected as the person to establish contacts with the small farmers of the area and to arrange the terms of purchase for agricultural products. Everything possible was done to hide the fact that the army was the buyer of agricultural products because it was feared that the French peasant would be unwilling to sell his produce at a fixed price and would resist any request which appeared to originate directly with the military hierarchy. It was con-

[63] Laporte, *Mobilisation économique*, p. 147.

sidered wiser to utilize a civilian "front" because, as one military writer observed,

Any one who knows the defiant French peasant knows that he is very susceptible to the influence of people who fulfill the dual condition of being well known to him and of representing authority in his eyes.[64]

The men who originated this procurement system were also aware that the whole scheme might collapse if war broke out in a year of bad harvests. The plan they devised to circumvent this contingency took advantage of the readily observable phenomenon that the "economic man" finds that war, or the threat of war, makes it highly profitable to buy up commodities which will soon be in short supply. Consequently, in 1906 Ducuing persuaded the legislature to enact a law which authorized the removal of tariff barriers on grain in time of war. The theory behind this legislation was that importers, realizing that the outbreak of war would boost the price of grain, would find the removal of tariffs a sufficient incentive to purchase large quantities of foreign grains. These imports, in turn, would make it possible for the army to buy the food supplies it needed even if domestic harvests were insufficient.[65] Thus the means of procuring military food supplies were essentially worked out within the framework of traditional economics.

One of the most serious problems faced by the French people and their military leaders during the First World War was the fact that their armies seemed always to need far more material than their factories could produce. Consequently, in any discussion of the extent to which pre-1914 French thought on the nation in arms dealt with economic phenomena, the arrangements made for the wartime employment of industry form one of the most central problems.

[64] *Ibid.*, p. 145.
[65] *Ibid.*, pp. 150-52. Ducuing wanted a law which would make tariff removal automatic with the declaration of war and which would be applicable for only a fifteen-day period, but the well-organized protectionist interests in the Chamber were not willing to concede that much.

The plans made to utilize French industry have provoked more than a little controversy. To some, blessed with the hindsight which came from the wartime experiences, it seemed that there had been nothing which resembled an industrial mobilization and that, indeed, neither public nor military officials had appreciated the importance of French industry. Fernand Engerand, the deputy whose memory jogged the Chamber into the Briey investigation, felt that French ignorance of the military value of their industrial system was so prodigious that it would forever stupefy the historian;[66] former War Minister Adolphe Messimy emphasized in his memoirs that industrial preparations had at best amounted to the creation of vast peacetime stocks;[67] and the wartime secretary of the Comité des Forges, Robert Pinot, observed that "no one had foreseen that along with the military mobilization we should have organized the mobilization of our industry."[68] A textbook on the problems of industrial mobilization, published in 1925, flatly stated that "Our mistake in it [war preparation] was due to the erroneous conception we had made of the nature of war. We had not foreseen the industrial mobilization of the country."[69] A contrary thesis, and one taught in French war academies in postwar years, was that, while the lacunae in the 1914 preparations were great, the plans put into operation at the outbreak of war were of sufficient detail and scope to be correctly described as an industrial mobilization in miniature.[70]

---

[66] Engerand, *Bataille*, p. 9.

[67] Adolphe Messimy, *Mes Souvenirs* (Paris: Plon, 1937), p. 318.

[68] Pinot, *Comité des Forges*, p. 177.

[69] Lt. Colonel Frédéric Reboul, *Mobilisation industrielle* (Paris: Berger-Levrault, 1925), p. 190. This list could be greatly extended. See Joffre, *Mémoires*, I, 78 or Baquet, *Souvenirs*, p. 45.

[70] Menu, *Applications*, I, 352 and *Influence of Industrial Production*, pp. 2-3; Lt. Colonel Delavallée, *Quelques Considérations sur la mobilisation industrielle* (Centre d'Études Tactiques d'Artillerie de Metz, 1923), p. 4 and *Cours de fabrications de de guerre* (Paris: Imprimerie nationale, 1922), p. 9. For similar statements see Laporte, *Mobilisation économique*, pp. 139, 157 and Herr, *Artillerie*, pp. 276-77.

To reconcile these viewpoints is perhaps less a problem of historical research than one of semantics. Whether one defines prewar preparations as a miniature industrial mobilization or maintains that there was no genuine anticipation of the role of industry, in either case the pattern which emerges is the familiar one that has already been discussed in connection with the wartime role of the railroads and the operations of the agricultural procurement program. The French army did indeed draw up many and specific plans, but they were all founded on the assumption of a short military campaign. The planners did pay attention to French industrial resources, but these were valued for the peacetime stocks they could furnish and the assistance they could provide to the process of mobilization. There were also contracts with private industry and deferments of skilled workers, but these were held to a minimum and affected but a small fraction of the total number of French industrial establishments and workers. In short, the French drew up a set of war plans which, because of their basis in the short-war psychology, proved within sixty days to be so inadequate that critics could honestly believe there had been no planning at all.[71]

The essential characteristic of the pre-1914 relationship between industry and the army was that both the military and civil leaders of France expected that the war could be fought with the stockpiles of material already accumulated at the time of mobilization. They did not anticipate that private industry

[71] For an excellent example of how a fair-minded critic was led to such conclusions, see Pierre Bruneau, *Le Rôle du haut commandement au point de vue économique de 1914 à 1921* (Paris: Berger-Levrault, 1924), pp. 10 ff. Bruneau attempted to show that the High Command had not completely neglected economic considerations prior to 1914. He argued that many pre-1914 courses in French military academies had focused attention on the nation's mineral resources and, consequently, had at least "implicitly posed" the problem of economic mobilization. Likewise, he noted that such military writers as Serrigny, Mordacq, and Delaperriere had paid attention to the economic, financial, and social aspects of war. Nevertheless, in his conclusion, Bruneau stated that the prevailing short-war thesis had prevented any real consideration of economic factors by the French command, that there had never been any prewar liaison between government and business officials, and that neither army nor political leaders had ever approached economic problems from any point of view except the purely military.

would have any significant role in the manufacture of armaments. In a course given at the École Polytechnique in 1911-
12 there was a special section devoted to problems of mobilization which made this clear. The course outline, for instance,
showed that particular attention was given to the mobilization
of the armies and the transportation facilities, but the portion
entitled "Matériel" contained little more than the bare statement, "As far as storage space will permit, the materiel required
at mobilization is manufactured and stored, in time of peace, in
the magazines or docks and as near the place of its intended
use as is possible." [72]

In the prewar Chamber and Senate when legislators raised the
much-discussed question of French artillery preparations, their
purpose was simply to increase the number of guns and rounds
of ammunition which would be on hand at the hour of mobilization. General Hippolyte Langlois, a Senator of particular
competence in military affairs, was tremendously impressed by
the enormous consumption of shells in the Russo-Japanese War
and even more alarmed by reports he had heard concerning German artillery preparations. Langlois constantly tried to prod
the government into making greater efforts. But—like Senator
Charles Humbert, the Senator who, on the very eve of the war,
shocked his colleagues with the revelation that German artillery
was superior to the French—General Langlois believed that the
solution was to have on hand a stockpile of 3,000 rounds per
gun at the hour of mobilization. Yet neither he nor the others
even touched upon the question of continuing production after
a war had actually started. [73] Indeed, when war did break out

72 See École Polytechnique, "Cours d'art militaire,—notions de droit international
. . . législation . . . organisation de l'armée . . . mobilisation," (4 conférences, Aug.,
1911), p. 83.
73 General Hippolyte Langlois, *Questions de défaut* (Paris: Berger-Levrault, 1906),
pp. 208-09; Charles Humbert, *Les Voeux de l'armée* (Paris: Librairie Universelle,
n.d.), pp. 279-86. See also Joseph Reinach, *Mes Comptes rendus* (4 vols., Paris:
Alcan, 1911-18), III, 79-85. Reinach was another leading political figure who
agitated for more artillery but did not discuss the question of wartime production.

in 1914, existing contracts for the construction of new artillery materiel were cancelled on the grounds there would neither be the time to complete them or, for that matter, to put them into use before the conflict was over.[74]

The task of providing the essential military stocks was a job for the state-owned factories and arsenals rather than a function of private enterprise. In 1914 the production of ammunition, explosives, and fieldpieces was a state-controlled operation; it was carried out by ten powder factories and sixteen artillery manufacturing centers under the control of the *Direction d'artillerie*, itself a bureau of the Ministry of War.[75] Though some manufacturers were equipped to handle such work and did produce armaments for foreign governments, they had long since ceased to occupy a position of any prominence in French military plans. When shortly before 1914 it was at last proposed to develop new and heavier artillery pieces, the idea of including such a firm as Creusot in the competition for acceptable models was, in the words of General Frédéric Herr, France's principal post-1918 artillery expert, "a measure which was radical and a departure from previous practice."[76]

Though the army intended to wage war with accumulated stocks, limited plans were drawn up to replace certain materials expended in battle. In these plans—the nature and scope of which will be considered in following paragraphs—an extremely modest role was assigned to private industry. A few plants

---

[74] Baquet, *Souvenirs*, pp. 44-45; Culmann, *Tactique*, p. 40. Even in early 1915 there were a number of industrialists, still unable to believe in a long war, who were reluctant to undertake the manufacture of heavy fieldpieces because of the time and expense involved in converting their plants for such work. However, the hesitancy to initiate programs for the manufacture of fieldpieces was at least in part caused by the fact that by this date the shortage of shells was so grave that of necessity it received first priority.

[75] Menu, *Applications*, I, 350; Pinot, *Comité des Forges*, pp. 172-74.

[76] Herr, *Artillerie*, p. 17. The insufficiency of the facilities of the great Schneider and Creusot works is described in Baquet, *Souvenirs*, pp. 37 ff. On the hostility of the French government and the technical services of the army toward the granting of artillery contracts to private industry, see Messimy, *Souvenirs*, pp. 82-88.

were given contracts to manufacture a total of 3,500 rounds of '75 ammunition per day. Some iron and steel mills were assigned the task of furnishing semifinished metals to the government arsenals and plants which, in turn, were to produce the war material in its final form.[77] These contracts were allotted only to fabricators in central France, for the artillery directors believed that those mills were the only ones which produced the high quality steel which suited rigid military requirements. In the production of '75 ammunition the only private industrialists included were those whose plants already contained the necessary machinery.[78] The *Direction d'artillerie,* aware that it would take many months to convert a factory to war production, believed that existing facilities were more than sufficient for the envisaged short war.[79] Moreover, in February of 1914, even those private manufacturers who were to furnish the 3,500 daily rounds of '75 shells during the course of a war were informed, according to Joffre, that when their present contracts expired, they would not be renewed.[80]

Since private industry was to play such a circumscribed role, and the army relied upon its stockpile of war materials, the wartime manufacturing programs were exceedingly restricted. Yet —and this is what has furnished the principal argument for those who believed that these arrangements constituted at least an embryonic industrial mobilization—the plans were drawn well in advance and included a multitude of provisions to insure adequate personnel, equipment, and raw materials for the carrying out of the programs. Plans for the manufacture of '75 shells had been drawn up in 1909 and called for a daily production of 11,800 rounds by the fifty-first day after mobilization, with a maximum daily output of 13,600 rounds to be attained thirty days later. In addition, by this latter date there

[77] Joffre, *Mémoires,* I, 77; Menu, *Applications,* I, 350.
[78] Menu, *Applications,* I, 361; Pinot, *Comité des Forges,* pp. 74-75, 173-74.
[79] Delavallée, *Considérations,* p. 4.
[80] Joffre, *Mémoires,* I, 78.

was to be a daily output of 465 rounds of '155 ammunition. Arrangements had been made, as noted, to procure the steel necessary to carry out this program, and the basic plan foresaw the need to stockpile large reserves of certain basic chemical ingredients, produced only in Germany, which were essential in the manufacture of explosives. A series of decrees issued by the government in the two years preceding the war had provided for hiring as well as deferring a total of 50,000 skilled workers to carry out this manufacturing program—35,000 in the government arsenals, powder factories, and artillery establishments and 15,000 in private industry.[81]

By way of contrast, it might be observed, in 1918 French industry, both private and state-controlled, was producing each day a total of 230,000 rounds of '75 ammunition and 50,000 of '155. At the same time there were some 1,700,000 men and women employed in war industry.[82]

What in retrospect appears even more striking is the confidence that the men who drew up these plans had in their system. Many of the deferments granted to industrial workers were valid for only a three-month period. This was particularly true in private industry, for the military authorities believed that the job of providing the semi-finished iron and steel products would be completed within ninety days and that the best interests of France demanded that industrial workers of military age, like railroad employees, should rejoin their units at the front as soon as possible. The administration of the *Direction d'artillerie* was so confident that its wartime operations would be little more than the routine execution of the procedures and plans already drawn up that most of its officers had been ordered to report to combat units on the day of mobilization.[83]

---

[81] Descriptions of these arrangements are to be found in many sources: convenient accounts are Menu, *Applications*, I, 351 ff. and Delavallée, *Cours de fabrications*, pp. 9 ff. See also Colonel Joseph de la Porte du Theil, *Cours d'artillerie* (Courbevoie: Chenove, 1930), pp. 411-18.

[82] Oualid and Picquenard, *Salaires*, p. 45.

[83] Menu, *Applications*, I, 351-54.

In developing personnel policies, French military authorities had permitted far more deferments in the years before the passage of the three-year law of 1913 than they did afterwards. In the 1890's there had been more than 30,000 *agents de maîtrise* in government plants who would have been deferred in time of war; after the 1913 law there were but 3,600. Creusot at the same time had the number of its deferred workers reduced from 11,600 to 7,000.[84] And when on the eve of war Messimy asked the head of the artillery establishments if more deferments were needed, he was told that sufficient men were available for the programs that were planned.[85] The desire to have every man of military age under arms—the same desire which had been so much a part of the three-year law itself—meant that front-line soldiers were more important than factory workers.

With such a system of war plans, to return to the question asked by M. Engerand, it was not difficult to understand why the French did not defend Briey. In a war which all believed could last but a few months, it was felt that a region which produced raw materials and semifinished iron and steel products could furnish but little appreciable support in the conduct of the war. And with war production centered around a few selected plants and government arsenals whose limited output would supplement the basic stockpiles, there could be no role for the factories of Briey. With a General Staff imbued with ideas of the offensive, desiring a war of movement with light, maneuverable equipment, confident that a few "great battles" would lead to military decision, and insistent upon mobilizing the maximum number of able-bodied men—with such a staff, Briey could have only a tactical, military significance.

In 1914, therefore, the concept of the nation in arms did not mean—as it did to postwar generations—that the economic and industrial resources of the French nation should be mo-

84 Culmann, *Tactique*, p. 42.
85 J.O.C. Doc., 1919, No. 6026, Part I, p. 271.

bilized along with the men of military age. Rather, the contrary was true: it was believed that because of the nation in arms—that is, because all men would go forth to battle—the resultant economic and social dislocations would be of such severity that a general European war must be of short duration. It was almost an axiom that no nation's economy could long withstand the shock of twentieth-century mass warfare. Thus, the French staff—not only for these reasons but also because of its firm belief that mass armies could achieve early victories—had worked out a set of detailed plans for the transportation, feeding, and supply of its troops which proved to be completely inadequate when it became evident in 1914 that the assumptions of the planners were erroneous. The men who wrote these plans were not unaware of the importance of railroads, agriculture, or industry in producing military strength. But because of the theories they held, they did not believe that these economic resources would be of any further significance once the armies had begun to march. Whereas Americans in 1941 believed that the Second World War would be won in the factories, Frenchmen in 1914 believed that what was to be the First World War could be won only on the battlefield. These men overestimated the abilities of their armies to achieve immediate victory just as they placed too much reliance upon the offensive. At the same time they underestimated the survival power of the modern state just as they did not realize that, under the pressure of grim necessity, the government could mobilize all French resources in the struggle to avoid collapse.

Thus, too, the theory of the nation in arms, so carefully elaborated and developed since 1870, came close to leading the French to military disaster. Because it carried along with it the belief that war must be short and the assumption that the way to win was to put every available man in uniform—in short, because the concept of the nation in arms concerned manpower only and was founded upon purely military reasoning—it failed to prepare Frenchmen for the war which was to develop, a war in which the production line was as important as the battle line. And if the Marne was a "miracle," certainly an even greater miracle was the one which enabled the French to produce the materials, armaments, and food necessary not only to supply the army but also to preserve the civilian life of the nation. Postwar French military thought was to begin at this point. Generalizing from war experience, a new generation of theorists, insisting that war had become "total," was to develop a concept of the nation in arms in which soldiers, factory workers, and farmers all performed a vital role in national defense.

IV

The Reorganization of the Nation in Arms, 1919-1928

AFTER THE DISASTERS of the Franco-Prussian War a defeated French nation needed but a few short years to complete the reorganization of its military establishment. By 1875 the new conscription system was three years old, there were laws providing for the organization of the army and the composition of its cadres and effectives, and an anxious Bismarck was becoming fearful of the revival of French military power. But after the successes of the First World War the victorious French required more than a decade to bring about the transformation of their military institutions. And even ten years after the Armistice much of the work remained to be done—an all-purpose bill designed to insure the organization of the nation in time of war still lay buried in parliamentary committees. Thus, in direct contrast to the era in which the Third Republic was founded, in the years after 1918 the transformation of the French nation in arms was slow and halting.

Psychologically, of course, it is perhaps easier for a defeated nation to discover a real purpose for reviving its military power, analyzing its theories of war, and reshaping its armed forces. But the lethargy of the French after Versailles was conditioned by something deeper than the loss of incentive and the tacit smugness which comes with the knowledge that one's army has achieved a great victory and has been heralded as the world's finest fighting force. In the first place, though victorious, the French had lost almost a million and a half in dead alone, to which was added the staggering total of three million wounded. France was bled white by a conflict which had cost billions of francs and left her northeastern regions a devastated area of ruins. To this war-weariness there was also added a chronic financial instability in the twenties which made many persons think that the costs of armed preparedness must be held to a minimum.

The French military problem had been so completely altered by the destruction of the German army that in the immediate postwar years the mission of the nation in arms remained uncertain. Though the possibility of a revival of German military power was never overlooked by either military or political leaders, the threat was potential rather than actual. After Versailles the German army was not a menace which could provoke such a military response as the three-year law of 1913. And with Germany occupied to the Rhine and the army of the Weimar Republic composed of the hundred thousand professionals of von Seeckt, there appeared to be every excuse to temporize and to delay the consideration of military questions. Certainly, as war memories dimmed and new expectations appeared on the horizon, there was no apparent reason for French legislators to believe the Republic in immediate danger. The public, too, was similarly inclined. The French people eagerly grasped at any proffered reduction in the length of military service, and to many observers it seemed that they once again felt that conscription was a *corvée* rather than a sacred obligation—an attitude which obviously did not fail to have its influence upon the deputies.

Consequently, post-1918 discussions of the nation in arms were more often static than dynamic. There were, as a matter of fact, no serious parliamentary debates on military policy (with the exception of the 1922 law) until the somewhat halcyon days of Locarno treaties and Kellogg-Briand pacts, an era when men throughout the world were persuading themselves that war could be legislated out of existence. Thus, for a Socialist to quote the immortal words of Jaurès on the militia appeared, to the Left, to be the summit of wisdom. Nor did moderates or conservatives undertake a fundamental examination of their own military beliefs. Instead, throughout the first postwar decade, parliamentary debates on the nation in arms—with the notable exception of the Paul-Boncour project for national organization in time of war—were phrased in traditional arguments presented in traditional forms.

These factors—economic difficulties, a lack of immediate military incentives, the *malaise* resulting from four years of war—provided the background for postwar military theory and, indeed, established the limits beyond which theory could not extend. Less negative in character were a number of other influences which had much to do with the shaping of French military thought in the twenties: the desire to preserve the international *status quo* and guarantee national security as well as the wish to establish postwar military organizations upon the "lessons" of the recent conflict.

France, having won a war, was uncertain of the permanence of victory. Vividly conscious of the fact that their country had been invaded in 1870 and again in 1914, men in the immediate postwar years were perhaps too conscious of the "German menace." No parliamentary debate on foreign or military policy was complete without frequent and pointed reference to the war potential, secret armaments, and lust for revenge of the hereditary enemy—though, to be sure, the deputies were still slow to enact military laws, and the pressure to reduce the length of service never abated. Only the radical fringe questioned German war guilt or innate aggressiveness, and a Poincaré could threaten to resign his office because the terms of the Versailles treaty were not sufficiently strict.[1] For though Germany was now prostrate, Frenchmen recognized that she possessed far greater resources in men and material than France did. Typical of the dominant attitude was the statement in the Senate report on the 1920 Treaty of Saint Germain:

[1] Frederick L. Schuman, *War and Diplomacy in the French Republic* (New York: Whitesley House, 1931), p. 256.

The Germany of Versailles is doubtless a conquered Germany, but she is also a Germany remaining compact, conserving—even reinforcing—her unity; she is a Germany able, no matter what the pretenses made, to pay the reparations which justice demands and capable, if she is not watched, of preparing the revenges which her power permits.[2]

The result was that, more than ever before in its history, the French nation became "security conscious." In a world where Britain and America appeared unwilling to guarantee French borders or to regard German intentions with sufficient scepticism, French military and political thought turned inwards, and the quest for security became a national fixation.[3] And the outcome of this quest was that France became wedded to the *status quo*. Fearful of her own position, she realized that more than any power she had the most to lose by any reshuffling of the building blocks which formed the European state system. Through treaty enforcement and alliances she sought, often in desperation, to prevent any changes in Europe because change might be detrimental to her security. Whether French governments were dominated by nationalists or by the moderate Left, and whatever the particular policies which were put into operation, the ultimate objective of preserving the European *status quo* and guaranteeing French security remained the same. In a very real sense the Briand policy of rapprochement with Germany was no different from the earlier Poincaré program of armaments and alliances.

This extreme solicitude for security and reverence for the *status quo* had its effect upon military thought and upon the evolution of the concept of the nation in arms. As a result of the new national outlook, French military thinking became defensive in character. The abject failure of the *offensive à out-*

---

[2] *J.O.S. Doc.*, June 23, 1920, No. 266, p. 257.

[3] Many observers, both before and after 1940, have noted this French fixation with security. Arnold Wolfers, *Britain and France Between Two Wars* (New York: Harcourt Brace, 1940), Chapter I, is the best and most detailed. But see also Schuman, *War and Diplomacy*, pp. 258 ff. and the excellent summary in L. B. Namier, *Europe in Decay* (London: Macmillan, 1950), pp. 1-8.

rance in the summer of 1914 and the four-year stalemate of unbroken trench lines had already done much to destroy French confidence in the cult of the offensive and to give a new validity to theories of defensive war. Postwar preoccupation with security and stability completed the orientation of French strategic doctrines toward the defensive and made the nation in arms into a concept for purely defensive warfare. "On to Berlin" became "They shall not pass"—and, symbolically, the crack troops of the Maginot Line were to have this motto emblazoned on their helmets.

Prior to 1914 the followers of Jaurès and Caillaux had been the men who wished to interpret the nation in arms in purely defensive terms. But in post-1918 France doctrinaire admiration for defensive warfare became the *mot du jour* of French military circles and received the apostolic blessing of the ruling dignitaries of the General Staff. Occasional nationalist spokesmen, like Colonel Jean Fabry or André Maginot, might speak of the need to create an offensive spearhead for the French army —might even broach the "forbidden" subject of preventive war—but their ideas had little in common with the offensive theories of a Joffre or a Grandmaison. At the most they wanted France to possess a striking force of trained soldiers on active duty who would be available at a moment's notice to undertake military operations which would prevent Germany from gaining the time to mobilize its overwhelming war potential.[4] Such a concept was more like the plan of a lightweight fighter who realizes that unless he lands the first blows he will be hammered into submission by his heavier opponent than it was like the theories of pre-1914 years. Eventually, as the events of May, 1940 were to demonstrate, the theory of the defensive was to have bitter consequences.

[4] For this point, which will be discussed further, see *J.O.C. Doc.*, June 2, 1921, No. 2710, pp. 1719 ff. (Fabry report on 18-month conscription bill). For Maginot's arguments: *J.O.C. Deb.*, March 16, 1922, pp. 860-62.

No less important in their effect upon the development of French theories of the nation in arms were the supposed lessons derived from the experience of the war years.

The total war effort in which eight million men had been mobilized and in which soldiers of the active, reserve, and territorial armies had fought and died in the successful defense of France made it impossible to question the policy of universal manhood conscription. The principle that national defense rested upon a mass army in which all served for a short and equal length of time and in which the reserves played the principal military role was simply not to be challenged after 1918. At the conclusion of the Franco-Prussian War republicans had been able to argue that the professional soldiers were responsible for the defeat, and the conservatives, in turn, could allege that the raw levies of Gambetta had turned defeat into disaster. But after the achievements and sacrifices of French soldiers of all ages not even the most die-hard advocate of the professional soldier could say that the victory had been anything but the victory of the whole nation. Hence the first lesson of the war was, to use the words of Joseph Monteilhet, the champion and historian of the French citizen-soldier, that the nation in arms *"avait fait ses preuves."* [5]

For confirmed believers there was, of course, no argument. As early as 1920 the Socialists were reintroducing a project to achieve the militia army of Jaurès. It was one of their arguments that such an army, in which there would be no distinctions between regulars and reservists, would have prevented all the disastrous defeats of the summer of 1914.[6] Another spokesman for the Left—M. Raiberti, a radical reformer of 1905 and,

---

[5] Joseph Monteilhet, *Les Institutions militaires de la France (1814-1932)* (Paris: Alcan, 1932), p. 382.

[6] *J.O.C. Doc.,* February 5, 1920, No. 277, p. 180. See also the writings of the Socialist officer, General Alexandre Percin, *1914-Les Erreurs du haut commandement* (Paris: Michel, 1920), Introduction. Percin's argument was that the three-year law and the staff's distrust of the reserves were responsible for the fact that the war lasted four years—an argument which the French Left was frequently to put forth.

for a brief moment in 1920, Minister of War—observed that the lesson of the war was that it was imperative to enact legislation which would make the nation and the army truly one.[7] When the Chamber of Deputies first began discussing conscription legislation in 1922, deputy after deputy spoke with admiration of the military prowess which the reserves—the citizen-soldiers—had demonstrated in the course of the war.[8]

Typical of the way in which wartime experience had affected traditional outlooks was the fact that conservatives were far less outspoken than in 1913-1914. While the Rightists maintained that, as they had predicted, the reserves had in fact lacked cohesion and military bearing in their first engagements, they were also quick to add that within but a few short months the reserves had proven themselves soldiers of as high quality as any in the French army.[9] And when Marshal Joffre came to write his memoirs in 1922, he could take the tolerant, charitable view that the question of the military value of the reserves had, in prewar years, been judged too severely.[10]

But the greatest lesson of the war was that it had not been the soldiers alone who had won the victory. The resources of industry and agriculture, the men and women workers behind the lines who had exploited them—these had been of equal and inestimable value. Hence it became a watchword, if not a platitude, of French military thought that future wars would be wars of materiel, and military writers devoted much attention to explaining the "revolutionary" character of the new warfare. The effect of the machine, as a Chamber army commission report of 1921 pointed out, had been to transform the army itself; in 1914 over seventy-one per cent of the soldiers had

7 *J.O.C. Deb.*, December 24, 1920, pp. 3779-80. "The army of France is formed of all the reserves of the nation, trained and cadred by themselves."

8 *Ibid.*, March 10, 1922, pp. 747-48 (Jean Ossola); March 14, pp. 777-78 (Patureau-Mirand), p. 781 (Colonel Picot); March 15, pp. 827-30 (Daladier); March 28, pp. 1182 ff. (Paul-Boncour).

9 *Ibid.*, March 16, p. 866 (Maginot); March 21, p. 964 (de Castelnau).

10 *Mémoires du Maréchal Joffre* (2 vols., Paris: Plon, 1932), I, 8-9.

been in the infantry, but by 1918 the importance of materiel was so great that foot soldiers numbered but half of the army, while the number of artillerymen had doubled. And the deputies reached the conclusion that the evolution was toward an even greater importance of material factors in warfare.[11] Or, as the prewar champion of native troops, General Mangin, observed, in no preceding war had the role of material been as crucial—it had determined the length of the conflict, established the pattern of tactics, and transformed the composition of armies.[12] A popular conclusion of many a writer was that while the pre-1914 military theorists had believed morale more important than materiel, the lesson of the war was that now it was the converse of this proposition which was valid. In the words of a Colonel Julien Brossé, "Morale alone can accomplish nothing against machines. On the contrary, it is confidence in machines which fortifies and strengthens morale."[13]

Military writers drew the lesson that the materiel of modern war had produced a long stalemate which, paradoxically, had not been resolved until the Allies had been able to produce and accumulate overwhelmingly superior concentrations of weapons, ammunition, and equipment. The war of position, with its endless line of trenches that prevented movement and maneuver on the battlefield, was—as the victorious Generalissimo Foch observed—the direct consequence of the machine guns, artillery, and other new materiel manufactured in huge quantities by the factories of the belligerents. Consequently, the defense had held the upper hand until the closing months of the war. But at that time, when the superior Allied productivity at last made itself felt on the battlefield, and when such new weapons as the tank were available in quantity, the ultimate victors pos-

---

[11] *J.O.C. Doc.*, June 2, 1921, No. 2710, pp. 1724-27.
[12] General Charles Mangin, *Des Hommes et des faits* (Paris: Plon, 1923), p. 136.
[13] Colonel Julien Brossé, "Notre Théorie de 1914 sur la conduite des opérations et les leçons de la guerre," *Revue militaire française*, X (Nov., 1923), 268.

sessed materiel in such overwhelming quantities that an effective offense was finally possible. As Foch wrote in later years:

As a matter of fact, the offensive never recovered its full power until we had increased more than tenfold the number of our heavy pieces and the allowance of ammunition of all natures. . . . Once an offensive was plentifully equipped in this fashion, it was no more restricted to a war of position than in the days of Napoleon. . . . Proof was thus again furnished that the aspects of war are ever a function of the engines placed at its disposal. Man alone, however gallant he may be, cannot change them; for without his machines he is powerless. . . . Consequently, in making preparations for the next war, we must not fail to take fully into account the varied and formidable materiel which will be employed in battle. . . . [14]

In the twenties French military schools added courses designed to furnish conclusive proof of the dominance of material factors in modern warfare. Students were taught, among other lessons, that the French failure to achieve a full exploitation of the battle of the Marne resulted from no strategic oversights but simply from a lack of materiel. They were informed that the stalemate of the trenches had been inevitable until the hour when the factories behind the lines had been able to produce great quantities of equipment and ammunition. Without this materiel there could be only local successes of limited tactical importance. One of their instructors, Colonel Charles Menu, made it a point in his course on the military applications of industry to excuse the failures of the High Command to achieve any great offensive victories until 1918 on the simple grounds

[14] Ferdinand Foch, *The Memoirs of Marshal Foch*, trans. T. Bentley Mott (New York: Doubleday, Doran, 1931), pp. 178-79. See also General Maxime Weygand, *Mémoires: Idéal vécu* (2 vols., Paris: Flammarion, 1950-53), I, 296-97. According to Weygand, who was perhaps Foch's greatest admirer, the future Allied Commander-in-Chief recognized as early as 1915 that the Allies did not have sufficient materiel to undertake an all-out offensive, but he always believed that victory would be achieved when sufficient materiel made it possible to break the stalemate of trench warfare. For similar views by less well-known military writers, see B.A.R., *L'Armée nouvelle et le service d'un an* (Paris: Plon, 1921), pp. 8-10 and "L'Organisation militaire," *Correspondant*, CCLXXXII (Jan. 25, 1921), 201; Lt. Colonel Émile Mayer, *La Guerre et l'armée de demain* (Paris: Garnier, 1921), pp. 10, 188 ff.

that all plans were doomed to be unsuccessful because the French GHQ did not have sufficient materiel to implement them until the closing months of the war.[15] The ultimate conclusion of these courses, like the opinions of Foch, was that victory had been the result of the final and irrevocable industrial and economic superiority of the Allies.

Most indicative of the new military outlook was the prominence accorded to materiel in the first postwar statement of official war doctrine. In 1921 a board of the highest ranking officers, among whom were Pétain and the Chief of Staff, Debeney, issued a document which laid down the principles and theories upon which the French army of the twenties was to be established. The opening sentence of these instructions was the outright assertion, "The salient fact of the war is, unquestionably, the progress realized in the armament of troops, the consequences of which were immediately felt in the domain of strategy as well as in that of tactics." [16]

All of the general forces that have been mentioned so far in this chapter—such as French economic problems, war-weariness, and the quest for security, as well as the increased respect for the reserves and the widespread awareness of the importance of materiel—shaped French military thought in the twenties. In short, while they often worked at cross-purposes or canceled each other out, at the same time they operated not only to nar-

15 Colonel Charles Menu, *Applications de l'industrie* (2 vols., École Supérieure de Guerre, 1928-31), I, v-vii, 6 ff. Menu's course, incidentally, dealt intensively with the history of the war from the battle of the Marne to the period eight or nine months prior to the Armistice. He omitted detailed discussion of the opening and closing phases since his aim was to show how the factor of materiel had imposed trench warfare until the problems of industrial mobilization could be solved.

16 Ministère de la Guerre, État-major de l'Armée, *Instructions provisoire du 6 Octobre 1921 sur l'emploi tactique des grandes unités* (Paris: Charles-Lavauzelle, 1925), p. 9. Despite its "provisional" nature, this document retained its force until 1936. Since it concerned "grandes unités"—that is, units of at least division size—and was written by a special board of high-ranking officers, it was considered the principal and "official" guide to strategy and tactics. Other "instructions" were issued in the form of regulations for a given arm or branch and were concerned almost exclusively with detailed tactical problems. Hence they were not as important as this document which dealt with general theories.

row the areas of disagreement over basic principles but also to enlarge the scope and definition of the concept of the nation in arms.

War exhaustion, financial difficulties, restrictions on German arms, and popular apathy created a situation, recognized by both friend and foe of short-term service, which made it mandatory to reduce the length of military service far below the three years established by the 1913 law. Throughout the decade which followed the war—and in fact until the time when even the dull-witted could realize that Hitler was a serious threat—all the various social pressures operated to abbreviate the term of conscript service to a basic minimum. Under such circumstances the traditional argument between those who favored and those who opposed short-term service became a pointless dispute.[17] Like the age-old controversy focusing about the Church, it was something which only occasionally simmered actively but which could be dredged up from the past and made to simulate a live issue whenever there were votes to win.

The desire to reduce the length of service was so strong in the immediate postwar years that, regardless of the angry charges hurled back and forth across the Chamber, the only genuine argument in the first parliamentary debates was be-

[17] Of the two dozen deputies who spoke in the debate of 1922 only André Lefèvre, speaking as a private member and not as a government spokesman, openly advocated a two-year service. See his speech, *J.O.C. Deb.*, March 17, 1922, pp. 894-902. Public impatience and social pressure for a reduction in the length of military service were specifically mentioned by Jean Fabry in his report for the Chamber's army commission, *ibid., Doc.*, June 2, 1921, No. 2710, p. 1712. Among the military authorities who saw the handwriting on the wall were General Charles Maitrot, *Le Nouvel État militaire de la France* (Paris: Berger-Levrault, 1919), who wrote that while France needed a strong army, it must be "gentle on the nation in order to permit it to raise itself from the ruins" (p. 5); General Maurice Duval, "La Crise de notre organisation militaire," *Revue de Paris*, II (Apr. 15, 1926), who wrote, "To tell the truth I doubt that our financial capacities will permit us to keep a well-equipped army of more than 400,000 men, and I believe that for this reason the length of service will be reduced to twelve or fifteen months" (p. 792). Public lassitude, extending into the ranks of the Chambers, was one of the particular worries of Lt. Colonel Frédéric Reboul, "Le Malaise de l'armée," *Revue des deux mondes*, XXVI (Mar. 15, 1925), 378 ff.

tween those deputies who desired an eighteen-month service and those who believed that a year would be sufficient.[18] The difference between the two traditional schools of thought, long-term versus short-term, was thus the narrow margin of but six months. Moreover, the legislation of 1923 which created an eighteen-month service was the work of the cabinet of Raymond Poincaré. And Poincaré was, of course, not only the individual who most desired to maintain French military power against Germany but also the same man who, a decade earlier, had insisted that a soldier was not properly trained until he had served a full three years in the army. To those who had heard Poincaré's earlier speeches, it must have been a distinct shock to witness his confession in 1922 that he was at heart an advocate of a one-year service and that he deeply regretted the fact that political necessities made him insist on a term six months longer.[19]

Thus, in the immediate postwar years France was to construct a nation in arms which, based upon an eighteen-month service, would have appeared a mere militia to even the moderate republicans of the previous decade. And at the same time the forces which produced this abbreviation, powerful enough to make a Poincaré express devotion to a one-year term, reduced the differences between "short-term" and "long-term" advocates to a matter of months and, consequently, made their traditional arguments of minor significance. Yet, even in such an atmosphere, the quest for national security was such that the French could never willingly turn their conscript army into a militia on the Swiss—or Jaurès—pattern as the Socialists would have desired.

That France must maintain an army suited to her political situation and her foreign policies was a constant theme in mili-

18 When Lefèvre proposed a two-year service, there were only nine of the 560 deputies voting who approved the plan. The *rapporteur*, Fabry, argued that as long as France controlled the Rhine and the results of the war were so clear, there was no need for a two-year service. *J.O.C. Deb.*, June 22, 1922, pp. 1941-42.

19 *Ibid.*, April 4, 1922, p. 1404.

tary debates and one which never disappeared amidst the furor over service reduction. At every delay there were men like Poincaré who, pointing to the east, would insist that "Time, in passing, has already worked against us." André Maginot, champion of nationalist causes, bluntly observed that French military policy must be the maintenance of an army which would "permit France to retain the world position to which she has a right." [20]   And to Colonel Jean Fabry, for many years *rapporteur* of the Chamber army commission, a strong French army was a vital necessity if Germany was to be kept in check. "The sole way to avoid war," he informed the deputies, "is simply to maintain France in the precise position where the treaty placed her, with her superiority clear, visible, and complete with regard to Germany." [21]   Others, like Foch and Clemenceau, constantly proclaimed the doctrine that France must maintain a strong army to prevent German rearmament, assure the payment of reparations, and enforce the Versailles settlement.[22] And the mere mention of disarmament—particularly any scheme not made absolutely conditional upon irrefutable proof of German disarmament as well as international pacts of mutual assistance—produced fulminations from conservatives who observed that disarmament would mean not only the loss of reparations but also, and more ominous, an impairment of French security.[23]

Such opinions, indicating that the nation in arms was not to be dissolved by a hasty disarmament nor turned into a powerless militia, were of course the traditional responses of conservatives

[20] *Ibid.*, March 16, 1922, p. 867.

[21] *Ibid.*, March 2, 1922, p. 600.

[22] The theme of maintaining the watch on the Rhine was constantly put forth in the Chamber army commission report of 1921, *ibid., Doc.*, June 2, 1921, No. 2710, pp. 1718 ff. See also such secondary accounts as Irving Gibson, "Maginot and Liddell Hart: The Doctrine of Defense," in E. M. Earle, ed., *Makers of Modern Strategy* (Princeton: Princeton University Press, 1943), pp. 365 ff. and Schuman, *War and Diplomacy*, pp. 274 ff.

[23] *Ibid.*, February 28, 1922, p. 594 and March 22, p. 1007.

and nationalists who firmly believed that superiority of armaments provided the only answer to the German problem. But such viewpoints were not the sole property of the French Right in the early twenties. Aristide Briand, the statesman whose name is always associated with Locarno Pacts and Franco-German *rapprochement,* informed the Washington Conference on Naval Disarmament in 1922 that the troubled world situation made it impossible for his country to disarm. The world, he averred, must realize that the French army was the guardian of European peace and that an unarmed France would be a constant temptation to German chauvinists.[24] And even when the Socialists officially presented their own militia schemes, their spokesmen were equally insistent about the need to guarantee French military security. Joseph Paul-Boncour, for instance, constantly laid emphasis upon the threat of German rearmament and potential military strength and maintained that only the Socialist system of armaments was adequate to meet the challenge.[25] Auriol, Boncour, and Thomas, in presenting the first Socialist project in 1920, argued at great length that Germany was insufficiently disarmed and insisted that the great lesson taught by their patron Jaurès was that France must always be militarily prepared.[26]

At the same time that the debate over the length of conscription was becoming less vital, the concept of the nation in arms was itself acquiring a far broader scope and meaning. This development was, of course, the result of the lesson brought home by the events of 1914-1918 that military manpower was not the sole decisive factor in war, and it reached its logical fruition when in the middle twenties the Chamber and Senate began debate upon a bill designed to provide for the total organization

[24] United States, Department of State, *Conference on the Limitation of Armament, Washington, November 12, 1921-February 6, 1922* (Third Plenary Session) (Washington: Government Printing Office, 1922), pp. 116 ff.

[25] *J.O.C. Deb.,* March 28, 1922, pp. 1189-91.

[26] *Ibid.,* Doc., February 5, 1920, No. 277, pp. 179 ff.

of the nation in time of war. But even in the proposed conscription legislation of the immediate post-Versailles era both
government and private projects indicated that the newer interpretation of the nation in arms involved more than the military relationship between the citizen and the state. In fact,
when the eighteen-month project was examined by the Senate
army commission, that body expressed a doubt about the wisdom of continuing to use the phrase, *"la nation armée."* It was
a phrase, the senators contended, which might no longer be
meaningful. In pre-1914 France it had signified only a military
mobilization, and it had been valid only for a war of limited
duration. But in postwar France all citizens must realize that
while "all of the nation is called to the defense of the country,
the entire nation is not placed under arms." Hence the senators
thought it might be wiser to substitute the phrase "the nation
on a war footing" because these words indicated, not that every
man was to serve in the army, but that every one was to serve
in the job best suited to his talents whether that be in the military services, the fields, or the factories.[27]

Consequently the characteristic feature of French military
thought after the First World War was the attempt to develop
a concept of the nation in arms which would embrace far more
than strict military considerations and which would assume the
meaning desired by the Senate committee. The official army
doctrine of 1921, for example, after explaining the importance
of material in modern war, went on to state:

They [war materials] have required an industrial and economic production, an increase of workers so great that gradually nearly all the
living forces of the country were made contributors. It then appeared clearly that the very life of the population was intimately
associated with that of the army and that the formula of the nation
in arms was being realized in all its amplitude. It is now the people
as a whole which wages war, which suffers from it. . . . [28]

---

27 *J.O.S. Doc.*, December 19, 1922, No. 518, p. 198.
28 *Instruction provisoire du 6 Octobre 1921*, p. 9.

The point need not be labored. Almost all writings on military problems in the postwar period started with the assumption that the importance of materiel and the need to increase its production in time of war had made modern warfare a phenomenon which embraced every aspect of the national life. Hence the concept of the nation in arms became, in turn, a theory for organizing the total resources of the French nation for the time of war. It involved the drawing of careful balances between the needs of industry and the army, planning the mobilization of factories as well as of soldiers, determining allocations of manpower for industrial and military needs, establishing ways and means to maintain the civilian population, and, in general, preparing for all aspects of what was now widely heralded as "total war."

Various military writers drew up elaborate blueprints for total war. The gist of those plans was a subordination of the entire nation to the will of the wartime government, and their underlying objective was to avert any repetition of the disastrous unpreparedness of 1914.[29] Such plans were the complete antithesis of the prewar arrangements which had paid so little attention to long-range economic factors. It was, for instance, now maintained that the individual who worked to enrich the national economy was at the same time enriching the army and that the strengthening of the army, in turn, strengthened the nation. To build dams and to make a greater utilization of water power would benefit civilian producers and at the same time increase French military potential; to import raw materials from French colonies would benefit consumers and in addition enlarge the stockpiles of resources needed for war. "Formerly

[29] See, for instance, B.A.R., *L'Armée nouvelle*, pp. 44 ff.; Mayer, *La Guerre de hier*, pp. 188-91. Mayer drew up a ten-point program which provided that in time of war all French citizens regardless of age or sex would be at the disposition of the government, that all factories and their personnel would be placed under government direction, and that all citizens who were mobilized would be subject to military discipline. For interesting comments on these first postwar "universal drafters," see Alfred Vagts, *Militarism: Romance and Realities of a Profession* (New York: Norton, 1937), pp. 441-42.

there were military men who prepared war and civilians who worked for the prosperity of the country; now there are only citizens who combine the two functions. That is the basis of the new organization." [30]

At the same time, in the French military academies, the newly established courses which dealt with the importance of materiel in war sought also to instruct the officer corps of the future about the need for industrial as well as military mobilization. It was not necessary, as one of the teachers wrote, to train French officers to supervise production or to inspect finished war goods but simply to make them aware of what the home front had to accomplish in wartime and, above all, of the great length of time required to turn ploughshares into swords. [31] In short, when military writers spoke of the nation in arms or of the need to bring the nation and the army into close contact, they meant not simply a political or social fusion but an integration of military plans and organization with the economic life of the country.

The actual recommendations and provisions of post-1918 conscription legislation themselves bore evidence of this new line of thought. A particular version of the nation in arms no longer depended solely upon social, political, or patriotic reasoning. When, for instance, War Minister André Lefèvre introduced the first government conscription bill late in 1920, one of the changes he desired was to raise the period of total eligibility for military service to thirty years. The reasons he advanced for this increase were founded upon the economic and social experiences of the war. It was necessary, Lefèvre said, to extend the period of eligibility for recall to service in order to insure an adequate supply of industrial workers for the production of war goods and to satisfy the

[30] B.A.R., *L'Armée nouvelle*, p. 150.
[31] Lt. Colonel Delavallée, *Quelques Considerations sur la mobilisation industrielle* (Centre d'Études Tactiques d'Artillerie de Metz, 1933), p. 2.

demands of elementary social justice. From 1914 to 1918 labor shortages had been so grave, he pointed out, that many individuals had been able to draw high wages and escape military service entirely because they were needed in factory work. At the same time fellow members of their own military class had been subject to all the perils and privations of the front lines. The best way to offset such future labor shortages and to prevent such injustices would be to make every Frenchman eligible for military call for a total of thirty years. Then, in time of war if industry needed skilled men, the need could be met by requisition—a process which would insure a sufficient quantity of workers and at the same time prevent flagrant wage differentials. Modern war, Lefèvre wrote, dictated that "every one be in a state of permanent requisition in the service of his country, and in order that a man may be placed or replaced in his job, the best way to do so is to mobilize him." [32]

Lefèvre went on to insist that the relationship between the civilian occupations of French citizens and the functions which they would be called on to perform in time of war must be considered in all future plans. He felt that the cadre of a reserve unit should be carefully determined in peacetime on the basis of the civilian employments of its members—that is, every reservist should hold a military grade and assignment which corresponded to his position, whether that of a manager or a simple worker, in the hierarchy of the factory system. Hence when a man was called to duty in time of war, his military function would be to perform the type of job which corresponded to his civilian occupation and for which his peacetime employment had prepared him, and he would hold a military rank based upon his civilian status. [33] Lefèvre's scheme was thus based upon the idea that the citizen practicing his trade or profession was not only increasing his own personal earning capacity but also making himself of more value to the army. By pointing out and

[32] *J.O.C. Doc.*, December 14, 1920, No. 1813, p. 488.
[33] *Ibid.*

recognizing this interrelationship, he hoped to achieve a real fusion between civilian skills and military needs.

In similar fashion, the first postwar report on conscription legislation by the army commission of the Chamber indicated that the deputies had enlarged the scope of their military thinking. Jean Fabry, as *rapporteur*, laid down three basic postulates upon which the new military establishment must be founded: to the traditional idea that the principle of absolute equality must be observed in all conscription practices, Fabry added a second rule that the new organization must absolutely guarantee the inviolability of the frontier and, a third, that the conscription system must take into account the need for industrial mobilization.[34] The demand for secure frontier defenses reflected the awareness that in any future war the loss of vital industrial areas adjacent to the French borders might cause decisive, if not fatal, shortages in essential war production. The insistence on industrial mobilization reflected the knowledge that the length and conditions of military service could no longer be considered solely in terms of the needs of the army but must also take into consideration the wartime manpower needs of industry and agriculture. Fabry observed that the essential problem in organizing the nation in arms was to create a system in which there would be an equilibrium between the soldiers at the front and the workers behind the lines. And he warned that unless France, a nation with limited resources in manpower, could work out such a precise balance between the needs of both army and industry, there could be little hope of victory in another world war.[35] The all-embracing character of modern war was such, Colonel Fabry later told the deputies, that France must have a military organization which guaranteed the nation would not "lose a square meter of our soil . . . a cubic meter of coal, nor a hectare of grain, not a single man in a single vil-

[34] *Ibid.*, June 2, 1921, No. 2710, pp. 1720-22.
[35] *Ibid.*, p. 1718.

lage" and which, in addition, would "not leave unproductive any of the resources of the country." [36]

Thus, the economic experiences of the war years tended to alter the outlook of the legislator upon the conscription practices which formed the very basis for the nation in arms. As a result of such thinking, when the new legislation establishing an eighteen-month service finally did become law in 1923, two clauses raised the period of total eligibility for active duty to thirty years and gave the government the authority in time of danger to requisition the services of any and all men who were subject to the jurisdiction of the recruitment law.[37] The idea that in time of war every Frenchman of military age must serve in the capacity, whether military or civilian, for which he was best suited thus became a part of the concept of the nation in arms.

These were the principal forces which shaped the broad outlines of French military thinking in the twenties. But the actual reorganization of the French army and the enactment of concrete legislation embodying these broad principles was an exceedingly slow, lethargic process which consumed the greater part of a decade.

The government did not introduce its first project for an eighteen-month service until the closing weeks of 1920, the Chamber did not begin its debates on the measure until the spring of 1922, and the promulgation of the law did not occur until the first of April of the following year.[38] Yet even this

[36] *J.O.C. Deb.*, March 18, 1924, p. 1342.

[37] General Bourgeois' report for the Senate army commission specifically singled out these two clauses as of particular importance. *J.O.S. Doc.*, December 19, 1922, No. 518, pp. 198, 206.

[38] However, although the three-year law remained nominally in force, the government instituted a system of furloughs and other arrangements shortly after the Armistice and, by this practice, reduced the actual length of service to two years. This was undertaken as a temporary measure pending new legislation but was continued till the eighteen-month bill became law. See Monteilhet, *Institutions militaires*, p. 405 and Shelby C. Davis, *The French War Machine* (London: Allen and Unwin, 1937), pp. 60 ff., the best over-all account of French military legislation in postwar years.

law was at best a temporary expedient. The pressure to reduce the length of service to an even shorter period was so great that a clause was included in the bill which stated that in 1925 the entire military situation would be reviewed to see if a further reduction was feasible. And the eighteen-month service did in fact satisfy no one. By 1926 a one-year service bill was in the legislative hopper. In March of 1928 it received final legislative approval and was soon promulgated by President Doumergue, although its provisions did not actually go into effect until the autumn of 1930.

It took a similarly extensive period for the other legislative fruits of victory to ripen. In March of 1924 the Chamber at length began debate upon a measure designed to replace the fifty-year old law of 1873 which had determined the basic organization of the French army. It required only two days of debate for the deputies to approve the bill, but the onset of recurrent political crises effectively prevented any further action by either Chamber or Senate. In the year following, General Charles Nollet, War Minister of the *Cartel des gauches,* introduced a modified organization bill, one more in line with the military theories of the Center and the Left. But there was never any debate upon the Nollet proposal.

Finally, in 1926 the organization bill—and, indeed, the whole program of military reform—was rescued by Paul Painlevé, a political leader of the moderate Left who held the post of War Minister from 1926 to 1928 and who had also served as Premier for a short period in 1917. In addition to reintroducing the organization bill and securing its passage as the law of July 13, 1927, Painlevé was responsible for the government project, which has previously been mentioned, to reduce the length of service from eighteen to twelve months. He also did what was possible to save a measure, more commonly associated with the Socialist leader, Joseph Paul-Boncour, intended to provide for the organization of the French nation in time of war, a bill which by 1926 had already languished in the legislature for over two years. Finally, Painlevé completed his task with a law, promulgated after little or no discussion on March 31, 1928, which organized the cadres and effectives of the army.

Painlevé, a disciple of Briand and a supporter of his foreign policies, was thus the minister most responsible for the creation of the postwar nation in arms. The resultant form of the French military establishment—with respect to conscription policies, the organization of army units, the policies concerning cadres and effectives—was clearly marked with his personal stamp. Without his initiative it is also more than likely that the long-delayed process of revamping the French military structure might never have been accomplished.[39]

The debates, reports, and extraparliamentary discussion of these various military measures, both before and during the Painlevé period, were indicative of the tenor of French military thought in the 1920's. All of these projects, with the exception of the somewhat technical legislation dealing with the subject of cadres and effectives, provoked widespread and extensive discussion—although much of it, to be sure, amounted to little more than the constant repetition of familiar ideas and theories. Yet despite the lack of dynamism in French military debates of the twenties, both the lengthy discussions and the variety of counterprojects, which were introduced by political groups dissatisfied with government-sponsored measures, were at least indicative of the importance of the legislation and of the varying concepts of military organization which were held by different groups of Frenchmen. Furthermore, and of greater importance,

[39] There is little published material available on Painlevé and his policies in the twenties. The one exception is a collection of his speeches and minor writings, published as Paul Painlevé, *Paroles et écrits* (Paris: Rieder, 1936). Painlevé was particularly interested in the program of fortifications on France's eastern frontier, and, indeed, at a later date Édouard Herriot proposed that the Maginot Line should be renamed the Painlevé Line. See Pierre Belperron, *Maginot of the Line,* trans. H. J. Stenning (London: Williams and Morgate, 1940), p. 83 and Gibson, "Maginot and Liddell Hart," p. 371. Gibson believed that Painlevé deserved credit for originating these fortifications—but in view of the events of 1940 it is doubtful if this is a controversy which will ever assume any significant proportions.

out of these debates there ultimately emerged the military establishment with which France went to war in 1939.

Though there was a wide area of agreement and though, in
addition, the controversy over the length of service had lost
much of its real significance, when debate opened on the first
conscription bill in the spring of 1922, there was the old and
familiar split between those deputies who desired to interpret
the nation in arms as a school and those who desired to maintain
a large, trained force of soldiers on active duty.[40] The former
was the viewpoint of the Socialists, Radical Socialists, and their
minor allies, while the latter represented the opinions of conservatives and nationalists and, in particular, of the Poincaré
cabinet which sponsored the legislation. In addition, furnishing heat if not light, there was by now a small but highly vocif-
erous group of Communist deputies whose approach to the
nation in arms was to reject it *in toto* as yet another fraud per-
petrated by malignant capitalists and social chauvinists upon
the toilers of this world.

The general intent of the government and its supporters was
to try to salvage as much as possible from the pre-1914 system
of conscription. The fear of a resurgent Germany and the desire to maintain French hegemony in Europe had a strong influence upon the ministerial project. The government spokesman,
War Minister Lefèvre, at the very first presentation of the
eighteen-month service bill argued that the troubled international situation had prevented earlier action and went on to
postulate a series of prerequisites for any reduction in the length
of compulsory military service. Among them: an increased recruitment of professional soldiers, the addition of a hundred
thousand native troops, the enactment of premilitary training
laws, and the transfer of many military tasks to civilian employees. To the great distress of the Left, the government appeared to think first of the total number of men that were

[40] The debate began on the last day of February, 1922, and lasted until the 23rd
of June, though discussion was not continuous.

needed on active duty to meet both present and potential military requirements. Upon these calculations they then determined the possible length of military service.[41] Lefèvre and his colleagues believed that French security required an army of 675,000 men of which 443,000 would have to be conscripts. It followed from this logic that, even with the additional recruitment of native soldiers and professionals, an eighteen-month service was necessary to provide a sufficient number of conscripts. Moreover, government spokesmen maintained time and time again that only an army of this size and composition could assure French security, provide six divisions to mount the watch on the Rhine, insure the enforcement of the Versailles Treaty, and furnish a force of trained men ready to operate quickly in any eventuality.[42]

The very essence of this conception of the nation in arms was the insistence that a force of trained and equipped soldiers should be ready and available at all times. There was, as earlier noted, no deliberate attempt by government spokesmen to minimize the wartime value of the reserves, and in fact they were paid many a flowery compliment. But a War Minister like Raiberti, a momentary occupant of the Rue St. Dominique in 1920, did not reflect the sentiments of the men who wrote the eighteen-month bill when he stated that "the French army is composed of all the reserves, trained and cadred by themselves." [43] Rather, the government attempted to convince the country that it should not rely solely upon the reserves—though it was freely admitted that in any major war they would play an even greater role in national defense than when the period of

---

[41] *J.O.C. Doc.*, December 14, 1920, No. 1813, pp. 487-92. See also the bitter remarks of Monteilhet, *Institutions militaires*, pp. 405 ff.

[42] *J.O.C. Doc.*, June 2, 1921, No. 2710, pp. 1734-35.

[43] *Ibid.*, *Deb.*, December 24, 1920, pp. 3779-80. Raiberti was one of the more ardent reformers of the era of the 1905 law, and he charged that the government project amounted to nothing more than an attempt to continue the age-old and "discredited" theory that the active army was to be a permanent cadre which would organize the reserves. However, the remainder of his speech makes it doubtful that Raiberti was as "advanced" a theorist as such a writer as Monteilhet has claimed.

service had been three or even two years. Men like Fabry emphasized, among other arguments, that the present age of specialization made it unlikely that, as the years passed, the reservists would be sufficiently in touch with the latest military techniques and improved weapons to be able to conduct a successful defense of the nation without the assistance of regulars and actives.[44]

More serious were the arguments designed to show that the very nature of the short-service conscript army made it necessary to keep in readiness a strong force of actives and career soldiers. If France relied solely upon her reserves and had no such forces in being, then it would be necessary to resort to a full-scale mobilization to carry out even a simple police action against any violation of the treaty. Worse yet, if war arose with Germany, the reserves might not be able to complete their lengthy mobilization processes in time to check the sudden onslaught of an *attaque brusque* launched by Germany's army of a hundred thousand skilled professionals. Hence both to carry out simple operations without disturbing the normal life of the people as well as to guard against the much-dreaded and often anticipated *attaque brusque*, it was essential to maintain a strong element of active soldiers in the French military organization.

To General Antoine Targe, onetime member of the *Conseil Supérieur de la Guerre*, the fact that modern warfare was a struggle between peoples—between vast nations in arms—was in itself a powerful reason for the creation of a strong frontier force of regulars and men on active duty, or *couverture*, as it was called. Targe argued—and his views were representative of military opinion—that only such a force could defend the threatened French frontiers throughout the long period which would be required to organize the military and economic potential of the country.[45]

---

[44] *Ibid.*, February 28, 1922, pp. 563-64.

[45] General Antoine Targe, *La Garde de nos frontières* (Paris: Charles-Lavauzelle, 1930), pp. 11-12.

There were others, perhaps less worried by the possibility of a German attack out of the blue, who painted a more enticing picture. These men claimed that if France created a powerful *couverture* of actives and professionals, the nation would possess a military force strong enough to take offensive action in the earliest hours of war and to do so without interrupting French civilian life by a mobilization of reserves. This was Maginot's argument, and it was carried further by de Castelnau, the president of the Chamber army commission. The latter was equally insistent that if a strong force of actives and career soldiers formed the core of the nation in arms, then the country might well be spared involvement in a long and costly war of attrition. Such troops could smash any German preparations in a minimum of time and prevent a full-scale war from developing. But if, on the contrary, the French placed all their reliance upon the reserves and had to wait for them to complete their necessarily time-consuming mobilization processes, then the Germans would have the opportunity to build up their military strength to such a point that they could wage a long war. It would seem, indeed, that at this date in the early twenties there were some French leaders who felt that, in view of Germany's potential strength, the only military security for France lay in having an army which could act on a moment's notice and prevent a long war from developing.[46] In any event, the corollary of all these arguments was, of course, that despite pressures for shorter service and for greater reliance on the reserves French conscription policies must enable the nation to maintain an army capable of carrying out such operations.

Opposed to this conception of the nation in arms was the familiar Leftist program for a militia army. As early as 1920 the Socialists had entered the parliamentary scene with a legislative project which amounted to little more than a restatement

---

[46] For Maginot, see *J.O.C. Deb.*, March 16, 1922, pp. 860-62, and de Castelnau, *ibid.*, March 21, pp. 960-65. See also the discussion in W. M. Jordan, *Great Britain, France, and the German Problem, 1918-1939* (London: Oxford University Press, 1943), Chap. 13.

of the measure which Jaurès had first introduced in the preceding decade.[47]   As in the past they started from general principles and insisted that the length of service was not to be deduced simply from a calculation of presumed military needs. Rather, the Socialists maintained that the emphases in any French military policy must be upon the shortest possible length of service, reliance upon the reserves in all military eventualities, and the ideal of the army as a training school and no more. The Socialists believed, after all, that during the war the reserves had more than lived up to all pre-1914 expectations, and they claimed, in addition, that if only the High Command had possessed the foresight of Jaurès and relied upon the reserves from the outset, then the battle of the frontiers might not have been lost nor would the ensuing conflict have been so interminable.   In the words of one of the most highly regarded military experts of the Left, a general officer of Socialist leanings, "The nation in arms saved France from the perils which the promoters of the three-year law made her endure." [48]

In all of the Socialist arguments there was both a considerable and a sincere concern about German military potential.   The 1920 project, for instance, clearly stated that until the day when the ideals of the League of Nations had been transformed into realities, France would have to maintain her own defenses. But the Left believed at the same time that the sole way to preserve security was to create a militia organization in which the length of service was but eight months—a period which Socialists believed sufficient to train a recruit but not long enough for the military hierarchy to make any other and presumably wasteful use of his time.

---

[47] *J.O.C. Doc.*, February 5, 1920, No. 277, pp. 179-81.

[48] General Alexandre Percin, *L'Armée de demain* (Paris: Bibliothèque Socialiste, 1920), p. 35.   For a summary of Percin's views, see some earlier articles he wrote for the Socialist daily, *L'Humanité*, which were published as an appendix to Jean Jaurès, *Democracy and Military Service*, ed., G. G. Coulton (London: Simpkin, 1916), pp. 142 ff.

Though the Socialists remained true to the heritage of Jaurès throughout the entire era of postwar military reorganization, they did differ from their mentor in one significant respect. Because the war had clearly demonstrated the need to safeguard the frontier regions, they placed far more stress than Jaurès had done upon the need for a *couverture,* itself capable of preserving the border regions intact. But the French Left still believed that the solution was to be found within the militia framework. The Socialist project outlined a complicated, if not unworkable, scheme to guard the frontier without resort to a large standing force of trained soldiers kept under arms solely for this purpose. The two hundred thousand annual recruits would be divided into two groups of equal size which would be called to the colors at intervals of six months. Then, after the recruits had received a basic training of three months, they would be transferred to units of the *couverture* situated on the frontier and receive the remaining five months of military instruction in such organizations. Thus, they would guard the nation at the same time they were completing their training. The borders of *la patrie* would have available defenders, under this system, for all but two months of the year. To assure the necessary protection in the remaining two months—June and December—the Socialists planned to recall various reserve units, particularly those whose members lived in border regions. It therefore seemed feasible—given the facts of German military strength in the twenties—to entrust the entire national defense to the citizen-soldiers, to make the only function of the army the training of recruits, and to forestall the alleged necessity of maintaining a strong force of regulars and conscripts who had already received all the military training they needed.[49]

A somewhat similar view was taken by the Radical Socialists who, led by Daladier and Antériou, presented a project for a one-year service. Though this measure did not follow the Socialist interpretation of the nation in arms as a militia, its main

[49] *J.O.C. Doc.,* February 5, 1920, No. 277, p. 181.

contention was that a greater reliance upon reserves—plus an added recruitment of colonial soldiers—would insure the security of France. Édouard Daladier summed up the Radical Socialist view when he charged that the victory of the government-sponsored measure marked the triumph of the "barracks army" over the nation in arms and that, if war broke out while the law was in force, the nation would once more be shunted aside, and the battle waged by an *"armée de facade."* [50] Throughout the long debates, the Radical Socialists joined forces with the Left in alleging that the eighteen-month proposal was an attempt to subordinate the reserves to the active army, to recreate a military force which separated the nation from the people, and to establish a *couverture* of regulars which would be a standing temptation to plunge the nation into military adventures. [51]

In the 1920's the newly formed Communist party, product of the internal split of French Socialists, turned the oratorical guns of Marxism upon the concept of the nation in arms. The theories of the Socialists were rejected as completely and defiantly as those of the nationalists. Renaud Jean, then spokesman for the twelve Communist deputies, fulminated against militarism and conscription. He claimed that the aim of all the disputing parties was war and that he himself could understand none of the fine distinctions drawn between offensive and defensive armies. Capitalism, he insisted, was the true cause of war—and if the deputies sincerely desired to solve the problems under discussion, they should immediately abolish the capitalist system in its entirety. The Communists would never recognize the necessity for any form of war preparations, and they would steadfastly refuse to approve any and all systems of conscription. Hence, until the days when Stalin became worried

[50] *Ibid., Deb.,* March 29, 1923, pp. 1664. For the Radical Socialist counter-project see the discussion, *ibid.,* April 6, 1922, pp. 1412-15.

[51] *Ibid.,* March 2, 1922, speech by Bénazet, pp. 602-06, and March 10, pp. 737-46. How these paralleled the Socialist viewpoint can be seen by a comparison with Boncour's speech of March 28, pp. 1182 ff.

by the Fascist threat, French Communists would have no part of the nation in arms.[52]

Yet despite the bitterness of parliamentary debate—and except for the attitude of the twelve Communists—these various interpretations of the nation in arms were not in fact as divergent as party politicians pretended. In the first place, as previously noted, the dispute over the length of service was basically between those who desired a year and those who insisted upon eighteen months. And even government spokesmen felt it necessary to apologize for their demand for the longer period. Both Poincaré and Colonel Fabry, whatever their personal sentiments, went on record as favoring an ultimate reduction to a one-year service. Likewise, as in prewar years, there was no question about observing the principle of the absolute equality of service for all.

Of even greater significance were the statements which the supporters of the government project made concerning the mission of the reserves in any future war. While denying that a viable military regime could be founded exclusively upon the citizen-soldiers, they recognized the fact that an eighteen-month service placed an even heavier responsibility upon the reserves than heretofore. The original Lefèvre project created a special category which was called the *disponibilité*. Every conscript, after he had completed his eighteen-month tour of duty, was assigned to the *disponibilité* for the next two years. Men in this category were subject to immediate recall to active service at the discretion of the Minister of War and could be summoned back to duty without the issuance of general mobilization orders. The *disponibilité* meant, simply, that the conscript, instead of being retained in the ranks after his training was over, was returned to civilian life on a stand-by basis.[53] And the idea underlying its creation was, as Colonel Fabry observed,

[52] For the "official" views of the Communists, see the long speech Jean delivered, *ibid.*, March 15, 1922, pp. 832-37.

[53] *Ibid., Doc.*, December 14, 1920, No. 1813, p. 491.

the recognition that the strength of the army no longer rested merely with the regiments on active service but also in the trained soldiers who had most recently left the ranks. This development, in turn, indicated a new definition of the active army. In the words of the army commission of the Chamber,

the more the time of service is reduced, the more it will become evident that the real power of the army resides not only in the classes with the regiment ... but above all in those who have just left it ... [thus] the active army comprises not only the effectives in the barracks but also all those of the three or four youngest classes. On this the viewpoint of the commission has been unanimous.[54]

Indeed, as the Senate *rapporteur* himself recognized in a subsequent report, the creation of the *disponibilité* and the assumptions on which it rested were a recognition of the principle so dear to the heart of the French Left that the basic military strength of the nation rested in its trained citizenry.[55]

The ultimate law of April 1, 1923 did not prove permanent. The fact that there was a large bloc of deputies who had favored a one-year service in 1922 was in itself a harbinger of the reduction to come. The Radical Socialists and the parties to their Left were particularly dissatisfied with the eighteen-month service, and, as a result, their electoral victory in 1924 foreshadowed the enactment of yet another conscription bill. Furthermore, France had entered an era of intense financial difficulties, a period when the so-called "fall of the franc" made the problems of the military budget particularly acute. The emergence of a "Locarno spirit" in the mid-twenties also tended to reduce French preoccupation with national security—at least to the extent that the army seemed somewhat less vital than heretofore.

[54] *Ibid.*, June 2, 1921, No. 2710, p. 1732.
[55] *J.O.S. Doc.*, December 19, 1922, No. 518, p. 207. A particularly joyous reception was accorded this provision by Monteilhet, *Institutions militaires*, pp. 380-82, because it appeared to him to mark the end of the concept of the actives serving as cadre for the reserves and to mean that the role of the latter was at last being recognized.

No less important was the fact that the eighteen-month system did not prove viable. Since Chamber and Senate failed to enact new organization laws, the army was forced to rely upon outmoded statutes. It was necessary, for instance, to try to apply the new conscription system to an army whose basic organization had been established at a time when recruits served five years in the ranks. Consequently, little could be done to correlate the number of existing units with the number of available soldiers—the result being an organizational chaos in which many units existed only on paper or with skeleton cadres. Low pay and retarded promotions reduced the morale of officers and regulars to a low ebb. Friends of the army spoke of a state of affairs so grave that it could be described only as "the military crisis," and wide circulation was achieved by a book bearing the title—ominous to those who held the army dear—*Feue l'armée française.*[56] Factors such as these, combined with the legal necessity to review the whole problem of the length of conscription, led in 1926 to the introduction by Painlevé of a bill to reduce the term of military service to twelve months.

That the one-year law would be passed was a foregone conclusion—in fact the normally talkative Chamber, in contrast to its usual lengthy and passionate debates on military affairs, approved and passed the measure in the record time of two days.[57] The new law added little that was new to the concept of the nation in arms. There was a pronounced tendency, indicated

[56] Captain Lucien Souchon, *Feue l'armée française* (Paris: Fayard, 1929), published after the final reorganization was achieved but typical of the attitude of many junior officers. The thesis of this book was simply that for a decade French military policies had been completely chaotic and that inept politicians were forcing their misguided views upon the army. For contemporary comment on the breakdown of the eighteen-month law, see General Charles Arthur Duval, "La Crise de notre organisation militaire," *Revue de Paris*, II (Apr. 15, 1926), 756-95 and Lt. Colonel Frédéric Reboul, "Le Malaise de l'armée," *Revue des deux mondes*, XXVI Mar. 15, 1925), 378-95. See also the report of Colonel Fabry, *J.O.C. Doc.*, June 22, 1926, No. 3040, pp. 836-37, which describes the condition of the army as "une crise grave." No less valuable is the book written by Paul Bernier, the Chamber *rapporteur* for the subsequent one-year service bill and one of its most ardent advocates: Paul Bernier, *La Loi d'un an* (Paris: Charles-Lavauzelle, 1931), pp. 8-10.

[57] *J.O.C. Deb.*, July 4 and 6, 1927, pp. 2256 ff. and 2324 ff.

by the statements of Painlevé himself, to consider the abbreviated service "as a great democratic reform [which] respects the principles of the national army and equal military service and prevents the military charge from being too heavy upon us." To which the afterthought was appended that the legislation would be a "grand economic and social benefit" since it would provide additional time for the young men of France to continue their educations or to earn money in their civilian jobs.[58] As in 1905, domestic considerations were more important than foreign policy or national security.

Both Painlevé and the majority of the Chamber army commission believed that a single year of military service would provide a sufficient guarantee of French security. At the same time all appeared confident that the dangers of a German *attaque brusque* were overrated and that, in any event, France would soon possess a system of eastern fortifications which would fulfill her security needs.[59]

The extent to which ideas had changed since 1913 was indicated by the fact that the Minister of War himself believed that it was theoretically possible to train a conscript in only eight months. But despite his beliefs Painlevé was not prepared to put them into operation. He contended that it was still necessary for France to keep at least a minimum number of trained soldiers under arms and available for a sudden emergency and that an eight-month service could never meet this requirement. Indeed, if such a policy were enacted, the army would have to recruit a large number of additional professional soldiers to meet its needs and the net result would be to impose new and ruinous financial burdens on the nation. Hence Painlevé would approve nothing shorter than a one-year term of service.

[58] Painlevé, *Paroles,* pp. 393-94, speech delivered in October, 1929, at the Sorbonne.

[59] This was the gist of the *exposé des motifs* submitted by Painlevé and the report of Bernier's commission Both claimed that French security could be maintained without difficulty under a one-year term. *J.O.C. Doc.,* August 11, 1926, No. 3372, pp. 1201-02 (Painlevé), and June 28, 1927, No. 4659, pp. 1038-40. (Bernier).

Yet even in the atmosphere of 1926 it was still not possible to adopt a twelve-month service simply and directly. On the insistence of the General Staff, Painlevé laid down a set of prerequisite conditions which had to be fulfilled before the one-year law could go into effect. Among these were: the enlargement of the professional contingent to 106,000, the hiring of more civilians to assume jobs heretofore handled by soldiers, the expansion of the *Garde républicain* (whose function was the preservation of internal security and order), and the re-establishment of the age of induction at twenty-one.[60] To be sure, these prerequisites reflected a political desire to make the "reform" more palatable to army officers and conservatives in general. But at the same time they indicated that neither the cabinet nor the War Minister were willing to turn the nation in arms into a pure militia. Though domestic considerations prompted service reduction, a lingering concern for security—something which the French legislator could never completely forget—postulated that at least a minimum number of safeguards should accompany a one-year military service.[61]

Although the length of service was henceforth to be but a year and although the proponents of the new law clearly stated their desire to expand the role of the reserves, the doctrinaire Socialists were as usual not completely satisfied.[62] The list of *"conditions préalables"* appeared to them as an indication that

[60] Bernier, in his later book, claimed that the army hierarchy insisted upon these conditions and argued that the law itself was not to be put into effect until they had been applied and were operating. Bernier, *Loi d'un an*, pp. 17-18.

[61] These conditions were in fact important. One of the reasons why the more conservative Senate accepted the bill was because, even with a one-year service, it seemed to provide guarantees that there would always be some permanent units in a state of readiness. Davis, *War Machine*, pp. 72-73. It should be noted also that for some time many military writers had indicated that the army's "price" for a reduction of service was the recruitment of more professionals. As early as 1919, General Maitrot had written that a one-year service was permissible if 150,000 career soldiers were maintained. Maitrot, *Nouvel État*, pp. 16 ff. See also General Charles Duval, "La Crise de notre organisation militaire," *Revue de Paris*, II (Apr. 15, 1926), 793.

[62] *J.O.C. Deb.*, July 4, 1927, p. 2262, speech by Sérol.

the sponsors of the one-year law, like those who had written the 1923 legislation, still desired to maintain a "barracks army" at the expense of the true nation in arms. Hence they introduced their own counterproject, a bill which called for a national militia whose members would serve for nine months and receive all their military instruction in specially created training centers rather than in line regiments. As would be expected, the Socialists hoped to entrust the duties of the *couverture* not to any standing force of trained conscripts or professionals but to the reservists who lived in the endangered areas.[63] But the Socialist variant of the nation in arms failed to create a stir. Indicative of the ridiculous ease with which the government-sponsored measure passed through the legislature was the fact that the final vote of the Chamber in December of 1927 was 410-23 —with the only opposition ballots coming from the Communist deputies.

Although the two conscription bills enacted during the twenties provoked by far the greatest controversies, there was additional though subordinate legislation which was of no little importance in the history of postwar French theories of the nation in arms. Among the significant laws which were connected with the military reorganization were those which concerned the organization of the army, the status of the colonial army, and various stillborn projects to establish premilitary training.

The issues connected with army organization were primarily technical and military in character, but the legislative debate, carried on sporadically from 1924 until 1927, revealed the same basic differences of opinion between Right and Left. When, for instance, Colonel Fabry introduced the first government project for army organization, he outlined a system which differed but slightly from the familiar structure originally established in 1873. The cabinet of 1924 desired to maintain a force

---

[63] *Ibid.*, July 6, 1927, pp. 2324 ff., speech by Renaudel. A convenient summary of their project is Bernier, *Loi d'un an*, pp. 23-26.

of thirty-two active divisions and to create an army which, as Fabry stated, would guarantee that if war broke out, "It would no longer be the cathedral of Rheims but the cathedral of Cologne which would be in the front line." [64] To implement this policy Fabry presented plans for a decentralized, regional military organization in which the necessary coordination of economic, military, and administrative efforts would be the responsibility of local military agents. [65] But to a Radical Socialist like Daladier this was a system which seemed to be founded on a desire to imitate German theories of aggressive and offensive warfare. And the Socialists naturally introduced their own system based upon civilian rather than military controls—and, in addition, pressed continuously for amendments which would have made it impossible to use the army in industrial disputes or to call the reserves into active service without the prior approval of the legislature. [66] In short, it was the same old argument centering around slightly different issues.

When the Senate failed to act on the original organization bill, the *Cartel des gauches* produced a new measure in the following session. Indicative of what was expected of it was the fact that its presentation by General Charles Nollet was the signal for cheers to rise from the benches of the Left. What distinguished the Nollet proposal was its emphasis upon the need to create facilities for more rapid mobilization and to provide more efficient training methods for both recruits and reservists. To accomplish his purposes the War Minister wanted to create a system in which there would be special centers to handle the mobilization of the reserves and also special training centers to manage the training of conscripts. Furthermore, as War Minister for the *Cartel des gauches*, Nollet insisted that the only function of the professional soldiers in the French army was to

---

[64] *J.O.C. Deb.*, March 18, 1924, p. 1355.

[65] *Ibid.*, p. 1349.

[66] *Ibid.*, p. 1358 (speech by Daladier) and, for the Socialist views, March 19, 1924, pp. 1371 ff. and March 20, p. 1424.

train recruits, and his organization bill attempted to put this idea into practice.[67] Thus, if the Nollet plan had been accepted, the organization of the French army would have been based upon the long-established premise of the Left that the active army was simply the school of the citizen; recruits would have been trained, not in existing regiments, but in special centers, and the career soldiers would have been, not the elite of the fighting forces, but simply instructors in the military arts. However, as so frequently happened in these years, the Nollet project was but another military measure which never received even the benefit of parliamentary discussion.

Painlevé, in introducing his own scheme for army organization, actually followed the main lines of the Nollet scheme. To be sure, he placed more emphasis upon rapidity of mobilization than the training of recruits and reservists (and, for this, was criticized by the parliamentary commission), but his bill was designed to establish an army organization which was geared to the system of twelve-month conscription. Hence, while Painlevé took into account and insisted upon an increased number of professionals, at the same time he drew up an organization law which was founded upon the assumption that the peace-time army could not provide a secure defense of the French frontier without the assistance of the *disponibilité,* that is, the men who had completed training and were returned to civilian life on a stand-by basis.[68] Thus, the provisions of the army

[67] *J.O.C. Doc.,* April 7, 1925, No. 1530, p. 587.

[68] For the revised project, see *ibid.,* January 28, 1926, No. 2500, pp. 121-23, and the parliamentary criticism in Sénac's report, April 8, 1928, No. 4355, pp. 631-40. Within the scope of this book there is no reason to discuss the many other—and more technical—aspects of the army organization law. The same is true of the other law which Painlevé succeeded in getting passed by both chambers—the law which pertained to the cadres and effectives of the new army. It dealt with the disposition of manpower among the various troop units, and even the usually voluble Colonel Fabry remarked that, in view of the legislation already enacted, its passage was virtually mandatory. Parliamentary discussion of the bill was in fact almost negligible. One item, however, might well be mentioned, for it showed in concrete form how the development of French military institutions was continuing to minimize the role of the active peacetime army: the cadres and effectives law provided

organization bill gave official confirmation to the fact that the reserves occupied the key position in the French military structure and that the peacetime army was becoming a school for conscripts instead of the basic fighting force.

In the debate on the postwar colonial army there was a resumption of earlier discussions on the advisability of extending the principle of the nation in arms to the French colonies. In the original Lefèvre conscription project one of the concerns of the government had been to increase the enlistment of native soldiers as a prerequisite to the eighteen-month service, and a number of counterprojects had emphasized the necessity of applying compulsory service to the natives of the Empire. Thus in postwar France the question originally posed by General Mangin was once more brought up for consideration: should the nation in arms include colored as well as white soldiers, and should its basic premise—equality of service for all—be extended to men of all races? [69]

There were many deputies, remembering the services rendered by African soldiers on the Western Front, who pointed out that the French colonies contained a vast unexploited potential of military manpower. On practical grounds they observed that if conscription were extended throughout the Empire, then it would be possible to shorten the length of military service for the young men of metropolitan France without at the same time weakening national defense. And, it was added, compulsory military service in the colonies would more than offset any military problems created by the French birth rate. As in the past these were arguments which had considerable appeal. Clemenceau, for instance, apparently believed that native conscription was essential to guarantee French security, while

---

that the newly established mobilization centers should not only be staffed with a special cadre but also that these centers were to be maintained separately from the regular structure of the army.

[69] The best secondary source which deals with this subject is Shelby C. Davis, *Reservoirs of Men* (Chambéry: Imprimeries Réunies, 1934), a work to which this and subsequent paragraphs are heavily indebted.

Maginot, when he served as Colonial Minister, inaugurated a program of economic and educational reforms in the colonies primarily because he was interested in improving the physical standards of native soldiers.[70] The common slogan which united all was "The Colonies—inexhaustible reservoir of men."

But such a policy ran counter to the wishes of those Frenchmen whose primary interest was the economic *mise en valeur* of the colonies. In their opinion economic exploitation and development were more important than military conscription. Since the colonial labor supply was short, it appeared wasteful to conscript natives for military service and deprive the colonies of manpower needed for economic development. Nor did military leaders themselves unanimously approve of the theories of a Mangin. To General Serrigny, now an important authority in matters of economic mobilization, it seemed wiser, in the event of a future war, to plan on utilizing native labor in industry rather than on the battlefield.[71]

The viewpoint of the opponents of native conscription triumphed as early as 1921 with the enactment of the Sarraut colonial bill and remained dominant throughout the decade of military reform. Indicative of the policy actually pursued was a decision made in 1926 that those natives who were assigned to the second portion of the annual contingent of their colony were to be employed on public works projects rather than actually drafted into the army.[72] There continued to be, as in the past, a form of colonial conscription, but it was based upon ministerial decree, and the practices varied from colony to colony. Moreover, no government of the 1920's ever presented a bill designed to regularize the conditions of native recruitment or to apply conscription in the colonies in the same fashion as in metropolitan France. When in 1928 the term of service for French youth was reduced to twelve months, it remained at two

[70] *Ibid.*, pp. 167-71; Belperron, *Maginot*, p. 58.
[71] Davis, *War Machine*, p. 137.
[72] Davis, *Reservoirs*, pp. 179-82.

years in Algeria and Tunisia and at three years in Indo-China, Madagascar, and Senegal.

Any attempt to bring the colonial and metropolitan armies closer together met with immediate opposition. Though there were few who ever advocated a merger or "fusion" of the two armies—that is, a heterogeneous mixing of colonial and French troops in a single armed force—important political groups like the Radical Socialists tended to believe that even the mildest attempts to break down the separation between the two armies were excessive and dangerous. When Colonel Fabry proposed to establish an interchange of cadres between colonial and metropolitan armies, his plan encountered opposition from those who apparently feared that the native soldier might, under these circumstances, come to consider himself the equal of the French citizen.[73] As the newspaper *Le Temps* once editorialized, native troops were particularly expensive, reliance on colored soldiers would lower the prestige of the white man, and the existence of large bodies of native troops posed the danger of pretorian guards. "It was the Roman Empire in its decline," the newspaper warned, "which replaced the legions with bands of barbarians."[74]

The net result of these economic and social criticisms was that the concept of the nation in arms was never fully extended to the colonies. The colonial army maintained its independence and remained a military force apart from the army of metropolitan France. There was conscription in the colonies, but it was applied by decree. The length as well as the conditions of service continued unequal, and the numbers of men who were conscripted remained small. In the French colonies military service continued to be a blood tax unequally apportioned.

[73] See the unfavorable report in *J.O.C. Doc.*, January 11, 1924, No. 6959, pp. 103 ff. The Fabry suggestions were contained in *ibid.*, April 12, 1921, No. 2477, pp. 1236-37 (original project introduced by Barthou for an interchange of personnel), and May 31, 1923, No. 6087, pp. 929 ff., a report in which Fabry argued that in military matters "the sense of the word 'country'" must be extended to "bring the whole of the colonial empire into it."

[74] *Le Temps*, April 23, 1926, p. 1.

Another subject which occupied the mind of postwar legislators and which formed an important aspect of French military
thought was the old and familiar question of premilitary training. In the decade of reorganization its desirability was officially
recognized by all parties, but, as in the past, there was little
concrete achievement. Premilitary training remained a particularly important aspect of the Socialist concept of the nation in
arms, for the followers of Jaurès maintained that if the young
men of France were already partially trained at the time of
their induction, it would never be necessary to create any special
military caste. Indeed, the Socialist General Percin would have
imposed strict penalties on any and all men who, upon reaching
the age of induction, were found physically unfit because they
had neglected their health.[75]

Programs for premilitary training were frequently proposed
as prerequisites for plans to reduce the over-all length of service.
Immediately after the war, for instance, Lefèvre indicated in
his first conscription project that such a system would permit a
more intensive and rapid training of French youth after induction. And he wanted to make the establishment of premilitary
training one of the conditions which had to be met before an
eighteen-month service could be put into practice.[76] But once
again no legislature in the twenties was willing to approve any
such projects, and after Painlevé had encountered a similar
apathy in 1928, there were no more official attempts to establish
premilitary training on a compulsory basis. But as late as the
middle thirties General Maxime Weygand, at the time of his
retirement from command of the armies, was still insisting that
the only way to preserve short-term conscription and to guarantee national defense was to enact a thorough program of premilitary training.[77]

---

[75] Percin, *L'Armée de demain*, p. 56. See also Davis, *War Machine*, pp. 50 ff.

[76] *J.O.C. Doc.*, December 14, 1920, No. 1813, p. 487.

[77] *Proces-vèrbal* of the session of January 15, 1935, of the Conseil Supérieur de
la Guerre. Reprinted in France, Assemblée nationale, 1946, *Commission d'enquête*

The role of the government was restricted to that of lending assistance to various private societies which gave military instruction and of making advancement in the ranks more rapid for those young men who could present certificates of military aptitude at the time of their induction.[78] For while French theories of the nation in arms recognized the need to give premilitary training to young men before their induction into service, there was no demand to translate theory into practice.

The net result of the laws put into effect in the years of military reorganization was to achieve most of the goals which reform-minded republicans and even Socialists had desired for many a year. Admittedly, financial difficulties and the pressure of public opinion were more responsible for these developments than any theoretical considerations or the conversion of non-believers to the cause of the reformers.[79] Nor can it be doubted that, amid the heady atmosphere of Locarno and the gradual waning of wartime passions, neither conservatives nor liberals believed it necessary to make any fundamental re-examination of their traditional theories of military organization. But, regardless of the causes, the French military institutions which emerged after ten years of protracted debates bore a striking resemblance to the Radical-Republican-Socialist versions of the nation in arms which had so frequently been proclaimed and in part achieved before the First World War.

The new army, while not a militia on the Jaurès pattern, was, in the first place, based upon the assumption that a one-year service was sufficient, that the primary function of the active, or

---

parlementaire: Les Événements survenus en France de 1933 à 1945, Rapport de M. Charles Serre (2 vols., Paris: Presses universitaires de France, 1951), I, 125. This is a report prepared by a special parliamentary commission established in 1946 to discover "the ensemble of events which preceded, accompanied, and followed the armistice of 1940." Its special significance will be discussed in later chapters.

[78] For a description of the operation of these societies and their function as schools of French patriotism, see C. J. H. Hayes, *France: A Nation of Patriots* (New York: Columbia University Press, 1930), pp. 74-78.

[79] A fact recognized by even such an ardent advocate of the Jaurès-Socialist position as Joseph Paul-Boncour. See his *Entre deux guerres* (3 vols., Paris: Plon, 1945-46), II, 224.

peacetime army was to train the annual contingent of conscripts, and, above all, that if war broke out, it would be necessary to recall considerable numbers of the reserves to carry out even the most limited operations.[80]   Indeed, these facts were explicitly and officially recognized by the legal separation which was made between the "peacetime army" and the "wartime army."   The former was described as the organization whose primary mission was the instruction of troops and the preparation of war plans, while it was the latter which alone was described as the organ of execution.

The difference between the pre-1914 army and its postwar successor was not purely descriptive or theoretical.   In the years before 1914 men had remained in combat units for one or two years after they had completed their basic training.   But now, under the one-year system, they returned to their homes almost as soon as their instruction was completed.   Since the contingent was called up on a semiannual basis, at any given moment only half of the "active army" had received as much as six months training.   Likewise, in 1914 the peacetime army had mobilized the reserves—that is, each regiment had formed its own reserve and territorial regiments at the hour of mobilization.   And a regiment on active duty was so nearly a complete unit that it could undertake operations by adding only a bare minimum of reservists.   But under the newer concept of the nation in arms the role of the regiments on active duty had been minimized to such an extent that the entire process of mobilization was to be performed by independent mobilization centers which, under the direction of a special complement of personnel, were to assign incoming reserves to their fighting units.   Under the system that was established in 1928, as General Brindel ob-

[80] The following critique is based upon the excellent summaries of the military reorganization and its significance to be found in General Marie Eugène Debeney, *Sur la sécurité militaire de la France* (Paris: Payot, 1930), pp. 28-36 and General Brindel, "La Nouvelle Organisation militaire," *Revue des deux mondes,* LI (Jun. 1, 1929), 481-501.   See also the excellent summary in Gibson, "Maginot and Liddell Hart," pp. 368-70.

served, no operation could be carried out without the recall of some part of the reserves. In a very real sense the army of France was now the reserve army, and the men actually under the colors were not so much an active army as themselves a "reserve."

There were, to be sure, over a hundred thousand professionals provided for by law, but their role was essentially that of training the recruits. While their presence did much to allay the fears of conservatives and military leaders that the French army was fast becoming a militia, these career soldiers did not seriously affect the character of the French army. The French military establishment was in fact so much focused upon the fulfillment of training functions that even militant Socialists should have had little reason to fear that the army could be used in police actions or strike disturbances. For, to insure that the recruit would never be detailed for any task which was not directly related to his military training, the job of maintaining domestic order had been turned over to the regular police and the specially created *Garde républicain.*

Even more indicative of the transformation of the French military establishment was the fact that the conscript no longer received his training in a line unit. His instruction took place at special training centers, and, although the name "regiment" was retained to describe these centers, this was done not because they were organized, battle-ready units but solely for the psychological value of preserving the regimental associations and traditions.

Thus, after long years, the army of France had become, as republicans and Socialists had demanded, a training establishment rather than a fighting force. And, as all recognized— and as will shortly be made more apparent—these changes had made it a military force capable of undertaking only defensive operations. For, since the peacetime army comprised only recruits taking their basic training and since the reserves, unfamiliar with many new military developments, would be needed in any type of operation, the French did not possess an army which could undertake the offensive at the outset of a general European war. Thus, too, the army based upon the new concept of the nation in arms had at last given France a military force designed solely for the defensive.

A logical corollary of the domestic reforms was the attempt to apply French military theories at the international level. At the 1932 Conference for the Reduction and Limitation of Armament the French presented a scheme which, if enacted, would have created a European military system founded upon the military thinking of the French Left and which, in addition, would have been essentially an international version of what the French had already accomplished within their own borders.[81]

The gist of the famous *Plan constructif français*—a scheme by which France hoped to preserve her own security and at the same time move along the paths of disarmament—was the transformation of the armies of each participating state into militias and the creation of an international army, or "police force," in the hands of the League of Nations. The men who proposed this system—Paul-Boncour, Cot, Herriot, and Daladier—believed that every European nation should maintain only a short-service militia, a force which would be sufficient to defend the country from outside attack but which, by definition, would not be "adapted to the sudden offensives" which would threaten the security of any neighboring state. Conversely, to enforce the peace and punish any aggressor, the League would have its own army. But this would be an army composed of long-term volunteers, and, unlike the military forces of the individual

[81] See Édouard Herriot, *The French Plan* (Geneva Conference for the Reduction and Limitation of Armaments) (London: New Commonwealth, 1934) and the scattered comments in his memoirs, *Jadis* (2 vols., Paris: Flammarion, 1951-52), II, 352-57. See also the comments in Paul-Boncour, *Entre deux guerres*, II, 225 ff. and Pierre Cot, *The Triumph of Treason*, trans. Sybille and Milton Crane (Chicago: Ziff-Davis, 1944), pp. 29-30. A good discussion of the origins and collapse of the French scheme is John W. Wheeler-Bennett, *The Pipe Dream of Peace* (New York: William Morrow, 1935), pp. 76 ff.

nations, it alone would possess such offensive weapons as tanks, heavy artillery, and motorized equipment.[82]

This was indeed a system conceived within the traditional pattern of the military thought of the French Left. Pierre Cot, for instance, claimed that the citizen-militias of the individual states would be purely defensive, completely democratic, and free from all the dangers to European peace which were inherent in regular armies.[83] But, according to the French, in the unlikely event that the people of any country should prove unreliable and should sanction an aggressive policy, then the very character of their militia army as well as the slow mobilization which it necessitated would serve to prevent the country in question from undertaking any sudden military offensive. This, in turn, meant that there would always be time for the League army to intervene effectively before any irreparable damage had been done.[84] Hence with a system of European militia armies and a League striking force there were double checks against war.

Thus, the French Socialists and Radical Socialists, carried away by their vision of the citizen army, offered their own domestic system of a short-service army to the League of Nations as a means of insuring the collective security of the whole world. While this scheme marked in fact the final evolution of the age-old militia concept, at the same time the plan was in itself a confession of the inherent fallacies of much of the reasoning which underlay the prevailing French theories of the nation in arms. After all, these men had proposed a short-service or militia army on the assumption that such a military force, since

[82] Herriot, *French Plan,* pp. 8-9.

[83] Cot, *Treason,* p. 29.

[84] Paul-Boncour, *Entre deux guerres,* II, 228-29. Writing in 1945 and before the bubble of Gaullist-Socialist cooperation had burst, Paul-Boncour devoted considerable space to explaining that his ideas for the structure of the League army had been greatly influenced by conversations he had had with the young Commandant Charles de Gaulle. As will later be noted, de Gaulle was at this time formulating his theories of a professional army equipped to wage mechanized warfare.

it was slow to mobilize, could not initiate an offensive operation or win a decisive decision in a matter of weeks. The French Leftists, on the other hand, had argued that in the event European peace was violated, the international police force of the League should be a picked force of professional soldiers who were equipped with the latest armaments. And obviously they expected that the latter army would win any battles which took place. Yet, if this was the case, what was the military value of the short-term French army that had actually been established during the twenties? What would be the outcome if the postwar French army, established upon the prevailing theories of the Left, was thrown into battle against an enemy whose army was based upon another pattern? Or if, to give another example, a situation should suddenly arise—as it did, in fact, in 1936—when the swift and decisive intervention of French troops would be the only way to prevent a German military *coup*? It would seem, indeed, that the doctrinaire advocates of the nation in arms, like the republicans who wrote the two-year law of 1905, had revealed some of the inner contradictions within their own theories of military organization.

V

The Organization of the Nation
in Time of War, 1919-1928

"FROM 1870 TO 1914 the war organization of France was supposed to be based upon the principle of the 'nation in arms.' But, it must certainly be recognized, our various military laws had made only an incomplete application of the principle. The term 'nation in arms' was interpreted in a restricted sense; it meant only that in case of war the active army should be increased by the mass of reservists. The able-bodied men 'made war,' but the country remained in expectation of the military events which would assure victory." With such words could the pre-1914 evolution of French military thought be described by men who had lived through the war. But in post-1918 France the trend of military thinking was changed; it now became an object of government policy to discover an all-inclusive definition of the nation in arms, and to write legislation which would make a complete "application of the principle." The above quotation, for instance, formed part of the *exposé des motifs* for a proposed law, first introduced by the Poincaré cabinet in 1924, to establish a complete organization of the French nation in time of war.[1]

Continuing in the vein quoted above, the 1924 document proclaimed the need for a broadened definition of the concept of mobilization. In the modern world, the report said, mobili-

[1] *J.O.C. Doc.*, January 10, 1924, No. 6949, p. 88. The quotation is from the original *exposé des motifs* as presented to the Chambers by the Poincaré government through its War Minister, André Maginot. Because of the victory of the *Cartel des gauches* in the 1924 elections no action was ever taken on this specific measure. However, on July 7, 1925, the identical project, with the same *exposé des motifs*, was reintroduced by Painlevé. *Ibid.*, July 7, 1925, No. 1879, pp. 114 ff. The above quotation, for instance, occurs on p. 118 of the Painlevé project.

zation should mean not merely putting armies on a war footing but also organizing the entire country for the demands of war. Moreover, since the line between combatants and noncombatants had become blurred, and every individual could now play a participating role in national defense, it followed that every person of French nationality would henceforth have a new social duty to fulfill. "Above military service . . . [there] is imposed the 'duty of national defense,' an obligation imposed on all and which extends to every sphere of economic, social, and political activity." [2]

French military thought was thus entering a new phase. The concept of the nation in arms, no longer restricted to the narrow area of conscription policies or to the relationship between the citizen and the army, was fast becoming—as these citations indicate—a theory for the preparation and conduct of total war.

As noted in the preceding chapter, the French felt that they had derived many profitable lessons from the experiences of the years 1914-1918 and that these might serve as guides in the formulation of future military policies. That it was necessary to plan for a war of materiel was, of course, the most obvious conclusion—a lesson which was stated and restated in parliament, press, and periodical. French economists, whatever their general outlook, agreed that in time of war some form of government intervention in economic affairs was vital and necessary.[3] Military writers, whether partisans of the offense or of the defense, whether hopeful that the next war would be a war of movement or fearful that it would be one of position, agreed that only a strong *politique de matériel* could prevent a war of attrition and stalemated defenses. In the words of Colonel Charles Menu, an authority on industrial mobilization:

[2] *Ibid.*, No. 6949, p. 88 or No. 1879, p. 117.
[3] Shepard B. Clough, *France: A History of National Economics* (New York: Scribners, 1939), p. 289.

Any military leader who hereafter ignores the lesson of the late war, who persists is not taking account of the material obstacles which stand in the way of the free development of the conceptions of the mind, will be powerless to create a tactic and a strategy resulting in victory. The one who, on the other hand, is skilled in dealing with what constituted an insurmountable obstacle in 1914-1918 will be, perhaps, the master of fate in a future conflict.[4]

A similar situation prevailed in the Chamber and Senate. The nongovernmental parties, particularly the Socialists, continually criticized the cabinets of the early twenties for offering legislation dealing with conscription or army organization before presenting what the critics regarded as more fundamental projects dealing with the organization of the nation in time of war. And, just as frequently, ministerial spokesmen countered with the claim that organic legislation of this type was already under study and would soon be presented for parliamentary consideration.

The French had, to be sure, during the recent conflict erected a vast and complicated structure to gear an unprepared nation for the needs of a war of attrition. Once the initial battles had failed to achieve victory, the struggle to organize national production had begun. In all fields government planning replaced laissez-faire. By the time of the Armistice a vast assembly of two hundred and ninety-one different agencies, at every conceivable level of government, had regulated and controlled virtually every phase of French life. The list of government activities was endless: prices were regulated, food and other essentials were rationed, exports and imports were controlled, raw materials were allocated, nonessential production was curtailed, defense manufacturing quotas were assigned and checked, merchant shipping was placed in the hands of an inter-Allied agency, and military personnel were returned from the front to work in munitions factories.[5]

[4] Lt. Colonel Charles Menu, *Applications de l'industrie* (2 vols., Ecole Supérieure de Guerre, 1928-31), II, 107.

[5] Clough, *National Economics*, pp. 260 ff. and Pierre Renouvin, *The Forms of War Government in France* (HESGM) (New Haven: Yale University Press, 1927),

But from the vantage point of the twenties, the greatest single disadvantage of the entire structure was that it had been completely improvised. The French architects of the wartime nation in arms had been forced to construct their building from the ground up and without any pre-existing blueprints to guide their work. Day by day the edifice had changed its size and shape as additions were made or portions lopped off. There resulted a labyrinth of overlapping and interconnected organizations of such complexity that few, if any, of the builders could explain the relationship between the whole and any of its parts. An added complication was the fact that this crazy-quilt organizational structure was founded solely upon the exceptional powers which had been granted to successive wartime governments to rule by decree. Hence, with the decree of October 24, 1919, which officially terminated the state of war, the legal bases for the wartime organization passed out of existence.[6] As France plunged headlong into the problems of demobilization, the elaborate complex that had been the wartime nation in arms quickly withered away.

A multitude of other considerations, all arising from the experiences of the First World War, added to the pressure for legislation which would provide a complete wartime organization well in advance of any future conflict. There was, for instance, the important question of war potential—and by *potentiel de guerre* the French meant that of their own country as measured against that of Germany, the only possible enemy. As long as it had seemed possible to wage war with accumulated stocks of materiel, the fact that German industrialization and German natural resources were far superior to those of France had not appeared to be the decisive factor in estimating the mili-

---

passim. See also Frank Chambers, *The War Behind the War, 1914-1918* (New York: Harcourt, Brace, 1939).

[6] Renouvin, *Forms of War Government*, pp. 137 ff. Renouvin believed that the postwar demobilization had been so complete and that the new arrangements which had been made were so insignificant that in any future war France would again have to resort to improvisations at every level.

tary balance between the two countries. After 1918, however, the economic resources of the two nations which could be transformed into military power became of critical importance in estimating their relative military strength. Furthermore, it was now a military commonplace that no future war could be waged simply with the equipment and ammunition which were carefully stored up in time of peace. Even if France had not needed her productive resources to repair the devastated areas, the cost of stockpiling the complex weapons developed since 1914 was prohibitive. And even if such a policy had been economically feasible, the tempo of industrial and scientific development was such that within a short time stockpiled materiel would be obsolete or, at best, obsolescent.[7]

Under such circumstances the industrial backwardness of France became a critical military liability. And the deficiencies of French industry were so serious, it was frequently noted, that they could be alleviated only by a careful organization of the nation well in advance of any war. Hence, whenever Frenchmen considered the problem of a future war with Germany, they paid particular attention to the relative war potential of the two countries and stressed the need for a thorough organization of their own resources.

Even at Geneva, when the French approached the thorny problem of the limitation of armaments, they insisted upon raising the even thornier question of possible limitations upon the "ultimate war strength" of a nation. Their spokesman, Joseph Paul-Boncour, insisted that any League formula for arms reduction should at least take into consideration the possibility, at some indefinite date, of placing limitations upon national

[7] A convenient summary of these points is to be found in the writings of a later student of French industrial mobilization, Lt. Charles Ailleret, "La Mobilisation industrielle," *Revue militaire française*, LIX (Feb., 1936), 145-206. In addition to writers of the twenties, such as Menu or Delavallée, whose works have previously been cited, see Colonel Narcisse Chauvineau, *Cours de fortification* (École Supérieure de Guerre, 1925) and Commandant Duchemin, "Poudres et explosifs, 1914-1918," *Revue militaire française*, XVIII (Oct., 1925), 119 ff. All of these writers emphasized the "fallacy" of attempting to stockpile war materials.

war potential. Though freely admitting the impractibility of any such plan at the moment, Paul-Boncour maintained that the issue was of primary importance in the cause of world peace:

Suppose I have before me a nation which, in view of its resources, its railways, its economic machinery, can with extreme rapidity transform its peace industries into war industries. I could not limit these industrial resources; I could not begin to think of doing so. Yet I am bound to put forth the consideration and to say to the organization [the League] which is proposing arms reduction: "What can you do to help me when I am attacked?" [8]

Another argument which further reinforced the demand for legislation to organize the nation for war was that modern industrialism seemed to make the danger of an unprovoked *attaque brusque* even more serious than it had been before 1914. This was an argument based upon the self-evident fact that there was a time lag between the moment when industry was ordered to produce war goods and the hour when finished materiel came off the assembly line and was available for military use. Bitter experience had taught the French that the delay between order and delivery consumed at least six to eighteen months. It was further noted that this inescapable time lag might work to the advantage of an aggressor nation—particularly a country like Germany which had a well-developed industrial system capable of quick conversion to war production. The Germans, it was claimed, could in secret initiate a gigantic rearmament program and order their industries to turn to the production of war materiel. By correlating the date at which arms and equipment would be available with the time set for the opening of hostilities, they could strike without warning and thus open any future war with a tremendous industrial advantage. In other words, having decided to wage war at a particular date, the Germans could issue their industrial mobili-

[8] League of Nations, *Documents of the Preparatory Commission for the Disarmament Conference* (Series II, IX, Armaments 1926.IX.7) (Geneva: Imprimerie d'Ambilly, 1926), pp. 18-19, 23-24.

zation orders well in advance and be in a position to launch an *attaque brusque* at the very moment when their industrial capacity was fully converted to military purposes and war goods were being produced in quantity. The victimized nation, if it was caught off guard, would then face an unequal struggle. Having nothing but accumulated stores with which to fight, the nation under German attack would have to wage war with vastly inferior weapons and would have to get along with insufficient supplies for at least a year until its own war production became available. Here, again, the only remedy for France, to avoid being made such a victim, was to have her own plans for national organization in readiness so that if the Germans began a camouflaged rearmament, the Third Republic would be economically and industrially prepared to meet the threat.[9] Indeed, when the long-anticipated national organization law was presented to the Chamber of Deputies, the American military attaché reported to Washington that the fear of such German trickery was the very *raison d'être* for the project.

Although the government did not introduce a bill for the regularization of wartime organization until more than five years after the Armistice, the problem had not been completely ignored in the interim. That the cabinets of the early 1920's were clearly aware of the new character of war and the need to expand the concept of the nation in arms was, after all, evident during the conscription debates, the widened scope of which has already been indicated. And, as also noted, two clauses of the eighteen-month conscription bill had authorized the government to assign men subject to that law wherever their services might be required, be that in civil or military employments.

---

[9] The literature on this subject is voluminous. General Bernard Serrigny, "L'Organisation de la nation pour le temps de guerre," *Revue des deux mondes*, XVIII (Dec. 1, 1923), 585, made the possibility of such a German attack one of the principal reasons for the enactment of the national organization bill. Serrigny was one of the military leaders most responsible for the development of postwar plans for industrial mobilization. See also Lt. Colonel Frédéric Reboul, *Mobilisation industrielle* (Paris: Berger-Levrault, 1925), pp. v-xv and General Frédéric Culmann, *Reichsheer et milices* (Paris: Charles-Lavauzelle, 1933), pp. 62, 66 ff.

Though these provisions affected only persons of military age, they were a clear indication of a new approach.

More indicative of the government's interest in national organization for a possible future war was the revision of the prewar Superior Council of National Defense [*Conseil Supérieur de la Défense Nationale*] by a decree of November, 1921.[10] Composed of the three service ministers (War, Navy, and Colonies), four "civil" ministers (Foreign Affairs, Interior, Public Works, and Finance), a number of important officers of high military rank, and presided over by either the Premier or the President of the Republic, the new council was assigned the formidable task of bringing about interministerial coordination of all questions pertaining to national defense. In prewar years this council, by contrast, had been composed of fewer ministers, its meetings had been infrequent, and its competence had been confined to questions which concerned the combined employment of sea and land forces and the defense of coastal regions and colonies. But under the terms of the 1921 decree it was to concern itself with a vast range of activities. It was to supervise the study of the ideas and principles upon which the conduct of future wars should be based, and it was to draw up plans for organizing the entire country for war. It was to devise ways and means to attain a balance between the wartime needs of the army and the basic requirements of the civil population. A primary function of the revised council was to help each of the ministeries of the government to draw up the particular plans which each would carry out in time of war. To aid the council—which could meet only occasionally and whose members obviously had other tasks to fulfill—there was established, in addition, a study commission and a general secretariat, the latter the only organ of the three which was perma-

---

10 *J.O. Lois et Décrets*, November 21, 1921, pp. 12734-35. For a complete discussion of the new council and its subsidiary organs, see Commandant A. L., "Le Conseil Supérieur de la Défense Nationale et la 'guerre totale'," *Revue politique et parlementaire*, CXX (Aug. 10, 1924), 199-218.

nent and whose members had no other task but the study of defense problems.[11]

The council and its subsidiary organs—in themselves a recognition of the need to work out both theory and practice of the new nation in arms at the top echelons of government—performed important work. Various experiments and tests were conducted, and elaborate regulations were drawn up to control wartime labor and manpower allocations, the procurement of foodstuffs, and industrial mobilization. And, of the greatest importance, out of these deliberations and studies there emerged the ultimate project for a complete organization of the French nation in time of war.

Another sign of the postwar tendencies was the way in which the age-old French policies of national economics began to merge with the newer concept of the nation in arms. To the traditional arguments advanced in behalf of government intervention in or assistance to commerce and industry there was added a further set of reasons based upon the needs of the nation in time of war. When in 1918 the Chamber of Deputies was considering a bill dealing with the ownership and control of subsurface mineral resources, the government insisted that no leases should run for more than ninety-nine years. The war, it was claimed, had clearly indicated that the state possessed a "superior right" and private industry only "particular rights"; and, consequently, any law concerning mineral resources must consider the needs of national defense.[12] Similarly, the legisla-

---

[11] In the prewar organization there had been a study commission, but, like the parent body, its functions were purely military in scope and its civilian members of distinctly secondary importance. The first director of the study commission of the 1920's, a M. Colrat, was replaced in 1922 by Colonel Jean Fabry, the perennial *rapporteur* of the Chamber's army commission. In 1924, Joseph Paul-Boncour assumed the post. The military officer who headed the permanent secretariat was General Bernard Serrigny; his assistance in drawing up the national organization bill was specifically recognized by Paul-Boncour in his *Entre deux guerres* (3 vols., Paris: Plon, 1945-46), II, 145-46, 245-46. Charles de Gaulle, incidentally, was a member of the secretariat in the early thirties. For a discussion of the operation of the council and its subordinate groups, see Menu, *Applications*, II, 10 ff.

[12] *J.O.C. Doc.*, November 8, 1918, No. 5166, p. 1774 and August 2, 1918, No.

tion of the 1920's which concerned the oil industry tempered classic economic liberalism in the interests of national security. For a nation which lacked domestic petroleum resources and which had been forced to rely on imported oil supplies to wage the First World War, it was a vital necessity to build up reserve supplies of a commodity which, as Clemenceau had said, was more precious than blood. Hence the Chamber decided that if an importer of oil wanted to obtain the government licenses that were necessary to do business, his firm would have to agree to maintain a three-months supply of oil on hand at all times so that, in the event of a sudden war, the petroleum requirements of the armed forces could be met. This policy—described as one of "liberty with guarantees . . . guarantees for the national interest"—was typical of the way in which the postwar ideas of the nation in arms reinforced traditional French policies of national economics.[13]

Decrees establishing a revised Superior Council of National Defense or laws intended to guarantee a supply of oil were, however, only temporary and partial solutions. The French political and military leaders concerned with national defense believed that the country needed an over-all law which would organize the entire nation for the demands of war and which would provide the legal basis for every aspect of war planning. After extensive study by the *Conseil Supérieur de la Défense Nationale* and its subsidiaries, the long-awaited proposal was first introduced in the Chamber in 1924 by War Minister André Maginot.[14] When no parliamentary action followed, Paul Pain-

---

4928, pp. 1318 ff. See also *ibid.*, 1917, No. 4184, p. 1957 (Session of January 10, 1918).

[13] *Ibid.*, February 23, 1922, No. 3955, pp. 274-75. The quantity of reserves to be maintained varied in the different projects; see also, April 12, 1921, No. 2485, pp. 1237 ff. and February 3, 1928, No. 5449, p. 378. For further discussion of these questions, see Clough, *National Economics*, pp. 336 ff.

[14] However, when the project was first introduced, its proponents argued at length that the work of the Conseil Supérieur and its subsidiaries had already accomplished many of the objectives which the law was designed to achieve. Both Painlevé and Paul-Boncour insisted that the Chamber and Senate were being called upon merely

levé, as previously noted, reintroduced the measure as one of the four basic projects for military reorganization which he regarded as essential. In March of 1927 the bill was finally debated in the Chamber and, after a surprisingly short four-day debate, was approved by the near record vote of 500-31. Only the Communists cast their ballots against the measure. And as *Le Temps* somewhat wryly noted, the general debate on the national organization bill had produced the rare parliamentary phenomenon of virtual unanimity.[15]

The area of agreement among the deputies was in fact so broad that the discussions on the measure, unlike so many military debates, failed to touch upon basic assumptions. Except for the Communists, every party believed some such law was necessary, and the general objectives of the bill were equally acceptable. But this quasi-unanimity was deceptive. Despite the ease with which the measure won the approval of the Chamber, its provisions for the organization of the nation in time of war represented but one of several current and possible approaches to the problem. Conservatives and elements of the French business community had a system for wartime organization based upon somewhat different assumptions, and they

to give legal ratification to measures which had already been taken. *J.O.C. Doc.*, July 7, 1925, No. 1879, p. 120, and February 22, 1927, No. 4018, pp. 254-57. See also Commandant A. P., "L'Organisation de la nation pour le temps de guerre," *Revue politique et parlementaire*, CXXVII (Jun. 10, 1926), 348 ff., an article in which the claim was made that at least a skeleton wartime organization had already been established in most ministries. The author insisted that the national organization bill should be approved so that final plans could be made and so that there would be a legal basis for the appropriation of funds. The American military attaché, Colonel Mott, concurred in these views and even stated that the report on the proposed legislation by the Chamber's army commission was actually intended to be a discreet rebuke to those ministries which had not already drawn up their own mobilization plans. Whatever the validity of such arguments—and, admittedly they have some merit—it seems more likely that they were developed primarily to convince possibly hesitant deputies that they were not being asked to approve legislation for which there were no precedents.

15 *Le Temps*, March 5, 1927. The newspaper was particularly pleased by the fact that the Socialists supported the bill since this seemed to indicate that on questions of national defense the Socialists were Frenchmen first and party politicians second.

were able to obtain a hearing when the bill came before the Senate. Nor did all the military members of the Superior Council of National Defense approve of the legislation that emerged from the Chamber. And finally, although the principal advocate for the bill was the Socialist deputy Joseph Paul-Boncour, and although the Socialists warmly supported the project during the Chamber debates, the party as a whole was by no means agreed on the wisdom of the proposal. In fact, when the Senate put a conservative twist to the project, the Socialists—with almost indecent eagerness—branded the revised version a reactionary document and resolved their intraparty difficulties by a quick flight into the ranks of the opposition.

Thus, though Frenchmen agreed on the need for a wider definition of the nation in arms, when it came time to translate theories into practice, they began to encounter serious difficulties. The proposed bill for the organization of the nation in time of war, so widely applauded on the occasion of its introduction in the Chamber in 1927, did not actually become law for over a decade. It was not enacted until July of 1938, on the very eve of the Munich crisis. In the intervening years the orphaned project, forgotten by its sponsors, lay buried in parliamentary committees. After its initial and speedy approval by the Chamber in 1927, the Senate made a number of important modifications, and, for a variety of reasons, neither house of the French legislature believed it necessary during the next ten years to work out a compromise which would reconcile the differences. But the history of the attempt to enact a bill for the total organization of the nation in time of war was, if nothing else, an important aspect of French thought on the nation in arms.

The original scheme, as elaborated by the *Conseil Supérieur de la Défense Nationale* and sponsored by War Ministers Maginot and Painlevé, was general in nature yet broad in scope. It was founded upon an assumption which had become a commonplace of postwar military thought—the idea that since war had become total, it was necessary in time of peace to prepare for all of its ramifications. The *exposé des motifs* sketched the rough outlines of an organization which would give an all-powerful state direct control over every phase of French life in time of war. There were five subsections which dealt with the major aspects of the problem and which discussed the role of the government and its administrative agencies, the relationship between the civil authorities and the military high command, the function of regional planning and control organs, the role of economic and naval blockade organizations, and the operation of the vast complex of economic and industrial mobilization. This latter section alone dealt with such problems as manpower allocation, control of plant equipment and raw materials, the apparatus of public finance, and the utilization of transport facilities.[16]

At the head of this vast organization Maginot and Painlevé installed the state itself:

It is definitely the government—alone exactly informed and master of the organs of execution—whose function it is to decide upon an action and to regulate its development, taking account at all time of the resources which the nation possesses for its military effort.[17]

The government, in turn, was responsible for making sure that all the national resources and powers were fully utilized. It was to satisfy the needs of the armed forces and at the same time take care of the material and moral welfare of the country with a minimum of privation for the citizen. For the French citizen there was, as earlier noted, a new civic obligation—the so-called "duty of national defense"—which was, indeed, an obligation immeasurably greater than that of military service "since its object, no longer merely the expenditure of blood, is that of labor in all fields and privations freely assented to for the safety of the nation." Nor was this new civic duty to be performed

[16] *J.O.C. Doc.*, July 7, 1925, No. 1879, pp. 115-17, or January 10, 1924, No. 6949, pp. 85-88.
[17] *Ibid.*, No. 1879, p. 117 or No. 6949, p. 87.

merely in time of war; all persons, whether they were in government service, private agencies, or simply individual citizens, must consider it their responsibility "not merely 'to make war' but 'to prepare themselves' to wage it." [18]

Finally, as a way of indicating how the character of warfare had changed since 1914, the sponsors of the law insisted that it was incorrect to speak merely of "mobilization." This was a term, they said, which meant simply calling up the army reserves and putting the military establishment upon a war footing. Instead, the term "national mobilization" should be employed, for it was a phrase which indicated that, in any future conflict, the entire nation would go on a war footing and that all persons of French nationality, regardless of age or sex, were to participate in the national defense effort.

This Painlevé-Maginot project was far more important for its theoretical postulates than for its concrete recommendations or its specific provisions for national organization. Realizing that details would have to be worked out by individual administrative action and would take the form of decrees—a process which, in addition, would be subject to constant modification—the government desired only to establish a few basic principles for wartime organization. Thus, for instance, the proposed law stated merely that the government must maintain over-all political direction of any war and that the military hierarchy would be in charge of the conduct of field operations; it laid down the principle that there should be regional subdivisions within the national organization so that Paris would not have to be consulted on every specific problem; and it postulated that, in the allocations of manpower for industry, every effort should be made to use older men in factory work. But at the same time the original government project said little of how these goals were to be achieved.

Nevertheless, back of these general recommendations there was one firm principle: namely, that the plans for the organiza-

[18] *Ibid.*, No. 1879, p. 117 or No. 6949, p. 88.

tion of the wartime nation in arms should be established so thoroughly in the years of peace that, should a conflict suddenly break out, the transition from peace to war would be as smooth as possible. The "time lag" between the issuance of orders for war goods and their delivery must be kept to a minimum, and the whole procedure carried out without resort to the disheartening regime of improvisations which had marked the course of the First World War.[19]

The planners who drew up the national organization project expected to base their wartime regime upon the normal civil and governmental organs of France. They reasoned that, in time of peace, the country could not be subjected to a regime specifically designed to meet the needs of war. But at the same time they believed it impossible to construct on paper a totally different organization for the nation at war which, at the hour of mobilization, could suddenly be substituted for existing institutions. Hence they decided to start with the normal organizational and governmental structure of the nation. It was to be adapted and modified to suit the expanded needs of wartime, but even in time of war France would still be controlled by the same administrative bodies and the same governmental agencies which guided the nation in normal times.[20]

Thus, on these assumptions, the projected law established the basic principle that the government was to decide what tasks were to be assigned to each of the various ministries and, in

[19] For an excellent discussion of this point, see Watson Pierce, *Industrial Mobilization in France* (Washington, 1945), a study made for the Army Industrial College by its Department of Research. Pierce states that the central core of French thought was the realization that there was a vast time lag between the issuance of an order and the delivery of the finished product and the knowledge that this lag had been nearly fatal between 1914 and 1918. Because of such lags military operations were postponed time and time again. Therefore, to prevent future difficulties, the French desired to construct a vast machinery for industrial mobilization in which the various factors of labor, plant, and raw materials would be coordinated by the General Staff under cabinet supervision (pp. 2 ff.).

[20] *J.O.C. Doc.*, January 10, 1924, No. 6649, p. 88 or July 7, 1925, No. 1879, p. 117. This point, however, is made in greater detail in Commandant A. P., "L'Organisation de la nation pour le temps de guerre," *Revue politique et parlementaire*, CXXVII (Jun. 10, 1926), 349-51.

addition, which private and public agencies would come under the control of each particular ministry.   Then, once a ministry had been given a particular wartime function, it was legally responsible for drawing up its own specific mobilization plans and making a precise evaluation of its needs, resources, and ultimate objectives in time of war.   Moreover, unlike the pre-1914 system, all of the ministries of the government were to participate in war planning, not merely those classified as "military."   The principle was also set forth that, in so far as possible, a single ministry would be held responsible for all of the operations connected with the procurement, manufacture, and distribution of the specific articles of war production over which it had been assigned jurisdiction.   It was hoped that these arrangements would avoid interministerial competition for scarce items. At the same time it was believed that such a system would make the transition from war to peace a smooth operation because existing government agencies would be involved and because these organs would be prepared for their wartime functions. Moreover, this scheme might also obviate the necessity for creating any special wartime organizations, such as a Ministry of Armaments, which would have to supervise every phase of the production of war material.[21]

[21] The men who drew up these plans were, however, fully aware that the concept of the single-resource, single-ministry organization could not always be applied. For instance, they realized that all communications facilities would have to be centralized under one controlling agency and that, on the other hand, certain materials, such as steel, which were used by several ministries would require special consideration.   But at the same time they felt that it would be a clumsy solution to set up an all-powerful Ministry of Armaments to direct the whole industrial mobilization complex.   Moreover, the idea of an Armaments Ministry did not fit into the plan to have the regular agencies of government direct war preparations.   The result, therefore, was an attempt to devise an intermediate solution in which, while the need for larger administrative groupings was recognized, the basic orientation was around existing governmental agencies.   This intention to base the wartime organization on the institutions of peacetime government was noted at the time by the American military attaché as well as by Commandant A. P., "L'Organisation de la nation pour le temps de guerre," *Revue politique et parlementaire*, CXXVII (Jun. 10, 1926), 359-60. See also the later article by Lt. Charles Ailleret, "La Mobilisation industrielle," *Revue militaire française*, LIX (Feb., 1936), 152-54.

In essence, then, the new theory of the nation in arms was that the regular governmental agencies and ministries should provide the foundation upon which, with some necessary modifications, the organization of the nation for the time of war would be established. And, above all, the men who elaborated this scheme believed that such a system, if anticipated and carefully coordinated in peace years, was the best way to insure a smooth transition from the state of peace to the state of war.[22]

Some two years after the government outlined its project for wartime organization, the army commission of the Chamber presented its report on the proposal. The reporter for this important document was a Socialist, Joseph Paul-Boncour, a prominent leader of his party, one of the principal French delegates to the League of Nations, and, in addition, a man who had long taken an active role in the formulation of national defense policies.[23] Paul-Boncour saw no moral or intellectual conflict between his work as a member of the *Conseil Supérieur de la Défense Nationale* [he had become vice-president of its study commission in 1924] and his role at Geneva. In fact he approached the task of creating the nation in arms with considerable relish and found the assignment quite in character with his admittedly Jacobin tastes. To be sure, one of the

[22] Since the proposed law laid down general principles, an examination of its specific clauses is less important than the theories and assumptions on which these were based. Also, some of the specific recommendations take on added significance when contrasted with the provisions of later counterprojects. However, for convenience, the following are the more important clauses of the original project: Article One established the principle that in time of war all native-born and naturalized French citizens, regardless of age or sex, were to participate either in the defense of the country or the maintenance of its material and moral welfare. Article Two defined "mobilization" as taking all the measures deemed necessary for the defense of the country, and putting the entire country on a war footing. Article Four further defined mobilization as not merely the calling up of armies but also the "mobilization" of the communications, economic, social, human, and intellectual resources of the nation. Article Five added a generalized statement that, in time of war, the government was empowered to take "all measures necessary to guarantee the morale of the nation"—an elastic provision which, it would seem, would have given the state the right to do just about anything deemed "necessary."

[23] *J.O.C. Doc.*, February 22, 1927, No. 4018, pp. 254-66, and the extended commentary in his *Entre deux guerres*, II, 245 ff.

first changes that Paul-Boncour made in the project was to add a clause which provided that the entire machinery of national mobilization would come into play "in cases foreseen by the League," but, even so, he made it plain that he believed France could embark upon no program of arms reduction until she had completed the organization of her national resources for the time of war.[24] Moreover, he was always proud to have been associated with this proposal for the organization of the nation; writing his memoirs during the dark years of the Vichy regime, the veteran Socialist leader could proudly observe,

The longer the war is prolonged and extended, there isn't a single measure... [and] not a single initiative to which the countries at war have had to resort which, as far as I can see, wasn't anticipated in what the Chamber voted eleven years before 1939.[25]

Small wonder, then, that the bill to organize the nation in time of war, though formulated in the top-ranking defense council and originally presented by such men as Maginot and Painlevé, came to be known as the "Paul-Boncour law." [26]

In their broad outline Paul-Boncour's ideas on the nation in arms paralleled those in the original government project. The Socialist *rapporteur* concurred with Painlevé and Maginot in the belief that modern war necessitated a total organization of the nation and a rigorous preparation well in advance of any conflict. But, if Paul-Boncour did not modify the scope of the proposed legislation, he did envisage certain definite changes which gave it an entirely different tone. He deliberately set out to bring the law into line with the Socialist concept of social justice and to establish the system of wartime organization upon principles which would win the enthusiastic support of the French masses. "Materially and morally," Paul-Boncour wrote

[24] *J.O.C. Doc.*, February 22, 1927, No. 4018, pp. 255, 259.
[25] Paul-Boncour, *Entre deux guerres*, II, 253.
[26] See an appreciation of his work in a German study of French economic mobilization, Eberhard Grosche, *Der Einfluss des Weltkrieges auf die seitherige Entwicklung der französischen Wehrwirtschaft* (Hamburg: Hanseatische Verlagsanstalt, 1937), pp. 128-29.

in his memoirs, "the defense of the nation is weakened if the mass of the workers do not give it their support; the national sentiment is deficient if their hearts are not in it." [27]   That he succeeded, at least for the moment, in convincing his fellow Socialists that he had accomplished his purposes was indicated when Pierre Renaudel, official spokesman for the party, informed the deputies that the law, as modified by Paul-Boncour, fully lived up to Jaurès' dictum that *"la nation armée sera la nation juste."* [28]

One of the first modifications in the proposed law that Paul-Boncour made in the interest of "social justice" concerned the question of wartime profits by French industry.   The reporter insisted that the restrictions contained in the government bill were not nearly stringent enough.   In addition, he maintained that the role of the working class had been overlooked in this document and, furthermore, that civilian responsibility for the direction of the war effort had been incompletely achieved. These three matters were particularly important aspects of his ideas on national organization.

The original government project had, to be sure, given the state increased powers of requisition.   In pre-1914 France requisition had been limited to fulfilling the immediate needs of the army and navy, and the power to requisition had been granted to military officers as well as the War and Navy ministries.   The 1924 bill, however, conferred requisitory powers on all the ministries of government and made it possible for these agencies to requisition whatever might be needed by the nation as a whole.   The government could thus command the services of any person or object and could even requisition any new invention which was considered valuable for the national defense. [29]

[27] Paul-Boncour, *Entre deux guerres*, II, 241.

[28] *J.O.C. Deb.*, March 3, 1927, p. 614.

[29] *Ibid., Doc.*, January 10, 1924, No. 6949, pp. 90-91, 97, particularly Articles 10-13, or July 7, 1925, No. 1879, pp. 119-20. These provisions were, in turn, based on two articles in the eighteen-month service act as well as a decree of August, 1917 which had given the government sweeping powers of requisition in time of war.

Paul-Boncour, however, found that this power was neither broad enough nor sufficiently well defined. And what particularly perturbed him was the fact that it seemed to him that the government intended to use its power of requisition only as a second choice if it proved impossible to reach *"accords amiables"* with private industry. In this expressed preference for friendly agreements Paul-Boncour saw the danger of excessive wartime profiteering. Nor did he believe that it was necessary for the government to authorize the payment of bonuses or bounties to industrialists as an incentive to war production—as far as he was concerned, the spur of patriotism alone should suffice. Consequently, among the changes which Paul-Boncour introduced into the government-sponsored measure was a revision of the bonus clauses so that no private manufacturer would be able, in time of war, to receive financial compensation that would exceed the amount he could get from the normal rate of interest on his total invested capital.[30] Defending his bill before the Chamber, Paul-Boncour argued that this change had helped to achieve his purposes: "For the first time a law—and to my knowledge it is the only one with this provision in any of the different countries—has abolished every other wartime profit except the remuneration which is given for the thing requisitioned."[31]

The Socialist leader likewise sought to broaden the bases of popular participation in the war effort and at the same time to insure the supremacy of civilian control. The original project, in the hope of making government intervention in economic affairs more palatable as well as more efficient, had proposed that the planning of industrial mobilization should be carried out with the help of consultative committees composed of representatives of government and of private commercial and industrial associations.[32] To the relevant articles which established

[30] *Ibid.*, February 22, 1927, No. 4018, pp. 259-60.
[31] *Ibid.*, *Deb.*, March 3, 1927, p. 617.
[32] *Ibid.*, *Doc.*, January 10, 1924, No. 6949, p. 92 or July 7, 1925, No. 1879, p. 121.

these procedures, Paul-Boncour added provisions intended to provide for employee as well as management representation on the consultative committees.[33] By similar changes of detail he sought to make certain that control of the nation in time of war would remain in the hands of civilians—in his version the military leaders were given authority over "military operations" instead of "the general conduct of military operations," as the original had provided, and a civilian representative of the government was to be a member of every regional or departmental organization. He redefined the wartime function of the President of the Council so that the political head of the state would be free to devote all of his energies to the prosecution of a war. He added, in addition, special sections designed to maintain the ultimate authority of the Chamber and Senate in time of war and, even if many of their members joined the armed services, to keep them fully representative of the nation.

What Paul-Boncour had done was to blend orthodox Socialist theorems with the concept of the nation in arms. In pre-1914 France, Jean Jaurès had made the reconciliation between Socialism and the nation in arms on the basis of a strictly defensive militia army of citizen-soldiers; in postwar France, Joseph Paul-Boncour effected a similar reconciliation upon the basis of government control of economic affairs, a strict limitation of wartime profits, the representation of workers in the governmental processes, and the exaltation of civilian over military rule.

This was not an unexpected evolution of Socialist thought. For, notwithstanding their devotion to the cause of peace, French Socialists had been among the first to recognize that between 1914 and 1918 the government had instituted a regime which in practice achieved many of the objectives which they had long held dear. During the First World War the French government had not only been forced to call upon the workers and their unions for assistance but had also found it necessary to subject every phase of the national life to minute and thor-

[33] *Ibid.*, February 22, 1927, No. 4018, p. 263.

ough regulation. Under such circumstances there were in wartime France not a few Socialists who, in the words of Élie Halévy,

nourished the foolish hope that the war had produced a miracle and that, on the day of peace, a permanent regime of state socialism combined with syndicalism would have been achieved, if not without the horrors of war, at least without the horrors of a revolution.[34]

Hence, since men like Paul-Boncour realized that the state in wartime must replace laissez-faire with a planned economy, must give labor groups a role in the direction of public affairs, and, in short, must adopt many policies which would be broadly "socialistic," it was logical for them to sponsor a measure such as the national organization bill. Moreover, these French Socialists had, in fact, written a law which, if it had been enacted, would have made it apparent that many of the basic postulates of Socialism would govern the nation in time of war.

The introduction of this measure into the Chamber was, as previously noted, the signal for rejoicing on all party benches. There was no more than a minor diversion from a scattering of Rightist deputies who feared that the bill, as modified by Paul-Boncour and his commission, placed too much emphasis upon requisition, failed to envisage the possibility of cooperative accords between government and private industry, and ignored the value of bounties as a spur to increased war production. One such deputy, the Marquis de La Ferronays, for instance, informed his colleagues that while he believed the proposed legislation was too socialistic in content, he nevertheless intended to vote for it, even if the offending clauses were retained.[35] Paul-

---

[34] Élie Halévy, *L'Ère des tyrannies (Études sur le socialisme et la guerre)* (Paris: Gallimard, 1938), pp. 193-94. See also his *Histoire du socialisme européen* (Paris: Gallimard, 1948), pp. 252-53 for a similar discussion. It might be noted also that Halévy, a close student of European socialism, dated the beginnings of *"l'ère des tyrannies"* with the First World War which brought an unexpected "statism" with it.

[35] *J.O.C. Deb.*, March 4, 1927, p. 640. When another deputy argued on behalf of industrial bonuses for production, his suggestion was greeted with loud shouts of "profiteer," and he soon withdrew his amendment when it was pointed out to

Boncour later maintained that this near-unanimity was the result of "the solidarity of old soldiers" who remembered the experiences of the war.[36] But it would be more correct to observe that, in the years before the rise of the Popular Front and the onset of serious domestic discords, French conservatives remained true to their traditional, nationalist heritage. They still feared Germany more than domestic Socialism. Consequently, they rallied to support a law which, despite the implications of some of its provisions, was designed to guarantee the military security of their nation.

The tiny fraction of French Communist deputies in the Chamber was the only group which, from the outset, raised strenuous protests against the bill to organize the nation in time of war. In the columns of their Parisian daily, *L'Humanité*, and in the Chamber class-conscious Marxists mounted a virulent and sustained attack. For while French Socialists had long since accepted the concept of the nation in arms and adapted it to their own political objectives, the Communists remained firm in their belief that as long as capitalism persisted—and as long as Moscow so ordered it—both patriotism and national defense were no concern of the proletariat or its leaders. Scare headlines in *L'Humanité* announced the alarming fact that Socialist members of the Chamber were receiving cheers of approval from royalist deputies. Bitter cartoons depicted Paul-Boncour as a bloated capitalist and advocate for the General Staff. The key theme of the Communist attack upon the proposed legislation —described as "the organization of forced labor and white terror in the service of imperialism"—was that henceforth no French citizen, regardless of age or sex, would be spared in a future war. And it was added that the Communists were the only party protesting this moral outrage. As one *L'Humanité* editorial observed, the war of 1914-1918 had provided the

---

him that the government intended to try for peaceful accords with industry. *Ibid.*, p. 658.

[36] Paul-Boncour, *Entre deux guerres*, II, 256.

bourgeoisie with a new means to enslave the working class—the concept of the nation in arms. The bourgeoisie, realizing that the barracks army no longer sufficed as a guarantee of their supremacy, had turned to the idea of the nation in arms which, with its mobilization of all Frenchmen, made it a certainty that the capitalist would remain the master of the working class and the destinies of the nation.[37]

Once the legislation, after its approval by the Chamber, had reached the Senate considerable thunder arose from the Right. To be sure, the French conservatives—supported by spokesmen for business as well as by high-ranking military officers associated with the *Conseil Supérieur de la Défense Nationale*—had no desire to reject the proposed law, but, like the Socialists, they desired to give it a somewhat different tone. And they, too, were particularly concerned about the same aspects of wartime organization which had interested the parliamentary Left. By the time the bill reached the upper house, much of the criticism which was only implicit in the Chamber discussions had now become vocal.[38]

---

[37] *L'Humanité*, March 2, 1927, and succeeding editorials through March 8. The Red-dominated CGTU at the same time declared that the French working class refused to recognize the legitimacy of national defense under a capitalist system. Henry Ehrmann, *French Labor from Popular Front to Liberation* (New York: Oxford University Press, 1947), p. 82.

[38] Indicative of this development was the belated change in the editorial policies of *Le Temps*. At the outset (March 4) the newspaper was lavish in its praise and urged all deputies, regardless of party affiliation, to support it. Though somewhat critical of the Socialists' tendency to adopt the concept of the nation in arms as peculiarly their own, *Le Temps* observed that it was a nationalist concept which all should support. Two days later (March 6) the newspaper wondered if a measure of such importance was not being too hastily debated; its editorial maintained that Article Ten (the one which pertained to requisition) would impose an inefficient system and indicated that French private industry could make a system of limited free enterprise operate more efficiently. In succeeding issues (March 7, 9-10) *Le Temps* praised the bill for creating order out of chaos but at the same time maintained that many of its provisions were jumbled, that the arrangements for government-industry relationships were inefficient, and that the whole project was too hurriedly debated. This was a representative example of the attitude of conservatives and nationalists who desired modified changes but who also supported the main objectives of the legislation.

At the very beginning of the report by the Senate's army commission, the spokesman for that group, the conservative Senator Klotz, observed that the proposed law was too harsh and that it granted an excessive amount of power to the government. "France has given too many proofs of her spirit of sacrifice," Klotz wrote, "for any one to have the right to consider her as a nation of deserters and to envisage the need to employ the solution of authority to constrain her civil population." [39] The report then went on to criticize the tendency in the Chamber bill to rely upon requisition rather than freely negotiated contracts and to deny the validity of the principles of free enterprise in the organization of wartime industrial and economic relationships. The Senate commission of commerce and industry, reaching similar conclusions after making a separate study of the bill, observed that the intention to make industrial agreements on a "no-profit" basis would make it virtually impossible for the government to achieve voluntary agreements with French industrialists and that, as a result, the state would have to resort to requisition in its dealings with private industry.[40] Klotz, for the army commission, echoed a similar fear when he wrote that a nonprofit regime would automatically lead to plant seizures. His committee strongly recommended that the legislation be rewritten to make the first obligation of the government that of seeking free and voluntary contractual accords with industry. Prices and profits should be a matter of consent and not of compulsion.[41]

[39] *J.O.S. Doc.*, May 24, 1927, No. 274, p. 586.

[40] *Ibid.*, January 17, 1928, No. 8, pp. 3-4. It was also argued that if plants were requisitioned in time of war, it would be impossible for them to resume operations in peacetime or to adapt themselves to the new conditions of economic existence.

[41] *Ibid.*, May 24, 1927, No. 274, p. 591. At a later date Paul-Boncour stressed the fact that the Senate had been opposed to the limitations on wartime profits contained in his bill. He charged that a widespread campaign against the measure had been led by French industrialists. See his testimony before a post-Second World War investigating commission, in France, Assemblée nationale, 1946, *Commission d'enquête parlementaire: Les Événements survenus en France de 1933 à 1945, Témoignages et documents* (9 vols., Paris: Presses universitaires de France, 1951), III, 811 ff.

Another point of major contention concerned the idea, expressed in both the original and in the Paul-Boncour versions of the law, that in time of war there should be a "national mobilization" of all persons regardless of age or sex. Article One, as originally drafted, had read: "All French citizens . . . without distinction of age or sex are required to participate in the defense of the country or in the maintenance of its material and moral life." In the Chamber there had been criticism of this concept on the grounds that it would destroy the civilian status of nonmilitary personnel who were associated with the national defense work and cause them to lose the protection accorded noncombatants by the London and Hague conventions.[42] To meet this criticism, Paul-Boncour had rewritten Article One to read: "All French citizens . . . without distinction of age or sex, are required to participate . . . whether as combatants in the defense of the country, or as noncombatants in the maintenance of its material and moral life."

The Senate commission, however, believed that even this revision was still too harsh, if not impractical. Senator Klotz bluntly observed that it was impossible to mobilize an entire nation. And, he wrote, if it were attempted, the result might well be a complete militarization of the nation, a subjection of free citizens to military discipline, and a sterile intervention by the state into the moral and intellectual life of the country. Furthermore, the Senate commission, refusing to use the phrase "national mobilization," substituted the words "organization of the nation" throughout the bill, confined usage of the word "mobilization" to strictly military spheres, and spoke only of the "utilization" of the economic resources of the nation.[43] These were, to be sure, but verbal changes, but they indicated that Klotz and his associates held to a concept of the nation in

---

[42] *Ibid., Deb.*, March 4, 1927, pp. 641-45. See also Gilbert Gidel, "L'Organisation de la nation pour le temps de guerre et le droit international," *Revue politique et parlementaire*, CXXXI (Jun. 10, 1927), 314-16.

[43] *J.O.S. Doc.*, May 24, 1927, No. 274, pp. 581-2, 586-87.

arms according to which, even in time of war, every attempt would be made to preserve the traditional liberal values of private initiative and freedom from excessive governmental intervention as well as to maintain the distinction between soldier and citizen.[44]

Yet these modifications were changes of secondary importance, and the principal provisions of the legislation remained. Even if the Senators wanted the government to rely upon the attainment of voluntary agreements with industry, they did nothing to remove the power of requisition from the hands of the state in the event that such attempts were a failure. Though the Senate wanted to employ bonuses and to trust in the profit motive as a means of stimulating war production, at the same time it insisted that there were to be no excessive profits arising from the special circumstances of war. It was a particular concern of Klotz, both in his Senate speeches and in his report, to maintain that his version of the proposed law retained the essential provisions and remained true to the basic principle that, in time of war, every individual and every resource were to be utilized in the defense effort.[45]

To an even greater extent than the French senators, those military leaders qualified to speak on the subject of wartime organization were reluctant to approve the theoretical postulates of Paul-Boncour and the Chamber. On purely military grounds they questioned whether an excessive concern with the economic and industrial aspects of war might not cause the country and

[44] Colonel Mott, the American military attaché, believed that the heart of the Senate modifications was the revision of the articles which pertained to requisition and that the Senators, above all, desired to insure a regime of contract. At the same time he stated that the Senate made few other important changes.

[45] *J.O.S. Deb.*, February 9, 1928, pp. 120 ff. and *Doc.*, No. 274, pp. 579-80. The changes, he claimed, pertained only to requisition policies, voluntary agreements with industry, and a controlled use of the profit incentive. Painlevé, speaking immediately after Klotz in the Senate debate, expressed a similar opinion, agreed that the word "mobilization" should have a restricted meaning, and stated that he and his cabinet colleagues preferred voluntary agreements to requisition. *Ibid., Deb.*, February 9, pp. 129-30.

its leaders to give but secondary consideration to the military side of warfare. If this happened, they warned, the army, as a fighting force, might be so weakened that it would have to abandon any and all plans for rapid operations at the start of a war and, instead, sit idly by until such time as the factories began to produce military supplies. Even worse, they said, was the danger that if France placed too much emphasis upon industrial mobilization and, consequently, neglected her army, then the nation might be forced into fighting another war of attrition—the one type of war which France, above all other countries, should try to avoid.

Typical of the military attitude was the advice offered by General Bernard Serrigny, prominent member of the *Conseil Supérieur de la Défense Nationale* and the army's leading authority on matters of industrial mobilization. As he wrote,

It must not be overlooked that this organization, however, is to be used only in case of a war of long duration, and we shouldn't, therefore, consider it of such importance that, by tying us to a form of warfare which may not suit our operations at all, it might prevent a future change in our war plans.

And he went on to caution against those who "preach the wisdom of assigning the technician to the factories, the farmer to the fields, the scientist to the laboratory, regardless of the age of the men or the needs of the army." This, Serrigny said, "will thus place the defense of the country, at the most critical moment, in the hands of vagabonds." [46]   General Frédéric Herr, once Pétain's artillery chief and another officer who believed that strictly military factors should have first though not all-

[46] General Bernard Serrigny, "L'Organisation de la nation pour le temps de guerre," *Revue des deux mondes,* XVIII (Dec. 1, 1923), 593. He carried this line of reasoning to such an extent that, almost alone among military writers, he justified the French lack of industrial preparedness in 1914. He claimed that with her small population and her inferior birth rate, France had no alternative but to place every man in the line. And in rhetorical form he asked if it would not have been a mistake for France to have assigned men to factories in 1914, particularly since the Germans used every available man in the army and themselves did not think of industrial or economic organization.

inclusive consideration, argued that if France ever fought a nation with a much larger army, she should still plan to put all her able-bodied men in the field and withdraw them for factory production only when the fighting front had been stabilized and allied armies were fighting alongside the French.[47]

Perhaps more vehemently than the senators, these army officials insisted that only a regime of free contract and competition could fill the needs of the new nation in arms. Government intervention, they warned, was sterile if not positively harmful. To cite Serrigny, Secretary General of the *Conseil Supérieur,* once more:

At first there will be a temptation to organize a system similar to that of Karl Marx in which everything will be requisitioned and directed by state officials, and there will be no profits, salaries, liberty, or private initiative—creating, in short, an economic force closely resembling the organization of the military forces at the front.[48]

But, in Serrigny's opinion, the ignorance and incompetence of government were such that while the state might direct and guide general policies, only the management of private industry and such great industrial associations as the *Comité des Forges* could effectively control the processes of wartime production. Similarly, in the course on industrial mobilization which Colonel Delavallée gave at the *École Supérieure de la Guerre,* that officer insisted that a regime of free contract and competition for war orders would provide the most efficient system, and he was seconded by another military expert in the field of industrial mobilization, Intendant General Laporte, who wrote in like vein that

We must force ourselves, then, to act with regard for the mentality and habits of producers and commercial operations—by placing them

---

[47] General Frédéric Herr, *L'Artillerie* (Paris: Berger-Levrault, 1924), p. 278.

[48] General Bernard Serrigny, "L'Organisation de la nation pour le temps de guerre," *Revue des deux mondes,* XVIII (Dec. 1, 1923), 595.

under the regime of contract rather than that of constraint—and by working through the cadre of existing organizations.[49]

Paul-Boncour himself later maintained that the General Staff was, if not quasi-hostile, at least indifferent to his law and did not realize that military operations could be carried out far more successfully if the High Command possessed the same authority in industrial and economic matters that it had within the military establishment itself.[50]

The result of these differences of opinion about the national organization bill was that it was impossible during the 1920's to get final legislative approval for the measure.   The Senate, acting in the spirit of the Klotz report, made the changes that were recommended, but—despite the valiant efforts of Painlevé —there the matter stopped.   Thereafter neither the Chamber nor the Senate made any further efforts to iron out the differences between their respective versions of the law.   The reasons for this turn of events were many and varied.   In the first place, many French businessmen looked askance at a proposed wartime organization law which, even with the Senate modifications, might subject them to a regime of requisition and a strict control of their profits.[51]   Even more significant was the fact that as soon as the Senate began to modify the Paul-Boncour draft, the Socialists turned against the project they had formerly advocated so strongly.   Their official spokesman claimed that

[49] Lt. Colonel Delavallée, *Cours de fabrications de guerre* (Paris: Imprimerie nationale, 1922), pp. 134 ff. and Intendant General Ferdinand Laporte, *Mobilisation économique et intendance militaire* (Paris: Charles-Lavauzelle, 1931), pp. 302-03. A few years later, Lt. Charles Ailleret, writing on the same subject, took the view that "Only those who think that an organization à la Karl Marx will furnish the nation with a suitable economic system can envisage this socialization of circumstance as a good thing," and he went on to oppose the creation of a wartime economic regime based upon the ideas of state socialism. Lt. Charles Ailleret, *L'Organisation économique de la nation en temps de guerre* (Paris: Librairie technique et économique, 1935), p. 27. For some adverse comments, see also Menu, *Applications*, II, 95 ff.

[50] Paul-Boncour, *Entre deux guerres*, II, 254.

[51] *J.O.S. Doc.*, January 17, 1928, No. 8, p. 4, the report of the Senate commission of commerce and industry which registered some of these protests.

the changes made by the Senate had altered the law to such an extent that in a future war, as in 1914, only the army and not the nation would be mobilized, that the door would be opened wide for wartime profiteering, and that the entire country would be left at the mercy of the General Staff.[52] This, however, was far from being the real reason for the change in the opinions of the Socialists. The party was actually badly divided on the whole issue. Many intellectuals as well as many rank and file members of the party opposed the project. The Communist attack on the measure had made such labor organizations as the *Confédération Générale du Travail* not only hostile to the bill but also fearful that it might entail a labor draft and the loss of high wartime wages. Thus, the Senate changes provided the Socialists with a good excuse to avoid their dilemma by turning against the project.[53] A final reason why the bill was never enacted was simply that the approach of national elections in 1928 made it appear political wisdom for all parties to drop the now-controversial legislation from the agenda.

No further attempt was made to enact a law on the organization of the nation in time of war until the eve of the Second World War. And thus, though there was widespread agreement that the military security of France made it necessary to enact such a law, the conflicting ideas of Socialists, conservative senators, and military leaders prevented any concrete legislative accomplishments. In terms of theory, the French had developed the concept of the nation in arms to its furthest point, but they were still unable to translate theory into practice.

[52] *Ibid., Deb.*, February 7, 1928, pp. 105-07.

[53] Paul-Boncour, *Entre deux guerres*, II, 258 ff.; David J. Saposs, *The Labor Movement in Post-War France* (New York: Columbia University Press, 1931), pp. 459-60, a brief note on the schism in Socialist ranks; Ehrmann, *French Labor*, pp. 82 ff., the best account. Paul-Boncour's later break with his party occurred when, particularly in the early thirties, the Socialists turned to doctrinaire pacifism and rejected his ideas entirely.

VI

The Nation in Arms and the Coming of a Second World War

With the passage of the one-year conscription law and the unsuccessful attempt to enact legislation for the organization of the nation in time of war the era of military reorganization drew to a close. The bills which had been passed—or attempted—had not only laid down the bases for the postwar nation in arms but had also established the military pattern which was to remain until the outbreak of a new conflict in September of 1939. The one-year service legislation had finally institutionalized the dearly beloved principle of the moderate Left and its allies that the army was essentially a training school and that French military strength resided in the reserve of citizen-soldiers. The "Paul-Boncour law," though without parliamentary approval, had given express recognition to the principle that, in a world where war appeared to have become total, the military power of the nation was directly proportional to its organized economic and industrial strength. There was, to be sure, new military legislation in the years prior to the coming of the Second World War—the building of the Maginot Line, a return to two-year service in 1935, the partial nationalization of war industry by the *Front populaire*, and, in the last year of peace, the eventual enactment of the national organization bill—but while these modified and even expanded French military ideas, none of the later legislation produced any significant change in the fundamental military pattern established in the twenties. The war which was fought and lost in 1939-40 was in large part in its military phase a test of the theories elaborated and put into operation in the first decade after the Armistice of 1918.

The military organization and institutions established in the first postwar decade remained unchanged for another ten years not only because they were founded upon assumptions which represented the ultimate working out of a long theoretical development but also—and more simply—because French military thought became stultified. The principal French theorists became wedded to the doctrine of defensive warfare to the exclusion of other, and possibly more fruitful, military concepts. Equally important was the fact that this doctrine was accepted not only by the men who commanded the French armies but also by the political leaders of the Third Republic. Thus, by the outbreak of the Second World War both political and military command had come to place a firm, unwavering faith in the power of the defensive, to insist that it was a virtual impossibility to rupture a continuous military front, and to expect that any war between France and Germany would be a long relentless war of attrition. The acceptance of this credo was so widespread that it is not incorrect to speak of a national "Maginot Line complex." Moreover, the logic upon which the postwar concept of the nation in arms was founded became, in turn, the logic on which the theory of defensive war itself came to rest; the ideas which were fundamental in the development of the former concept were the same ideas which were employed to justify the latter. Thus, French thought on the nation in arms tended to become a closed body of static doctrine which provided a thorough justification for the adoption of defensive military strategies and the assumption that no German onslaught could achieve quick or easy victory.

The great lesson of the war of 1914-1918 had been that materiel was as important as manpower and that, consequently, entrenched infantrymen, armed with the weapons which flowed from mass production industries, had been able to maintain a continuous front from the North Sea to the Swiss frontier.

One result of this knowledge was, of course, the attempt by men like Paul-Boncour to enact legislation which would establish the proper balance between front-line soldiers and rear-area production workers and thus guarantee both a steady flow of war material and a sufficient number of soldiers. Another and equally significant conclusion was the belief that the offensive had become more difficult—and a static defense, by contrast, much easier—because the new materiel and weapons which had been developed worked to the advantage of the defender. Theorists of the immediate postwar years, like Marshal Foch, had not been entirely pessimistic about the future of offensive operations; they had argued that if an attacking army built up an overwhelming material superiority, it could break through the line of trenches and restore the war of movement. But the military writers of the thirties, particularly those associated with the upper strata of the military hierarchy, stressed the negative aspect of the wartime experiences: the virtual impossibility of a successful offense. Sceptical of the offensive potentialities of the tank and the airplane, these men continually emphasized the ability of current materiel to obstruct offensive operations, prevent a war of movement, and bestow tactical advantages upon the military force entrenched in fixed defensive positions. Hence they came to visualize the French army as a singularly defensive tool and to emphasize that France must adopt a defensive strategy for at least many months after the outbreak of any future war. The theorists who held such views could not, of course, envisage an immediate military victory for France or anticipate any type of conflict except a war of attrition, but they could at least retain the comforting thought that an attack by the German army could achieve no sudden or overwhelming success for the forces of the Third Reich.[1]

[1] On the strategical ideas of the French military leaders between the two wars, see Donald J. Harvey, *French Concepts of Military Strategy (1919-1939)* (Unpublished dissertation, Columbia University, 1953). At all stages in the preparation of this book I have gained immeasurably from conversations and associations with Mr. Harvey. Although it was written shortly after the defeat of 1940, an excellent

√ The other great lesson of the First World War had been that the reservist had proved his mettle. This belief, particularly comforting to a nation which desired a minimum length military service, was of course the especial favorite of the dominant political parties, but a chastened High Command—perhaps because it recognized the handwriting on the wall—seems to have accepted it with but little outward protest. In any event, the prevailing faith in the reserves provided the essential justification for creating a military organization which was suited almost exclusively for defensive missions and which could not, in view of its composition, undertake offensive operations at the onset of hostilities. To those Frenchmen who tended toward pacifism, of which there were many, a defensive army waging defensive warfare was the only legitimate type of military organization. Hence, when a minority of "advanced" thinkers like Charles de Gaulle and Paul Reynaud outlined plans for an armored corps of professional soldiers who would be able to act as an offensive striking force, these men were the first to cry out in protest not only because such schemes threatened to lay violent hands upon the sacred principle of the citizen-soldier but also because they anticipated offensive—and, consequently, immoral—warfare. Thus it was that many of the heirs of Jaurès and Gambetta, like those who emphasized the importance of materiel, also made the concept of the nation in arms into a theoretical justification for defensive warfare.

√ An equally powerful and somewhat more obvious reason for the stagnation in French military thought and achievement in the thirties was the serious economic and political crisis of these years. In France, as in so many other countries, its effect was to create at least a partial paralysis of the will to resist. The seemingly endless years of economic depression—becoming most

short summary of French military ideas is Irving M. Gibson, "Maginot and Liddell Hart—The Doctrine of Defense," in E. M. Earle, ed., *The Makers of Modern Strategy* (Princeton: Princeton University Press, 1943), pp. 365-87. See also Fred M. Greene, *French Security and Military Leadership against Germany, 1919-1940* (Unpublished dissertation, Yale University, 1950).

severe in France at a time when other European states appeared on the road to recovery—made many persons believe that money expended on national defense was a shameful waste.   In these years of depression the pipe dream of peace through disarmament, as well as a genuine fear of war and a sense of its futility, drove many men of good intentions into the ranks of the pacifists.   Hence it was small wonder that an advocate of preparedness like Paul-Boncour became a pariah to his fellow Socialists and that, while he resigned from the party in protest, his former colleagues once again resumed the practice of voting against military appropriations as a matter of principle.

Even more disheartening was the political disintegration of the French nation which came swiftly upon the heels of the deepening social crisis of the 1930's.   When the parties of the Left merged their differences in the ill-fated *Front populaire* of 1936, the French Right, fearful of a plunge into the murky depths of Socialism, began to lose some of its traditional anti-German nationalism and to see in Adolf Hitler a type of saviour who, after all, was reputed to have rescued his country from the tender mercies of the Leftists.   Although probably only a few Frenchmen actually operated on the assumption that—as the catch phrase ran—Hitler was better than Léon Blum, the number of nationalists and conservatives recruited for the strategy of appeasement was high.   To be sure, just at the time when the Right was becoming increasingly disaffected, the Popular Front parties, motivated by the desire to halt the spread of Fascism, at last took up an active anti-German policy.   Thus Socialists eventually came to approve increases in the military budget, and the Chamber itself came to witness touching spectacles of alleged Communist devotion to *la patrie*.[2]   However, the French Left, for a variety of reasons, had little more success than preceding governments in solving France's domestic prob-

[2] This switch of traditional attitudes is the theme of Charles Micaud, *The French Right and Nazi Germany 1933-1939* (Durham, N. C.: Duke University Press, 1943).

lems and restoring national morale. Whatever the causes, there can be no doubt that in 1939 the French people went to war with a listless reluctance that in no way resembled the spirit of any previous generation.

Thus the decade of the thirties—when military theories became stagnant and a divided nation became lost in introspection and party warfare—did not provide an atmosphere conducive to the development of dynamic concepts of the nation in arms. Hence the theory of *la nation armée* proclaimed the legitimacy of but one type of warfare: the defensive.

The outstanding military achievement of the years which immediately followed the basic military reorganization—to move from general to specific considerations—was the building of the vast series of underground fortifications, since known as the Maginot Line, along sectors of the exposed eastern frontier. There were many reasons for constructing these subterranean labyrinths of concrete: the tradition handed down from Vauban to Seré de Rivière, the almost legendary symbol of the battered but unconquered forts of Verdun, and the knowledge that France must soon evacuate the Rhineland buffer zone. Those who, like Painlevé or Maginot, believed in the defensive powers of modern armaments stressed the fact that fortifications would enable the defenders to pour forth a continuous and uninterrupted stream of fire from artillery and automatic weapons which would interdict all enemy movement on the battlefield.[3] But, in addition to these significant arguments, one of the im-

---

[3] See *J.O.C. Deb.*, December 10, 1929, p. 4235 (speech by Maginot) and Paul Painlevé, *Paroles et écrits* (Paris: Rieder, 1936), p. 391. On the influence of the Verdun experience, see *J.O.C. Doc.*, December 29, 1929, No. 2657, pp. 399-400. It is also a fact of importance that the first credits for construction were granted in the year which preceded the French evacuation of the Rhineland; a few years earlier Painlevé had been forced to sell surplus army barracks and property to obtain the money for experimental models. On this see Enno A. Kraehe, "Motives behind the Maginot Line," *Military Affairs*, VIII (Summer, 1944), 115, an article, based upon parliamentary sources, which is the best account of the building of the fortifications and the purpose they were to serve. The account in Pierre Belperron, *Maginot of the Line*, trans. H. J. Stenning (London: Williams and Morgate, 1940), pp. 76 ff. is interesting but superficial.

portant motives for building the Maginot Line was the belief that fortifications would answer the manpower needs of the army.

As long as France adhered to the principle of universal service and established her army upon mass conscription, the problem of manpower for her armed forces was always a primary consideration.   In all the discussions that preceded the building of the Line there was a keen awareness of the fact that Germany possessed a far larger population from which to recruit her soldiers than France did and that, when the so-called "lean years" arrived in 1935 (the time at which the young men born during the First World War, when the birth rate had slumped tremendously, would come of military age), the hereditary enemy would be in an even more advantageous position because of the sharp decline in the size of the annual French contingents. Consequently, to a nation which feared that too few men would be available for conscription, the Maginot Line won adherents on the simple grounds that it would enable fewer men to fight more efficiently.[4]

No less important was the fact that so many of France's industrial and mineral resources were located on a still-vulnerable frontier, a consideration which assumed an added military significance in view of the realization that in any future war every factor of production would be needed to maintain the nation in arms.[5]   After 1870 Seré de Rivière had constructed a defense

4 *J.O.C. Deb.*, December 27, 1929, p. 4774, a speech by Maginot in which he stressed the advantages of the fortifications after 1935. See also Enno Kraehe, "Motives behind the Maginot Line," *Military Affairs*, VIII (Summer, 1944), 114.

5 The same logic, it would seem, should have dictated extending the fortifications along the Belgian frontier to guard the equally vital industrial complex centering around Lille. Since the Sedan breakthrough many explanations have been offered: some have blamed Pétain, while others have insisted that such fortifications would have driven Belgium into neutrality even before 1936. However, it appears that the French staff had long anticipated moving into Belgium at the outbreak of war for the purpose of establishing a defense line on Belgian soil. It was believed that such a strategy would not only protect the area around Lille but would also prevent destruction of the vital manufacturing centers of northeastern France. On all of these points, see Theodore Draper, *The Six Weeks' War* (New York: Viking, 1944), pp. 3-10, André Géraud (Pertinax), *The Gravediggers of France* (New York:

line running from Belfort through Toul and Épinal as far as Verdun, a location which had been chosen primarily to take advantage of the defensive possibilities of the heights of the Meuse but which had been based exclusively upon purely military criteria. Now, however, fortifications were situated so that they could mount permanent guard over areas that produced war materials vital to the French armies and so that they could prevent much of the industrial heart of the nation from becoming, as in 1914, an easy acquisition for the German army.

Perhaps the most significant reason for the construction of the Maginot Line was the fact that, with the enactment of the one-year law of 1928, France adopted a form of the nation in arms which made fortifications appear a vital adjunct to national defense. As early as the debates in 1927 on the national organization bill Paul-Boncour had observed that the day was fast approaching—as war veterans ceased to be subject to military call —when the defense of the nation would rest squarely upon the shoulders of young, untested, short-service soldiers and reservists who had never been under fire. Consequently, however much the political parties in power might believe in the inherent military virtues of such soldiers, most deputies considered that it would at least be prudent to reinforce an army of reservists with bastions of concrete.[6] After all, whereas in 1914 there had been three classes under arms and available to guard the French frontier, the legislation of 1928 had officially recognized the fact that, even with Painlevé's additional professionals, the active army could not perform the *couverture* mission without the immediate aid of the youngest reserve classes. Moreover, it was realized that it would require considerable time to call up

---

Doubleday, Doran, 1944), pp. 11 ff., and, above all, Lt. Colonel Lugand, "Les Forces en présence au 10 mai 1940," and R. Villate, "L'Entrée des Français en Belgique," *Revue d'histoire de la deuxième guerre mondiale,* Nos. 10 and 11 (Jun., 1953), 14-27, 60-64. For various interpretations of the French failure to extend the fortifications along the Belgian frontier, see Paul Reynaud, *La France a sauvé l'Europe* (2 vols., Paris: Flammarion, 1947), I, 215-20 and General Maurice Gamelin, *Servir* (3 vols., Paris: Plon, 1946-47), I, 303-08 and II, 184-85.

[6] *J.O.C. Deb.,* March 3, 1927, p. 619.

these reservists—indeed, under the prevailing military system, the mobilization of the entire national army would be a particularly lengthy process.   Under such circumstances, then, fortifications appeared vital; acting as a steel and concrete *couverture,* they would not only reinforce the army but would also provide the nation with sufficient time to mobilize all of its military establishment.

Even if the Germans struck with the highly publicized *attaque brusque*—a theme which, incidentally, appeared in postwar French military literature almost as consistently as it had in the years before 1914—the advocates of the Maginot Line claimed that they could not penetrate the French fortifications despite the fact that the defenses would be manned by short-service recruits and reservists without experience.[7]   On the other hand, as Colonel Jean Fabry argued, without such fortifications, the French would not have the time, the space, or the freedom to organize their nation in arms.   In this same speech, it might be added, Fabry pointed out something which in later years many Frenchmen seemed quite readily inclined to forget: that the Maginot Line was intended to act as an auxiliary instrument of national defense, an inanimate *couverture* designed primarily to give France the time to mobilize the nation in arms.   It was not intended to be a Chinese wall which would hermetically seal the Franco-German frontier for the duration of a war.[8]

It might also be observed that if, in a sense, fortifications were the price paid for a system of one-year conscription, once the Maginot Line was constructed it served, by the same line of reasoning, as a powerful argument for the continuance of the existing military order.   When, for instance, the military budget of 1935 was under debate, the *rapporteur* advanced the thesis that France could continue to conscript men for a twelve-month tour of duty because she had a strong system of eastern fortifications. Despite the increasing threat from Germany and the coming of

[7] *Ibid.,* December 10 and 27, 1929, pp. 4217 ff. and 4766-77.
[8] *Ibid.,* December 27, 1929, pp. 4770-71.

the years of reduced contingents many believed that the Maginot Line not only tended to alleviate the chronic manpower problem but also permitted maintenance of the 1928 law.[9] Thus the Maginot Line enabled the French to have their cake and eat it too—its construction was made necessary by the creation of a military establishment based on a one-year service, but, once the Line was built, it also served to justify the continuance of the same recruiting system.

Even when it became apparent that Germany, under the dictatorial regime of the ex-corporal Hitler, was beginning a deliberate rearmament and had no compunctions about scrapping the military clauses of the Versailles Treaty, the French made no basic modifications in their own military organization. To be sure, in March of 1935 the French Chamber authorized the extension of the period of military service from one to two years, and at the same time, defense expenditures began a moderate upward spiral.[10] But the government relied on a technicality in the 1928 law to achieve the two-year service, and the increases in military spending were at first quite modest— indeed, throughout the early phase of rearmament there was a pronounced tendency to regard military expenditures as simply another means of economic recovery. The French government, like that of many other states, discovered that the money spent for rearmament acted as stimulant to the economic system. Hence the Blum cabinet, for instance, appropriated supplementary military funds "for the execution of national defense programs and great public works designed to aid economic recovery and fight the depression" and, in addition, found authorization for military expenditures under the provisions of a law designed primarily to combat the depression. Thus both

---

[9] *Ibid.*, November 22, 1934, p. 2573 and June 14, 1934, pp. 1489 ff.

[10] Charles Tiffen, *La Course aux armaments et les finances publiques* (Paris: Librairie Générale de Droit et de Jurisprudence, 1937), pp. 122 ff. In fact, the amount of money spent for armaments in 1935 was not as great as had been spent in 1932, but it did represent at least a moderate increase over the expenditures of 1934. From 1935 onwards, too, there was a steady increase in military expenditures.

rearmament and the two-year service of 1935 entered by the back door, and neither modified in any appreciable degree either the theory or the practice of the nation in arms.

The debate over the length of military service, coming at a time when the problems of depression still received priority and when the possibility of doing business with Hitler did not yet seem an absurdity, fitted into the customary pattern of Chamber military discussions. The conservatives and nationalists were the main supporters of two-year service, the Left was strongly opposed, and the Radical Socialists were, as usual, divided among themselves.[11] In 1935 French Socialists were still perilously close to doctrinaire pacifism. In these years, for instance, they regarded the allocation of funds for supplementary training periods for the reserves as financially ruinous, and they considered that rearmament of any sort was but the prelude to a European arms race from which none could profit.[12] During the two-year service debate Léon Blum, speaking for his party, maintained that the project was a form of political trickery, and he was scandalized that, at a time when the nation was just beginning to recover from Fascist-sponsored riots, the government could think of trying to militarize the French people.

The attitude of both Socialists and Radical Socialists remained intransigent throughout the course of the 1935 conscription debates. During these military discussions, Paul Reynaud, as unorthodox then as later, was attempting to secure parliamentary consideration for the military theories of a young colonel,

11 Micaud, *French Right*, pp. 41 ff., particularly valuable in showing that the conservatives—such as Fabry, Reynaud, Marin, Franklin-Bouillon—were unanimously in favor of the increase and hostile to Germany.

12 *J.O.C. Deb.*, February 21, 1934, p. 601, a debate in which the Socialists refused military appropriations and which took place barely two weeks after the famous Fascist-inspired riots of that year. Similar opposition was voiced to Pétain's request for additional funds to complete the Maginot Line., *ibid.*, June 14, 1934, pp. 1497-98, 1523. The Communists, of course, continued to remain in bitter opposition to "degenerate militarism" until the formation of the Popular Front and until Stalin indicated that French armaments were vital to the anti-Fascist front, at which time the party "line" went through appropriate convulsions. Alexander Werth, *The Twilight of France 1933-1939* (New York: Harper, 1942), pp. 40-41.

Charles de Gaulle, who believed that the French army should have added to it an armored force of a hundred thousand crack professional troops. Spicing his words with liberal quotations from the writings of Jaurès, Blum shrugged off the suggestions of Reynaud and de Gaulle as nothing more than misguided theories of the sort that were common to the upper brackets of a military clique which would relish an offensive war. And he warned that if France adopted the antidemocratic, aggressive system of de Gaulle, then the nation would re-establish the reactionary military system of the Napoleonic era and face the added danger of becoming involved once again in sterile and wasteful offensives like those of 1914.[13] Édouard Daladier, the spokesman for the Radical Socialists, seconded Blum with the allegation that the Reynaud plan for a mechanized army of professional soldiers was a concept "more dangerous than one might believe for the security of our nation." [14] Consequently, reaffirming their faith in the short-service army of hallowed tradition, Blum and his colleagues not only refused to authorize any increase in the number of professional soldiers but also opposed lengthening the term of military service.[15] Thus, as late as 1935, the form which the nation in arms had achieved in the 1928 law still retained all of its original validity for the French Left.

Nor in 1935 did the Flandin government approach the question of two-year service with any deeper insights. Perhaps be-

13 *J.O.C. Deb.*, March 15, 1935, pp. 1023-27. Blum restated his opposition to the scheme before a post-Liberation commission of investigation. See France, Assemblée nationale, 1946, *Commission d'enquête parlementaire: Les Événements survenus en France de 1933 à 1945, Témoignages et documents* (9 vols., Paris: Presses universitaires de France, 1951), I, 223 ff. (Hereafter abbreviated as Commission d'enquête).

14 *J.O.C. Deb.*, March 15, 1935, p. 1048.

15 Even after the formation of the *Front populaire*, there were some Socialists— dubbed the "irreconcilables" and led by a Marcel Pivert—who continued to attack the two-year service and to spread antimilitarist propaganda. See Hélène Modiano, *Les Militaires contre la nation* (Paris: Éditions du Parti SFIO, 1936), a violent attack on the two-year law which is documented by the speeches of a Communist deputy. See also Werth, *Twilight*, pp. 41-42.

cause Flandin and his colleagues feared a public outcry against doubling the conscript's tour of duty, they took refuge in an "escape clause" conveniently available in the 1928 legislation— Article Forty, which granted authority to the government, if circumstances warranted and if the legislature gave a formal vote of approval, to keep trained men in service for an indefinite period of time after their one-year term was over.[16]

This clause had been placed in the one-year law by the deputies of 1928 who, however much they might have been under the spell of doctrinaire military thories, were nonetheless aware of the triple problem posed by the French birth rate, the size of the respective French and German populations, and the fact that in the "lean years" of 1935-1939 the number of men available for induction would suddenly drop to a hundred and twenty-five thousand, or half the normal contingent. Such concerns, as in pre-1914 years, had in fact continued to command the attention of the deputies in the period after the war.

As early as the first postwar debates in 1922, for instance, there had been an extended discussion of the military problems connected with the French birth rate, and many deputies accepted General Serrigny's thesis that the key to national defense was to be found in the birth rate. Amateur demographers, as in the past, continued to prophesy doom, and even the sponsors of the eighteen-month bill had insisted that, because of the French birth rate, no conscription law could remain in force for more than fifteen years.[17] During the same debates a wide variety of amendments were offered as solutions to the problem; all would have juggled the length of service as a means of boosting the birth rate. For instance, one scheme would have reduced the term of service for young men who were members of large families, on the grounds that such a provision would

---

[16] *J.O.C. Deb.*, March 15, 1935, pp. 1021 ff.

[17] *Ibid. Doc.*, June 2, 1921, No. 2710, p. 1731. For a discussion of the influence of the birth rate on French military thought, see Shelby C. Davis, *The French War Machine* (London: Allen and Unwin, 1937), Chapter I, "A Bid for Babies."

be a strong incentive for Frenchmen to rear bigger families. Another proposal was that the length of time a soldier served in the ranks should be directly proportional to the size of the family of which he was a member—the deputy who made this suggestion argued that, as the Revolution had enshrined the Rights of Man, the government should now enshrine the Rights of the Family. The ultimate *reductio ad absurdum* was an amendment which would have enabled any conscript to obtain a release from the army if he could present his commanding officer with written evidence that his wife had become pregnant; the author of this amendment was sublimely confident that it would solve the problem of the French birth rate by making it highly advantageous for young men to assume the burdens of fatherhood.[18]

In the 1928 debates much of the same ground was covered, and many of the same fears were expressed. The remedy of the "escape clause" was added, and an additional scheme was formulated to maintain the size of the annual contingent at the steady, if somewhat reduced, level of 200,000 men by juggling the age of induction between nineteen and a half and twenty-one years.[19]

Therefore, because the Flandin cabinet knew that both the public and the deputies were well aware of the coming of the "lean years" and of the correlation between conscription policies and the birth rate, the ministry approached the problem of extending the length of service on this level. Making deliberate use of the aforementioned Article Forty, the cabinet restricted its conscription policy to the simple request for authorization to double the term of service during the years from 1935 to

18 *Ibid. Deb.*, June 15, 1922, p. 1817. For the preceding schemes see June 8, pp. 1696 ff. and June 13, pp. 1777-78. The number of amendments was so great and their combined effect would have been so crippling that Fabry was correct in believing that they threatened the entire project's effectiveness. See also Joseph Spengler, *France Faces Depopulation* (Durham: Duke University Press, 1938), pp. 128-29.

19 J.I.R.G.I., *L'Armée française vivra* (Paris: Librairie de la *Revue française*, 1929), pp. 50-51; Paul Bernier, *La Loi d'un an* (Paris: Charles-Lavauzelle, 1931), pp. 50-51.

1939 in accordance with the provisions of the law of 1928.[20] This procedure was adopted despite the fact that Article Forty had not been designed to serve as the basis for a permanent system but simply as a means of keeping trained men under the colors in the event of a sudden emergency.[21]   However, Flandin apparently believed that the only way he could avert a bitter parliamentary battle over conscription policies was by relying on this article instead of introducing an entirely new project. Thus, in view of the government's tactics, the doubling of the length of service in 1935 reflected no significant changes in either the established theories or practices of the nation in arms. Since the cabinet argued its case on the carefully chosen ground of the imminent decline in the annual contingents, two-year service, like rearmament, arrived in a backhand manner and produced no appreciable difference in either the French military establishment or the assumptions upon which it was founded.

After the electoral triumph of the Popular Front in 1936 one of the first measures proposed by the new ministry of Léon Blum was the nationalization of French war industry.   Yet, like the two-year service project, arms nationalization was not a proposal of great significance in the history of French thought on the nation in arms.   Nor, for that matter, was it closely related to the increasing German threat which the reoccupation of the Rhineland had recently emphasized.   The principal reasons advanced in behalf of arms nationalization were political and social, and only incidentally was there any genuine consideration of its relation to problems of national defense.   The Popular Front was riding the wave of popular hostility towards the "merchants of death."[22]   Such organizations as the CGT

---

[20] *J.O.C. Deb.*, March 15, 1935, pp. 1021.

[21] Paul Reynaud was quite bitter about the use of Article Forty. He argued that it had been an imprudent step which the Left had been able to use to good advantage in the campaign of 1936 and, furthermore, that the original intention of the authors of the articles had been simply to provide troops to meet an emergency. Reynaud, *La France*, I, 308-10.

[22] Henry W. Ehrmann, *French Labor from Popular Front to Liberation* (New York: Oxford University Press, 1947), pp. 84-85. General Gamelin later claimed

had long demanded nationalization of the arms industry, and when the Popular Front parties were drawing up their 1936 election platform, the authors of their program placed considerable stress upon a plank which called for the nationalization of French armaments and the suppression of all private trade in arms.[23]   Moreover, in introducing legislation designed to achieve these election promises, the spokesmen for the Popular Front could argue that they were not proposing something entirely new and radical, for the manufacture and sale of powder had been a government monopoly since the 1790's and, more recently, Pierre Laval's ministry had been authorized to establish strict controls over the finances and the profits of private arms manufacturers.[24]

Almost all of the arguments advanced in behalf of the arms nationalization project related to the political and social advantages which the Popular Front ministry claimed would follow from its enactment.   The thesis advanced by War Minister Édouard Daladier was simply that the manufacture of armaments should be regarded as one of the public services and not as a source of profits for any one.[25]   One of his principal arguments was that the nationalization of war industries would be an important step along the road to eventual world peace.

---

the Controller General of the army, Robert Jacomet, had attempted to win his approval for the law by arguing that "the political current was toward nationalizations." Jacomet also contended that the army would have great difficulty getting appropriations for war materials if it failed to approve the government's nationalization program. Gamelin, *Servir*, I, 213.

[23] See Pierre Cot, *The Triumph of Treason*, trans. Sybille and Milton Crane (Chicago: Ziff-Davis, 1944), pp. 397-99. It is significant that the demand for arms nationalization was included in that part of the Popular Front platform which was entitled "Defense of the Peace."

[24] *J.O.C. Deb.*, July 16, 1936, p. 1931, and discussion in Kimon A. Doukas, "Armaments and the French Experience," *American Political Science Review*, XXXIII (Apr., 1940), 283, 287 ff.

[25] *J.O.C. Doc.*, June 26, 1936, No. 465, p. 1079, the original *exposé des motifs*, supposedly the work of Daladier, the Minister of War. Typical of the prevalence of this attitude was the fact that even at the Riom Trial Léon Blum insisted that arms nationalization had been widely demanded by a French public which refused to tolerate the consistent warmongering of the arms manufacturers. Pierre Tissier, *The Riom Trial* (London: Harrap, 1942), p. 88.

Daladier said that various studies by the League of Nations showed that international control of armaments was impossible until each of the individual members of the League had undertaken the job of regulating the manufacture and sale of arms within its own borders.[26] To the members of the Chamber army commission—a group which reached similar conclusions— arms nationalization would make world peace easier to achieve, help to check any worldwide armaments race, prevent private industrialists from reaping immoral profits, and help to alleviate the social conflicts then so evident throughout the country.[27]

In this quest for social justice both the cabinet and the deputies were inclined to minimize, if not overlook, the effect which nationalization would have upon defense policies and war production. To be sure, Daladier argued that state ownership would insure a more rapid production of war goods because private profits would not be a determining factor, and Chouffet, the Chamber *rapporteur*, maintained that a proper coordination of industrial mobilization plans could be obtained only if the armament industry was nationalized.[28] But these considerations were given but perfunctory attention. There was, for instance, no discussion in the project itself or in parliamentary debates of how such goals were to be achieved, and Daladier never went further into detail than to make the pious statement that nationalization would automatically increase production.[29] More-

[26] *J.O.C. Doc.*, June 26, 1936, No. 465, p. 1080. In his final pre-election speech Daladier had insisted that nationalization of the arms industry was vital to the "organization of the Peace." *Le Temps*, April 26, 1936.

[27] *J.O.C. Doc.*, July 9, 1936, No. 628, pp. 1258-60. For a highly critical account of the motives which underlay the arms nationalization program, see A. Bigant, *La Nationalization et le contrôle des usines de guerre* (Paris: Les Éditions Domat-Montchrestien, 1939), pp. 30 ff. Bigant, noting the prevalence of arguments designed to make it appear that nationalization was necessary for European peace, that it would eliminate an "immoral" industry, and that it would alleviate industrial disputes, concluded that the law was essentially "political" in character (p. 57).

[28] *J.O.C. Doc.*, June 26, 1936, No. 465, p. 1082 and July 9, 1936, No. 628, p. 1258.

[29] *Ibid., Deb.*, July 17, 1936, pp. 1993-94 and *J.O.S. Deb.*, August 7, 1936, p.

over, the War Minister apparently believed that in 1936 the French war industries were overexpanded. The government, he pointed out, was going to take over only those plants whose production was needed to maintain the projected rearmament program and to replace materiel which was consumed. Daladier maintained that if the state assumed control over the entire French armaments industry, then it would find itself the owner of much excess and idle plant capacity and would be forced to spend vast sums of money to convert these unused facilities for the production of normal civilian goods.[30]

Consequently the whole nationalization program received superficial consideration. Since most deputies were convinced of the need for some controls, even the principal counterproject called for the enactment of such measures as strict licensing of arms manufacturers, government supervision of their finances, and the prohibition of all exports of arms.[31] There were, to be sure, some conservative charges that the enactment of the law would be "a victory for the Marxist doctrine," but the Popular Front measure, never seriously challenged, passed the Chamber

---

1112. This, of course, has been one of the points most hotly debated after the French defeat. At Riom, and later, Daladier insisted that it would have been impossible to modernize French war plants without nationalization, and Pierre Cot argued that the production of tanks would have been less if such private industries as Renault had not been placed under government control (see Tissier, *Riom Trial*, p. 88; Cot, *Triumph of Treason*, p. 164; *Commission d'enquête, Témoignages et documents*, I, 18 ff.). Gamelin contended that the benefits of nationalization began to show themselves only after 1938 (Gamelin, *Servir*, I, 213). It should be noted, however, that Pierre Cot's scheme for nationalizing the French aircraft industry was not founded upon such narrow and essentially moral preoccupations. Cot hoped to set up a national organization which would modernize an industry that every one realized was backward and inefficient. Another of his goals was to decentralize an industry which was located almost exclusively in the vulnerable environs of Paris (Cot, *Triumph of Treason*, pp. 321-24; Werth, *Twilight*, pp. 272-74; and, particularly, the highly flattering estimate of Cot's achievements in Watson Pierce, *Industrial Mobilization in France* [Washington: The Army Industrial College, 1945], pp. 14-16, 24-25, an account based upon contemporary reports by the American military attachés).

30 *J.O.C. Doc.*, June 26, 1936, No. 465, p. 1082, and *Deb.*, July 17, 1936, p. 1994.

31 *Ibid.*, July 16, 1936, pp. 1939-43.

with only eighty-three dissenting votes and the Senate by a voice vote. The only major change was the addition of a time limit for expropriation—March 31, 1937—so that private arms producers would not feel themselves permanently in danger of losing their properties.[32]

When Hitler's diplomatic policies and German rearmament at last began to make it apparent that the nightmare of another world war was a devil which could not be exorcised by wishful thinking or nonaggression pacts, the French finally began to reconsider Paul-Boncour's long-dormant project for the organization of the nation in time of war. Unlike arms nationalization, this measure was specifically designed to increase French military security, but, like so many other military bills, its progress through Chamber and Senate continued to be slow. The national organization project was reintroduced in the Chamber in June of 1935, but the deputies did not resume their discussions of it until March of 1938—an hour when the threat of war was, or should have been, obvious to all.

Actually not all of the intervening period had been wasted, and more than a few accomplishments, all suggested by the initial bill of the late twenties, were made in the interim. A law of August, 1930, for instance, gave government ministries the authority to make special five-year agreements with various industrialists and to place "educational orders" for war goods with them. Under the provisions of this law manufacturers were to be granted the funds that were necessary to initiate research programs, expand production facilities, and install special equipment so that, at the hour of mobilization, their plants could be quickly converted to war production. The sponsors of this measure hoped that it would help them to find the proper assignments for the proper industrialists and that, through the

[32] Due to this provision and the financial troubles encountered by the Popular Front only 200 of the 400 million francs appropriated were ever utilized, and only a part of the program put into effect. Kimon A. Doukas, "Armaments and the French Experience," *American Political Science Review*, XXXIII (Apr., 1939), pp. 284-85.

peacetime orders which were made, it would smooth the transition from peacetime to wartime production.[33]

Another important legislative act, a law of January 21, 1935, modified the long-standing requisition procedures which dated from 1877. Under the provisions of the new bill, the government could, by a simple decision of the cabinet, assume broad powers of requisition "whenever circumstances should require it." [34] Enactment of this measure was at last a clear recognition of the fact, first officially proclaimed in the Paul-Boncour project, that under modern conditions of warfare the right of requisition should not be restricted solely to military commanders to fulfill the immediate needs of the army nor, in point of time, limited to the period of full mobilization.[35] The mere threat of war or the sudden outbreak of a period of international tension was sufficient and legal justification for the government, under the terms of this law, to begin requisition procedures without any general mobilization.

Finally, and perhaps of the greatest importance, was the fact that even while the national organization bill languished in committee, many of its objectives had been achieved through decrees and instructions of the *Conseil Supérieur de la Défense Nationale.* It is the opinion of a qualified American observer who studied French industrial mobilization procedures for the Army Industrial College [now, the Industrial College of the Armed Forces] that the delay in legal ratification of the mobilization law had not, in turn, delayed the development of the major parts of French mobilization plans since the various ministries could act on unratified legislation provided presidential approval was secured.[36]

[33] Lt. Charles Ailleret, "La Mobilisation industrielle," *Revue militaire française,* LIX (Apr., 1936), 165 ff.

[34] *J.O.C. Doc.,* June 29, 1934, No. 3727, pp. 1115-16, and June 5, 1934, No. 3499, p. 859.

[35] Both the above-cited *exposés des motifs* insisted that the 1877 law was no longer adequate since the powers of requisition could be utilized only at the time of full mobilization and only in the interests of the military services.

[36] Pierce, *Industrial Mobilization,* p. 4.

As early as 1930-31 there were in existence over a dozen different documents concerning the direction and control of industry, agriculture, labor, civilian population, transportation, exports and imports, and mines in the event of a future war. These instructions followed the recommendations and provisions in the as yet unratified national organization bill: French needs and resources for waging war were first determined at the departmental level under the guidance of the prefect; mobilization plans and schedules were drawn up by individual manufacturers, and control over their operations was assigned to particular ministries; over-all coordination of plans, particularly for products used in wartime by more than one ministry, was carried out by a special bureau of the War Ministry; and the whole program was under the supervision of and in accordance with the views of the General Staff.[37]

Undoubtedly much of this organizational structure existed only on paper, but at the same time the instructions were worked out in minute detail. Moreover, there is reason to believe that French industrial mobilization procedures suffered the most not from a lack of planning but rather from the reverse—that is, plans were drawn up in such intricate detail that the total organizational complex was inflexible and component parts could not be modified unless the entire structure was changed. When, for instance, Pierre Cot wanted to create new units for the air force and additional regiments of antiaircraft artillery, his plan was vetoed because it would have meant that there would be fewer men available for the infantry and because it would have required resources and finances already earmarked

---

[37] As early as 1930-31 Colonel Charles Menu was insisting that the bases for a future industrial mobilization were already established. He noted that the first set of regulations for the utilization of labor in wartime was issued in 1926 and that, in the following year, detailed instructions were laid down for procedures to maintain civilian and military food supplies in wartime. Colonel Charles Menu, *Applications de l'industrie* (2 vols., École Supérieure de Guerre, 1928-31), II, 10-11. For further details on the frequently elaborate mobilization plans, see Pierce, *Industrial Mobilization*, pp. 5-10.

for a naval construction program.[38]   But, in any event, when the national organization bill finally became law in 1938, it had benefited from more than fourteen years of experience and testing in the various government ministries and the *Conseil Supérieur*. And even though the French legislature did not approve the Paul-Boncour law until that time, the French had nonetheless been able to obtain a clear picture of the industrial and economic resources which they had available for war. Not only did they have a great deal of generalized knowledge about industrial mobilization but they had also experienced a psychological preparation for the tasks which they would be called on to perform in wartime.

As a result of this advance preparation, the previous discussions of the 1920's, and, above all, the urgency of the international situation, the national organization bill received quick approval when it was finally debated in 1938. Furthermore, for similar reasons, its provisions revealed little that was new or different in French thought on the nation in arms. Indeed, the *rapporteur*, Guy La Chambre, made it a point in his report that there was little if any difference between the version the Chamber was now asked to approve and the original measure of 1927, a contention he attempted to prove by making an elaborate comparison of the two.[39]   Similarly one of the keynote speeches in the Chamber had as its theme the argument that since the premises of the proposed law had long been a matter of common knowledge, the only task which remained for the legislature was simply to give the bill a speedy vote of approval.[40]   Neither the report of the Chamber's army commission nor the debate in the legislature was really thorough or rigorous. In the face of the obvious threat of Nazi Germany, both houses of the French

---

[38] Pierce, *Industrial Mobilization*, pp. 40-41. Pierce maintained, however, that "The French plan, in general structure and thoroughness of organization, may be regarded as a model of its type" (p. 8).

[39] *J.O.C. Doc.*, March 5, 1936, No. 6817, pp. 506 ff.

[40] *Ibid.*, *Deb.*, March 22, 1938, p. 871.

legislature unanimously passed the bill after only short debates and without making many significant changes in the versions which had emerged from committee study. The Chamber of Deputies, after two days of discussion, gave its approval by a vote of 603-0 with only its presiding officer, Herriot, abstaining; and a few months later the Senate, so recalcitrant ten years previously, made the measure into law by a 297-0 vote. Moreover, with the change in the party line, the Communists were among the strongest supporters of a law which, they said, would protect the nation from external aggression and prevent individuals from lining their pockets with wartime profits.[41] To Paul-Boncour, who was serving as Foreign Minister in the second Blum cabinet at the time of the Chamber vote, such unanimity must have been gratifying. And such speed must have appeared astounding.

There were, however, several issues which did provoke debate and which eventually led to certain modifications in the original measure. These concerned the problem of controlling and directing the complex organization of the French nation in wartime. There was, first of all, a group of deputies who consistently maintained that the law should give the Minister of National Defense greater authority to control the work of the three service ministries. Likewise, there was an equally persistent agitation in favor of nominating, in advance of any declaration of war, a wartime generalissimo who would have supreme command over army, navy, and air establishments. Finally, considerable pressure developed for the establishment of a Minister of Armaments who would have unquestioned authority in matters of war production. In the first two instances —the demands for an all-powerful Minister of National Defense and a wartime supreme commander—the issues had already been partially resolved by decrees issued during the regime of

---

[41] *Ibid.*, p. 957. French labor, at least as far as the CGT was concerned, no longer opposed the bill, but their attitude was more one of passive acceptance than of warm approval. Ehrmann, *French Labor*, p. 87.

the Popular Front, and the provisions of the national organization bill did little more than provide legal formalization for
measures which had been taken previously. In the latter case
—the agitation for an Armaments Ministry—the debate was
over an issue which had been raised many times since the end
of the First World War. And in all three, the eventual outcome was a middle-of-the-road compromise.

Well before 1938 there had been a trend toward establishing
a Minister of National Defense who would have widespread
powers over all French war preparations. As early as 1932 the
Piétri cabinet had experimented with a short-lived National
Defense Ministry charged with the function of coordinating the
work of subordinate Air, Naval, and War ministries. This,
however, had been largely a paper reform and had actually
amounted to little more than a reshuffling of the traditional
ministries. Its success was slight.[42] In June of 1936 Édouard
Daladier, then serving as Minister of War, was given the additional title of Minister of National Defense. As such, he was
to coordinate the work of the other service ministries which,
however, retained both their individuality and their independence.[43] Two years later, in early 1938, Daladier was given
additional powers over the Air and Naval ministries, and at all
times he was supposed to possess widespread powers in the determination of plans for economic mobilization. Hence, when
it came time to define the functions and responsibilities of the
Minister of National Defense in the wartime organization,
Daladier himself insisted that the decrees of the preceding
January had gone far enough. Both he and his government
rejected any and all attempts to create a "super" ministry which
would be solely responsible for the operations of clearly subordinate War, Navy, and Air ministries.[44] He desired no repeti-

[42] *J. O. Lois et Décrets,* March 30, 1932, p. 3279; Géraud, *Gravediggers,* pp. 109-10.

[43] For a discussion of the 1936 system, see Paul Bernier's report in *J.O.C. Doc.,* November 12, 1936, No. 1281, pp. 273-4.

[44] Representative arguments advanced in behalf of a clear-cut Ministry of National

tion of the 1932 experiment which, he claimed, had overcentralized the direction of French military affairs.[45]

There was a similar background and outcome to the demands for the nomination of a supreme commander-in-chief for all French military forces.   To be sure, General Maurice Gamelin had been apointed in January of 1938 Chief of Staff for National Defense, and he had been given authority over the army, navy, and air forces.   But Daladier hesitated to make him generalissimo of all the armed forces before the outbreak of war.   In fact, up to and including the defeats of May, 1940, there was considerable confusion over the extent and limits of Gamelin's authority.[46]   In the debates on the national organization bill, the government indicated that it wanted to have French war policies determined by a permanent committee formed of government officials and military officers and presided over by the President of the Republic.   On the contrary, those who wanted a generalissimo argued that only a single authority could make the quick, instantaneous decisions which were necessary in modern warfare, and they insisted that a committee would be unable to formulate effective policies.   Again Daladier rushed to the defense of the *status quo* and opposed the creation of a unified command.   He expressed the view that wartime control by a generalissimo would be undemocratic and that it might deprive the government of its control of policy.   To be sure, he hedged a bit and admitted that it might be necessary to appoint a com-

---

Defense are to be found in General Henri Mordacq, *La Défense nationale en danger* (Paris: Les Éditions de la France, 1938), pp. 26 ff. Mordacq, who favored the 1932 system, claimed that the arrangements made in 1936 permitted too much freedom to the Navy and Air ministries. See also Jean Fabry, "La Défense nationale," *Revue militaire générale*, II (Jan., 1938), 19-30. For a critique of the 1938 decrees, see General Paul Azan, "L'Organisation de la défense nationale," *Revue militaire générale*, II (Mar., 1938), 253-58.

45 *J.O.C. Deb.*, March 22, 1938, p. 892.

46 Géraud, *Gravediggers*, p. 39, and an important article by A. Reussner, "La Réorganisation du Haut-Commandement au mois de mai 1940," *Revue d'histoire de la deuxième guerre mondiale*, Nos. 10 and 11 (Jun., 1953), 49 ff. which indicates that even the appointment of Weygand as commander-in-chief of all the theaters of operations on May 19, 1940 did not end the confusion.

mander-in-chief once war had broken out, but he flatly refused to make such a nomination in time of peace.[47]

Under this interpretation—which was given legislative sanction in the provisions of the 1938 law—Gamelin remained Chief of Staff for National Defense with uncertain authority over the three military services, and the determination of wartime military policies was left in the hands of a joint committee of military and government representatives. Hence, in both the areas of military and governmental command, the national organization law confirmed pre-existing arrangements and, in addition, expressed the principle that no single military officer or cabinet official was to be solely responsible for directing the wartime nation in arms.

There were, in fact, a number of persons who were dissatisfied with the scope and content of the projected law for the organization of the nation in time of war and who felt that its provisions were not sufficiently stringent. One of these, the future Air Minister, Laurent Eynac, submitted a separate report for the Senate's air commission which, recalling the Socialist critique of the 1920's, maintained that the phraseology of Article Two—which spoke of the "utilization" of national resources and the "mobilization" of military forces—indicated that the government still thought in terms of a war which would be decided by the clash of mass armies rather than by war materiel, armaments, and industrial mobilization.[48]   Within the Chamber

[47] *J.O.C. Deb.*, March 24, 1938, pp. 946-51, and *Commission d'enquête, Rapport*, II, 254. Daladier apparently believed that the national organization bill was flexible enough to make it possible to appoint a supreme commander if such a step appeared necessary. His views, incidentally, received considerable support from air and navy spokesmen who, as in other countries, opposed unification, particularly under an army officer. The important military periodical, *Revue militaire générale*, plugged hard for a unified command during these years. See Vol. I (Jun., 1938) which alone contained three articles on the need for a *commandement unique*. Likewise, a former War Minister, General Joseph-Léon-Marie Maurin, was particularly critical of the 1938 law on national organization for its failure to create a supreme commander. See his *L'Armée moderne* (Paris: Flammarion, 1938), pp. 265-66.

[48] *J.O.C. Doc.*, June 9, 1938, No. 302, pp. 190-92. See also Maurin, *Armée moderne*, p. 266.

those who, like Eynac, wanted a more rigorous or all-embracing law tended to center their criticisms around the bill's failure to include provisions for a separate and all-powerful Ministry of Armaments within the framework of the national organization. The argument of these critics was that the experiences of 1914-1918 had indicated that it was necessary to establish such a ministry in time of peace so that there would be a constant flow of supplies as soon as mobilization had been ordered.[49] This, it might be noted, was an issue which had been discussed many times in preceding years.

But once again it was the Minister of National Defense, Daladier, who rebuffed such attempts to create a "super" ministry. A Ministry of Armaments, he insisted, would not only disarrange the plans which had already been made but would also deprive existing ministries of many of their legitimate functions. If it should turn out that such a ministry was necessary, there would be sufficient time, as in the nomination of a supreme military commander, to establish it upon the outbreak of war. Moreover, Daladier maintained, if the Chamber insisted on creating a Ministry of Armaments at this time, the result would be an excessive and unnecessary acceleration of war preparations: "If you follow the authors of this amendment, you would create in this country, from today on, a war economy." [Applause from the Right.] "You may applaud, gentlemen, you may show your enthusiasm. For my part, I am resolutely opposed to this conception."[50] His reply revealed much of the laissez-faire attitude which underlay French war preparations.

[49] *J.O.C. Deb.*, March 22, 1938, pp. 871-73 (speech by a M. Besse) and general discussion of Article Two, pp. 888-90.

[50] *Ibid.*, p. 888. See also the important testimony of General Rinderknech, pre-1939 Chief of the Section of Armament and Technical Studies of the General Staff, in *Commission d'énquête, Témoignages et documents*, V, 1487-88. Rinderknech maintained that a Ministry of Armaments should have been created at an early date and claimed that this had not been done because the government leaders didn't want to go on a war footing until the actual declaration of hostilities.

The threat of aerial bombardment and destruction from the skies, a fear which paralyzed the will of the Allies in the years of Hitler's "Saturday surprises," added a new dimension to the concept of the nation in arms. Article Seven of the 1938 organization law stated that "the organization of passive defense against aerial attack is obligatory throughout the entire national territory." The responsibility of preparing the measures for "passive defense"—a colorless yet ominous term which suggested an unarmed civilian population helpless against fleets of enemy bombers—was added to the functions of the Minister of National Defense. The government was given the power to requisition all men over eighteen for temporary service in this work, and older men who had just been freed from their obligations in the reserves were placed at the disposition of the passive defense authorities. All Frenchmen were henceforth ordered to participate in air raid drills. The responsible minister might order industries to take precautionary measures designed to minimize bomb damage to their plants and to protect the lives of their employees; he might even prescribe the methods and materials to be used in the construction of new buildings so that they would withstand attack from the air. Finally, the government assumed a heavy financial obligation to construct shelters, warning systems, and gas detection centers.[51] The rise of the heavy bomber had indeed provided a new set of responsibilities to the government and the citizen alike.[52]

With the final passage of the law for the organization of the nation in time of war, French thought on the nation in arms

---

[51] See *J.O.C. Deb.,* March 24, 1938, pp. 924-32 for a discussion of these provisions.

[52] Like the preceding issues relating to the command of the nation in arms, the provisions for passive defense were not entirely new. As early as April 8, 1935, the Chambers had approved a special law on passive defense, and in fact many of its clauses reappeared in the 1938 national organization bill. The original measure, however, made the Minister of the Interior the controlling agent, apportioned most of the financial burden to local communities, and made fewer demands on the individual citizen. It was also never really put into effect. See *J.O. Lois et Décrets,* April 9, 1935, pp. 3978-79; *J.O.C. Deb.,* March 24, 1938, p. 925; and Mordacq, *Défense nationale,* pp. 51-52.

reached its climax. The major provisions of the law, as previously noted, followed the pattern of the Paul-Boncour project of the preceding decade. The government retained its position as director and coordinator of all wartime activity. It could, in the hour of need, requisition persons as well as property; its range of authority in wartime included not only the military forces but also the entire civilian population in all of its manifold occupations; and it could begin to operate the wartime organization in periods of international tension and not merely after the order for general mobilization had been issued. In short, the new definition of the nation in arms meant that, unlike 1914, there was no sharp dividing line between civilian and soldier just as there was no clear separation between peacetime and war industry. All were to come under the authority of the government. Moreover, true to the egalitarian heritage of France, the wartime organization was designed—in theory rather than practice, as 1939 was to show[53]—to create an equality of sacrifice. Profits were to be limited, and, although the law recognized industry's need for specialists, it declared that the young were to serve at the front and the older men in the factories and on the farms.

Yet, notwithstanding these provisions which, if literally applied in time of war, could have moved France along the path toward totalitarianism, the government showed a noticeable reluctance to carry the concept of the nation in arms to ultimate and theoretical absolutes. The insistence upon the final responsibility and authority of an elected Chamber in time of war was one indication of this attitude—the national organization law was designed to prevent any repetition of the political abdication of 1914 and the long struggle of the legislature to regain its

[53] For a discussion of the breakdown of some of these provisions in 1939, see Ehrmann, *French Labor*, pp. 172 ff. and D. H. Popper and J. C. de Wilde, "The Wartime Economy of Britain and France," *Foreign Policy Reports*, XVI (Jul. 15, 1940), 119-20. By March of 1940 there were only 1.2 million workers in French industry, as compared with 1.7 million in 1918. There was also widespread dissatisfaction with the regulations which assigned some men to industrial jobs while others were assigned to the front lines.

authority over the military. Another clear sign of this same attitude was the hesitancy of the government to create an all-powerful Ministry of National Defense or a supreme commander who would be in charge of all wartime military planning. French thought on the nation in arms did not call for authoritarian solutions to national defense problems. Perhaps more important were Daladier's reasons for turning down proposals for an Armaments Ministry in 1938. He desired to maintain, just as long as it was possible, the traditional civilian ways of doing things and to preserve, up to the last moment, the normal civilian standards. As far as he was concerned the nation in arms should be created and put into operation only when the threat of war was overwhelming. Whatever conclusions one might draw from this attitude and the obviously harmful effect it had upon French war preparations, Daladier's view—and that of his government—at least had the merit of recognizing peace and not war as the normal state of society. Unlike the concepts of his German and Italian neighbors who spoke at length of the ethical beauty of war, Daladier's reading of the nation in arms did not postulate that French society must forever be kept in a state of readiness for armed conflict. Nor, though the concept of the nation in arms had vastly expanded, did it mean that French society was to be eternally geared for war or that peacetime enjoyments should be curtailed in the sole interest of the leviathan state.

The ideas and the laws which have been discussed in this and preceding chapters provided the accepted and official foundation for French military institutions between the two wars. There were always some persons who disagreed with the established military order even though they were, at best, a small if vocal minority. Even prior to the rebuilding of the German war machine, some suspected that all was not for the best in the best of all possible military worlds. After all, had not Hans von Seeckt, Germany's foremost theorist in the days of the Weimar

Republic, argued that the mass, conscript army was a clumsy relic of the past, a force doomed to become involved in sterile wars of attrition and stalemate? [54] And was his glorification of the 100,000 professionals permitted his country by the Versailles Treaty merely a rationalization of weakness? The professional army had, indeed, been wished upon Germany not by the Allied generals but by the Allied politicians who feared that a defeated enemy might employ short-term conscription as a means of building another huge army as it was commonly—and erroneously—believed Prussia had done after the defeat of Jena. [55] The warning of the victorious generals that a small but highly trained force of professionals might be even more dangerous went unheeded. After Versailles, however, the fear of an *attaque brusque* by von Seeckt's professionals was never wholly absent from French military thought. Maginot's demand for a strong *couverture* as well as the construction of the fortifications which received his name indicated the prevalence of this sentiment. Moreover, while the foremost French officers continued, whatever their private worries, to give public support to the existing French military institutions, an occasional writer arose to challenge both the theory and practice of the nation in arms.

In post-1919 France the clearest example of a writer who focused these fears of an *attaque brusque* and these doubts about the power of the mass army into a coherent, full-bodied critique of prevailing military doctrine was the one-time soldier, sometime statesman, Charles de Gaulle. Eventually canonized by a coterie of journalists and political admirers as a prophet who

[54] Hans von Seeckt, *Thoughts of a Soldier,* trans. Gilbert Waterhouse (London: Ernest Benn, 1930), p. 55.

[55] William O. Shanahan, *Prussian Military Reforms, 1786-1813* (New York: Columbia University Press, 1945), pp. 13-16. His introduction is a short but excellent account of how fear of a revived *Krümper* system led Lloyd George, Clemenceau, and the other Allied political leaders to develop their scheme for a German army of 100,000 professionals enlisted for a twelve-year period. One of the main themes of Shanahan's book is to show that, despite popular beliefs, this system was not responsible for the revived Prussian power of 1813.

labored for years without honor or recognition,[56] de Gaulle began criticizing French military institutions in the mid-thirties. In his various writings he developed an elaborate theory for successful offensive warfare based upon a contingent of 100,000 professional soldiers formed into half a dozen fully armored and mechanized divisions. De Gaulle's ideas—set forth in his now well-known *Vers l'armée de métier*, a special memorandum he addressed to the French military and political command in January of 1940, and in the parliamentary speeches and writings of his supporter, Paul Reynaud, an unorthodox financier turned military expert—were in fact neither wholly novel nor unrecognized, but they were at least a thorough criticism of the prevailing concept of the nation in arms.[57]

Notwithstanding the many persons who have attempted to credit the wartime leader of Free France with both omniscience and originality, there was nothing particularly striking about de Gaulle's demand for either a professional army or for mechanized equipment. As early as the mid twenties, for instance,

[56] Philippe Barrès, *Charles de Gaulle* (New York: Brentano's, 1941), pp. 11-17 claims that in 1934 he (Barrès) was told by von Ribbentrop that the French possessed an officer named de Gaulle who had showed the Germans how they would eventually break the Maginot Line! In his preface to a translation of de Gaulle's *Vers l'armée de métier*, Walter Millis described the book as follows: "Here are that precision and lucidity of thought, that ability to grasp the problem of modern war as a whole, backed by a real sense of the past, a real knowledge of military history and even a genuine literary grace, which are the glory of the French military tradition." *The Army of the Future* (New York: Lippincott, 1941), pp. 8-9. Both of these examples typify the general adulation which was accorded de Gaulle during the years when he was leading the Free French.

[57] Charles de Gaulle, *Vers l'armée de métier* (Paris: Berger-Levrault, 1934 and other editions), a work which was translated in English as *The Army of the Future* (New York: Lippincott, 1941). This is his principal work but see also "Comment faire une armée de métier," *Revue hebdomadaire* (Jun. 1, 1935) and "Memorandum adressé par le Colonel Charles de Gaulle aux généraux Gamelin, Weygand, et Georges et à MM Daladier et Reynaud " (Jan. 26, 1940), both of which are reprinted in full in *Trois Études* (Paris: Berger-Levrault, 1945), pp. 119-45 and 147-76. On Reynaud's relationship with de Gaulle and his advocacy of de Gaulle's military theories, see Paul Reynaud, *Le Problème militaire français* (Paris: Flammarion, 1937), a short work which Reynaud had reissued in 1945 and in which the only change appears to have been the addition of a one-page introduction that is reducible to the four words, "I told you so." See also Reynaud, *La France*, I, 312 ff.

such military writers as General Hubert Camon and Colonel (later General) Émile Alléhaut had written at length about the need for the motorization and the mechanization of French forces; and both had clearly pointed out that only through the adaptation of the gasoline engine to military purposes could a war of movement replace the war of trenches.[58]

Similarly, however restrained their criticisms, a certain number of officers had continued to emphasize the advantages which a professional military force could add to the French army. General Frédéric Culmann's *Reichsheer et milices*, a comparison of the German and French armies, was but one of a number of books which pointed out that a small but highly trained professional army might defeat an enemy whose military organization was based on the principle of "an armed mob, mediocrely trained, heavy to manage and whose mobilization will be slowed down by the induction of reservists in a very high proportion." [59] In the late twenties this undercurrent of fearful admiration for the army of von Seeckt had been sufficiently strong to provoke the French Chief of Staff, General Marie Eugène Debeney, to devote the entire first chapter of his *Sur la sécurité militaire de la France* to a criticism of those French writers who praised the German professional army and to a reaffirmation of his own faith in a national army founded upon the principle of the nation in arms.[60] In the same years the irrepressible Pierre Cot remarked in the Chamber, with some asperity, that the popularity of the professional army within French military cir-

---

[58] Colonel Émile Alléhaut, *La Guerre n'est pas une industrie* (Paris: Berger-Levrault, 1925), pp. 141 ff.; General Hubert Camon, *La Motorisation de l'armée* (Paris: Berger-Levrault, 1926), pp. 54-57. As Camon wrote, "We must not, above all, be hypnotized by the four years which the world war lasted. The nation which will have the advantage over its enemy of a motorized army will certainly finish the (next) war within a month."

[59] General Frédéric Culmann, *Reichsheer et milices* (Paris: Charles-Lavauzelle, 1933), pp. 170-171. For others of similar persuasion see the writings of Maitrot, Duval, Reboul, Souchon, cited in preceding chapters.

[60] General Marie Eugène Debeney, *Sur la sécurité militaire de la France* (Paris: Payot, 1930), pp. 9-24.

cles arose from the erroneous belief that only the Germans had a reliable army.[61]

But, be that as it may, the heart of the de Gaulle critique was his contention that the principle of the nation in arms was outmoded and obsolete. Worse yet, that it was dangerous. The logic of the nation in arms, he insisted, would condemn France to wage an almost endless, grinding war of attrition in which all of her resources both in men and in materiel would be pitted against those of her enemy. As in the First World War there would be a total mobilization of vast armies which would, in turn, re-establish the conditions of the military stalemate of 1914-1918 in which the immobile masses had been able to achieve nothing more than local advances at a tremendous cost in lives. "Indeed," de Gaulle wrote, "we must point out a frightening disproportion between the losses suffered by the nation in arms and the tactical, strategic, and political results that this system was able to procure." [62] Moreover, de Gaulle was convinced that huge conscript armies were suited only for defensive warfare—in fact, as he explicitly stated, the very organic laws on which the French army was based had created a purely defensive military machine—and that, for this reason, any future war between such armies could only be a war of attrition which would not terminate until one of the belligerents was utterly exhausted.[63]

The principal reason why de Gaulle believed that the concept of the nation in arms had lost its validity lay in the fact that it seemed to emphasize quantity rather than quality. The French Revolution, de Gaulle claimed, with its passion for egalitarianism had made the mass army a part of the democratic tradition— "there was something in this that appealed to the general passion for levelling." [64] Moreover, in contemporary France the theory

61 *J.O.C. Deb.*, December 10, 1929, p. 4217.
62 De Gaulle, *Trois Études* (Memorandum), p. 150.
63 *Ibid.*, pp. 157-58.
64 de Gaulle, *Armée de métier*, p. 56.

of the nation in arms was being pushed to its ultimate and most illogical conclusion:

On the pretext that in our age it is the whole nation which fights, some are anxious to deny that strictly military formations have any value. By the mere fact of its rising, the people will possess power, address and courage. And, therefore, to assemble permanent bodies of troops, to distract citizens from their work and their surroundings, to inculcate into them anything, whatever it may be, which is different from the ordinary professional life would be useless, even dangerous.[65]

Thus, while he may have been influenced by German military theorists, de Gaulle was certainly no stranger to the venerable French military tradition of du Picq and the Second Empire.

To de Gaulle there was no logical reason to have faith in the mass army. He was certain that the quality of the individual soldier was far more important than the quantity of men under arms. But unlike earlier writers who had followed this theme, de Gaulle based his theories upon the conditions of society in the modern age of industrialism. Prior to the coming of the machine, he pointed out, it had at least been theoretically possible to reconcile the conflicting elements of quantity and quality within a given military establishment. But the Industrial Revolution had made this impossible. The ever-increasing complexity of the machine had created an age of specialists without whom the industrial complex of the nation could not operate efficiently. This was a development which had affected the army as much as the factory, for no modern army could operate without specialists either. The army now possessed tanks, airplanes, and other highly complicated pieces of materiel, but only soldiers who had received a specialized and lengthy training in their operation could handle them efficiently. Moreover, to entrust these new weapons of war to the average conscript who had served but a year or two in the ranks would lead to inefficiency, improper use of these military tools, and, above all, to the creation of an army which was suited for nothing but

[65] *Ibid.*, pp. 60-61.

defensive missions. The nation in arms was, therefore, obsolete; the age of specialists had arrived.

A professional army, formed into highly mechanized units, appeared to de Gaulle to be the only system which would resolve the dilemma created by the nation in arms. He was convinced, first of all, that only armored divisions could restore maneuver and movement to the conduct of war and could break the hitherto impenetrable fronts of 1914-1918. In the second place, he was equally convinced that professional soldiers were the only fighting men who possessed the skill, knowledge, and training to operate the new weapons produced by the machine age.

To be sure, at least in the mid-thirties, de Gaulle still believed that the principle of the nation in arms was valid if the stake in war appeared to be unlimited. However, he doubted the likelihood of total war. "There are good reasons for believing that a war starting tomorrow would be only remotely connected, at the beginning, with the premature attack of mobilized masses." Wars of such nature had become too expensive a luxury for the European nations and entailed sacrifices every country wished to avoid. "On the whole, the ubiquity of wealth, the overlapping of interests, and the infiltration of ideas have created an interdependence which bids them [the nations of Europe] to limit their actions." [66]

In the future, de Gaulle stated, wars would be confined to lightning attacks by armored units which sought to gain only limited objectives. The victim of such an aggression would face the hard choice of accepting either the *fait accompli* or of waging an all-out "total" war involving all the resources of the nation in arms and from which neither side could emerge a real victor. Most nations, he thought, would choose the former, hard though it might be. France herself might some day be involved in such a situation in the event of a German attack, and, according to de Gaulle, the only way his country could avoid having to make such a choice—that is, between accepting

[66] *Ibid.*, p. 81.

the results of a German aggression or becoming involved in a total war leading to Pyrrhic victory—was to refashion its army along the Gaullist pattern. If the French did this, then, it would be a French mechanized corps of professional soldiers, itself seizing the initiative in the early hours of a war with Germany, that would roll up such impressive gains that the enemy would have to face the grim dilemma of surrender or all-out war. And, of course, under the circumstances which de Gaulle envisaged, the Germans would fear involvement in a long war of attrition and sue for peace. In short, the de Gaulle *armée de métier* was presented as a guarantee that there would be no need for France to engage in total war or to call into being the vast complex of the nation in arms. An army relying upon professional *esprit de corps*, making use of modern armor, and based upon the idea of specialization of function would relegate the concept of the nation in arms to oblivion.[67]

Although de Gaulle continued to agitate for his system until the 1940 defeat and although his cause was well served by Paul Reynaud in the Chamber of Deputies, his theories found little favor either with the political or military leaders of France. The political Left and Center, as previously noted, angrily rejected his professional soldiers as a reactionary scheme of great danger to democratic institutions. In fact, as a report by a commission of the post-Liberation National Assembly on the causes of the 1940 defeat clearly states, because de Gaulle hitched his mechanized chariot to a professional star, debates on the wisdom of his over-all scheme and the merits of mechanization inevitably became bogged down in the timeworn conscript-versus-mercenary

[67] How de Gaulle's theories were related to those of von Seeckt and how much the former was motivated by fear of an *attaque brusque* was shown by a British officer, Major E. W. Sheppard, "Two Generals,—One Doctrine," *Army Quarterly*, XLI (1940), 105-18. It is not without interest that in the same year de Gaulle's *Armée de métier* was published (1934), the same publishing house (Berger-Levrault) issued a short, anonymous pamphlet entitled *La Fin de la nation armée*. The tone of this pamphlet was far more harsh than anything de Gaulle wrote, and its principal point was that the Germans were the only people who had a real army. It went on to charge that the mobilization of the nation in arms would lead to a total war in which "le communisme pratique s'installe".

argument and proceeded no further.[68]   When Reynaud, a more astute politician than the colonel, presented the de Gaulle scheme, he was careful to dissociate himself from the charge that he thought solely in terms of career soldiers.   Reynaud argued, to be sure, that the situation in 1935 was the reverse of 1870 and that the current problem was to add quality to quantity, but at the same time he insisted upon maintaining the national conscript army.   All he wanted was to add a spearhead of professional and mechanized units so that the army as a whole would possess mobility and offensive possibilities.   "The armed nation in France," he wrote, "is the solid wood of the lance.   Let it be equipped with an iron tip, and let a single arm guide it toward a single goal." [69]

Nor did the de Gaulle program obtain the stamp of approval of the responsible French military authorities.   For this there were many reasons.   In the first place, men like Pétain, Weygand, and Debeney were sceptical of the military potentialities of the tank and the airplane.   Their military writings stressed, rather, what the counterweapons—the antitank guns and the antiaircraft artillery—could accomplish.   Debeney, for instance, wrote in 1935 that in any future war the mechanized land forces would find that their freedom of maneuver was much more limited than it had been in 1918.[70]   When several French military writers published translations of Douhet, the Italian theorist of airpower, Marshal Pétain pointed out in an introduction to one of these translations that it was a highly dangerous idea to expect very much from the independent operations of an air force.[71]   At the same time not a few of the French military

---

[68] *Commission d'enquête, Rapport*, I, 75.

[69] *J.O.C. Deb.*, March 15, 1935, pp. 1040-42.   See also Reynaud, *La France*, I, 312 ff. and *Le Problème militaire*, p. 105.

[70] General Marie Eugène Debeney, "Encore l'armée de métier" and "La Motorisation des armées modernes," both in *Revue des deux mondes*, XXVIII (Jul. 15, 1935), 279-95 and XXXII (Mar. 15, 1936), 273-91.

[71] Philippe Pétain, Preface to Colonel P. Vauthier, *La Doctrine de guerre du Général Douhet* (Paris: Berger-Levrault, 1935).

leaders of the thirties were particularly confident in the Maginot Line and convinced that modern weapons conferred all the tactical and strategical advantages to the defense. Naturally, to such men the de Gaulle scheme for offensive warfare was heresy pure and simple. General Maurin, the Minister of War, followed Reynaud's 1935 speech on behalf of a mechanized army with remarks that have become "classic": "How can any one believe that we are still thinking of the offensive when we have spent so many billions to establish a fortified barrier? Should we be crazy enough to go in front of that barrier to—I don't know what sort of an adventure?" [72] Thus, military scepticism about the new weapons like the tank and the airplane as well as the increasingly prevalent idea that the Maginot Line was a "Chinese Wall" combined to defeat the de Gaulle plan for a mechanized army.

Even more relevant, however, is the fact that the military hierarchy accepted the basic tenets of the nation in arms and, in fact, used the concept to oppose the idea of de Gaulle. Both Debeney and Weygand, to cite but two examples, claimed that the cost of recruiting professional soldiers would be so high that it would absorb far too great a proportion of the military budget. De Gaulle's *armée de métier,* they said, could be created only at the expense of the conscript portion of the army. It might indeed be possible to add the elite soldiers demanded by de Gaulle, but what would then happen to the annual contingents who would necessarily be deprived of money, materiel, and prestige? Wouldn't they fall into the category of a mere "resigned militia"—as Weygand put it—and hence make the military condition of France even weaker? [73] Even after the occupation of the Rhineland, when Gamelin was acutely aware

---

[72] *J.O.C. Deb.,* March 15, 1935, p. 1045.

[73] General Maxime Weygand, "L'Unité de l'armée," *Revue militaire générale,* I (Jan., 1937), 18. See also his testimony in *Commission d'enquête, Témoignages et documents,* I, 241. Debeney's principal theoretical statements were contained in his *Sur la sécurité militaire de la France,* which, although published in 1930, anticipated the type of argument put forth by de Gaulle.

that his armies were incapable of countering German aggression with an immediate response, the French commander was sceptical about creating a mechanized expeditionary force of professionals; in a note to the *Conseil Supérieur de la Guerre* he observed that the creation of such a force would, in turn, make it almost impossible to obtain funds and cadres for the existing army.[74] And Pétain also observed that if too much emphasis was placed upon one element in the national defense—such as armor or airpower—it would throw the entire structure out of balance and imperil the sum total of French security.[75]

The military reply to de Gaulle, in short, was based upon the total complex of the nation in arms—that is, the responsible army officials insisted that French security not only demanded a national army whose unity must be preserved but also required the utilization in war of all the resources of the nation. They doubted if war would take the limited form anticipated by de Gaulle. After all, as Debeney pointed out in a later book, all the European countries had organized their military forces upon the principle of the nation in arms, and the Germans, under Hitler, had quickly abandoned the 100,000 man army of the Weimar Republic. It was, therefore, more prudent to assume that any future war would take the form of the conflict of 1914-1918.[76] "Modern wars," Pétain wrote in 1935 in an article advocating a two-year military service, "imply the putting to work of the total resources of a people, and our national defense must be established upon the principle of the nation in arms. This concept exactly corresponds to the political and social state of a nation without territorial ambitions and which has no other aims but safeguarding her soil." [77]

[74] *Commission d'enquête, Rapport*, I, 54.

[75] Pétain, preface to Vauthier, *Doctrine de guerre.*

[76] General Marie Eugène Debeney, *La Guerre et les hommes* (Paris: Plon, 1937), pp. 354 ff.

[77] Philippe Pétain, "La Sécurité de la France au cours des années creuses," *Revue des deux mondes*, XXVI (Mar. 1, 1935), vii.

The concept of the nation in arms was thus the accepted doctrine of the French military leaders. They were, it would seem in retrospect, on solid ground when they pointed out the difficulties of recruiting a professional force, when they criticized de Gaulle for his conception of the nature of modern warfare, and when they insisted that it was necessary to think about all of the army instead of some of its components. Americans, who during the early stages of the Second World War were frequently propagandized by the fervent advocates of "victory through airpower" and by those who overpraised the military virtues of the tank, can perhaps now appreciate more of the French "official" doctrine than they could in 1940 when it seemed self-evident that de Gaulle had always been right and his opponents always wrong.[78]

Unfortunately, however, the French military theorists carried to extremes their belief that it was necessary to guard against overspecialization in particular weapons or instruments of national defense. Moreover, since this was combined with their scepticism about the value of planes and tanks and their trust in the powers of the defense, the result was that the concept of the nation in arms, in the hands of the Pétains and their followers, became an argument to use against those who wished to give special attention to aerial or mechanized forces. And the

[78] Certainly, from the purely theoretical point of view, the arguments of Debeney, Pétain, and others were as sound as those of de Gaulle. This latter, for instance, envisaged only ever-victorious offensives and never once dealt with the question of whether or not his mechanized forces might be stopped by a resolute defense. Whatever else they may have done, the official French theorists took this into consideration. Perhaps the best criticism of de Gaulle was written by the relatively unknown General Émile Alléhaut in his *Être prêts* (Paris: Berger-Levrault, 1935), pp. 178-79. Alléhaut, a theorist who believed firmly in the offensive power of armor, insisted however that it was possible to reconcile quality with quantity and that a conscript army could achieve de Gaulle's ultimate purposes. And he concurred with the highest-ranking officers in believing that there would be room for only a sketchy militia alongside de Gaulle's expensive professionals. Finally, he correctly prophesied that the Germans had no intention of preserving their professional army and argued that their ultimate forces, composed of career soldiers and conscripts, would completely engulf any French *armée de métier* no matter how well armed.

effect of this doctrine was to retard the development of French air and tank units. As such, it was a contributing cause of the 1940 defeat.

The basic concept of the nation in arms did not preclude the creation of an adequate "army in being." There was no logical necessity for postwar theories to lead inevitably to the creation of an army which would be unable to defend the nation against a German attack. But what happened was that the political Left, drawing its conclusions from nonmilitary reasoning, tied a host of political, economic, and psychological factors into the popular concept of the nation in arms and made it a stereotype. Conservative military leaders, arguing from the tactical and strategic lessons of 1914-1918, did the same. The result was that, whereas the general theory of the nation in arms led to no set military form, the particular post-1918 theory led to the creation of an inadequate military form and provided a rationale to preserve the *status quo*.

VII

1940: The Consequences of a Theory

EVER SINCE THE TOTALLY UNEXPECTED COLLAPSE of the French armies within a few short weeks in May and June of 1940, there have been a flood of official, unofficial, and "inside" explanations of that catastrophe. In the early spring of 1942 the Vichy government sponsored the much-publicized Riom trial in an attempt to demonstrate to the French people that their prewar political leaders, particularly the men of the Popular Front era, bore the chief responsibility. Shortly after the Liberation, and for totally different reasons, all the parties in the new National Assembly voted to establish a special investigating commission to discover "the ensemble of political, economic, diplomatic, and military events which, from 1933 to 1945, have preceded, accompanied, and followed the armistice." [1] It was, incidentally, more than ten years after the disaster of 1940 before the committee was able to render its report, and there is no reason to believe that this report has done much more than to scratch the surface of the problem. [2] A French public opinion poll,

[1] J.O. *Assemblée nationale, Deb.*, August 29, 1946, pp. 3389-401. Parts of this chapter, in different form, were published in my article, "The Military Defeat of 1940 in Retrospect," in E. M. Earle, ed., *Modern France: Problems of the Third and Fourth Republics* (Princeton: Princeton University Press, 1951), pp. 405-20.

[2] France, Assemblée nationale, *Commission d'enquête parlementaire: Les Événements survenus en France de 1933 à 1945, Rapport* (2 vols.) and *Témoignages et documents recueillis* (9 vols., Paris Presses universitaires de France, 1951). There is a great deal of information in these volumes of great interest to students of recent French military history as well as to those interested in French diplomatic and political history. The collected documents (such as heretofore unavailable *procès-verbaux* of meetings of the *Conseil Supérieur de la Guerre*) are more pertinent than the report. It should be noted, however, that much of the testimony given by such witnesses as Reynaud, Jacomet, Weygand, Gamelin, Paul-Boncour and others simply repeats what these men wrote in their memoirs. Likewise, the collection of documents is spotty rather than systematic. For a criticism of the accomplishments of

taken in 1945, indicated the wide range of opinions that Frenchmen held about the reasons for their defeat: thirty-one per cent of the people believed themselves guilty, eighteen per cent blamed their leaders, and thirteen per cent placed the blame on "politics" in general.[3] What is even clearer is that most of the explanations which have been published so far have been one-sided and partisan. A Swiss military writer, trying like a good Swiss to steer a neutral course through the conflicting testimonies of generals and politicial leaders, observed with obvious distaste that most of the books written to "explain" the 1940 defeat have actually attempted to prove only certain predetermined points of view.[4]

Indeed, many interpretations have been offered. The easiest way out was to advance the argument, maintained in later years by such dissimilar figures as the Radical Socialist leader Édouard Herriot and General Maxime Weygand, that, after all, France was but the advance guard of a world coalition which, in 1940, had not yet mobilized. Given but scanty support from the English, totally unable to obtain more than words of moral encouragement from the Americans, and deserted by the Russians, the French were inevitably doomed to military defeat.[5] On the other hand, in the first stages of surprise and shock, there was a tendency among popular writers, particularly in the United States and Great Britain, to consider the French defeat in moral terms—that is, to describe the "fall of France" in such

the investigation with particular reference to military affairs, see General Lestien, "La Campagne de France devant la Commission d'enquête parlementaire," *Revue d'histoire de la deuxième guerre mondiale*, Nos. 10 to 11 (June, 1953), 184-91.

3 Saul K. Padover, "France Today," *Social Research*, XVI (Dec., 1949), 493.

4 Major Édouard Bauer, *La Guerre des blindés* (Lausanne: Payot, 1947), p. 55, one of the best accounts of the use of armor in World War II.

5 For Herriot's theory see the preface he wrote for Albert Vallet, *Le Problème militaire de la IVᵉ République* (Lyons: Éditions Seguila, 1947), pp. 10-11. General Maxime Weygand, *Mémoires: Rappelé au service* (2 vols., Paris: Flammarion, 1950-53), 6-7, 275. The editors of the semiofficial publication of the Historical Section of the General Staff have also approved this thesis. See *Revue historique de l'armée*, II (Jan., 1946), 46-47.

a way as to suggest a crude Darwinistic interpretation in which a morally weak and corrupt nation had failed to survive the supreme test of its fitness.[6] It is, though erroneous, a profoundly human attitude to consider the issue of war in such a frame of reference, to believe that "good" nations do not lose wars so easily, and to think that the final outcome of military struggle sheds light upon the defects and failings of a civilization.

Moreover, the split among the responsible leaders of the Third Republic—a difference made particularly evident by the peculiar circumstances of the Riom Trial—has further compounded the difficulty of explaining the disaster of 1940. In general, the wartime military leaders and their supporters, with the notable exception of Gamelin, have steadfastly maintained that the responsibility was not theirs; the trouble, they say, was that the politicians failed to provide them with the requisite tools and that the army did not possess sufficient amounts of material.[7] The reply of the men who controlled the government of the ill-fated Third Republic—an answer compounded of many appealing yet, ultimately, unconvincing arguments—has been that they were in no way responsible for military decisions. Considering themselves as middlemen, they have consistently claimed

[6] For an excellent critique of this approach, see Denis Brogan, *French Personalities and Problems* (New York: Knopf, 1947), pp. 178-79.

[7] An excellent example of the unrepentant military view is Robert Darcy, *Oraison funèbre pour la vieille armée* (Paris: Boivin, 1947), a particularly bitter attack upon the French parliament for its neglect of the army. Memoirs by such general officers as Edmond Ruby (of the staff of the Second Army at Sedan) or E. Réquin (of the Fourth Army) place the principal emphasis upon the lack of materiel. Edmond Ruby, *Sedan, terre d'epreuve* (Paris: Flammarion, 1948); E. Réquin, *Combats pour l'honneur, 1939-1940* (Paris: Charles-Lavauzelle, 1946). Likewise, another officer, General L.-M. Chassin, in his history of the Second World War, presents a prevalent military interpretation when he claims that France had but 930 tanks with which to oppose the 4,300 of Germany, a virtual five-to-one German superiority which accounts for the magnitude and swiftness of the defeat. See his *Histoire de la deuxième guerre mondiale* (Paris: Payot, 1947), p. 48. Gamelin himself, it should be noted, sent a long report to Reynaud on May 18, 1940, in which his account of the disaster placed great emphasis upon the shortages of crucial equipment and weapons, but in his memoirs he specifically repudiated much of this report. General Maurice Gamelin, *Servir* (3 vols., Paris: Plon, 1946-47), III, 419 ff.

that they supplied the army with all the equipment and materials that its commanders demanded; the defeat, then, was the consequence of the faulty military theories and erroneous strategies of the military hierarchy.[8] In the words of the National Assembly report of 1951:

The general staff, having retired to its own Sinai among its revealed truths and the vestiges of its vanished glory, lived on the margin of events, devoted all its efforts to patch up an organization which had been superseded by the facts.[9]

Or as a Radical Socialist writer confidently maintained:

We demand once again that there be published—if any one dares—the complete list of the war materials of all sorts which fell into the hands of the enemy during the war or were destroyed to escape them. The astronomical figures at which we would arrive would remove the scales from the eyes of those whom the Riom trial has not yet convinced and would absolve the Third Republic.[10]

Obviously, for a disaster of the magnitude of the French defeat no one, single interpretation is adequate. Nor, for that matter, could it be maintained that deficiencies in military the-

---

[8] Former Finance Minister and postwar President of the Republic Vincent Auriol, for instance, has claimed that according to the constitution the formidable task of preparing mobilization plans, defining war doctrine, and formulating military strategy was in no way incumbent upon the civil authorities. It is, therefore, unjust to blame the military failure upon the political leaders. Vincent Auriol, *Hier . . . demain* (2 vols., Tunis: Charlot, 1944), II, 53. Controller General Jacomet has insisted that he and Daladier not only provided the army with a 14 billion franc credit for war material at a time when its leaders believed 9 billion sufficient but also completed a four-year armament program a full eight months in advance. Robert Jacomet, *L'Armement de la France, 1936-39* (Paris: Éditions Lajeunesse, 1945), p. 322. Daladier and Blum, in turn, relying upon a statement of Gamelin, have confidently claimed that in 1940 there was "an honorable equality" between German and French armaments. Such arguments, indeed, served as the basis of the defense at the Riom trial; in reply to the Vichy charge that they were primarily responsible for the defeat, the former government leaders (and Gamelin, afterwards) replied that the supply of arms had been adequate but that the shopworn doctrines of the high command had led to disaster. See Pierre Tissier, *The Riom Trial* (London: Harrap, 1942), pp. 35 ff. See also Daladier's and Blum's testimony in, *Commission d'enquête, Témoignages et documents*, I, 18 ff. and 224 ff.

[9] *Commission d'enquête, Rapport*, I, 67.

[10] Vallet, *Problème militaire*, p. 136.

ory were more important than other elements in contributing to the ultimate disaster. The origins of the French tragedy are deeply rooted in chronic, inherent weaknesses in the nation's political, economic, and social structure, and any historian must consider far more than the purely military record. Such considerations are, of course, beyond the scope of a book devoted to the development of military theory. Nevertheless, when the defeat of the French army in 1940 is analyzed, the outcome appears to have been materially affected by the French failure to develop a theory of warfare adequate for the needs of the struggle which began when Hitler invaded Poland. In pointing out how faulty theory contributed to the defeat of the French armies it is not as necessary to discuss French tactical and strategic ideas—a separate topic of itself—as it is to explain how the prevailing concept of the nation in arms aided in the development of an inadequate war doctrine and helped create an army suited solely for defensive operations. For, just as the dominant concept of the nation in arms in 1914 led to the French to send all their available man power to the front in the expectation of speedy military victory and left them unprepared for a war of attrition, so, too, in 1939-40 did their revised concept of the nation in arms lead them to anticipate a particular type of warfare which, except for a few short months, failed to materialize. And while this concept gave them a military establishment which avoided the errors of 1914, it provided them with an army unable to meet the new demands of a later generation.

One of the reasons why these theoretical issues are significant is simply because, contrary to the views which were widely held during the war itself, the disproportion between Allied and German war equipment was not so great that no other explanation for the defeat is necessary. To be sure, no re-examination of the facts will permit a revised estimate of the opposing aerial strengths—German superiority in the air remains clear and overwhelming.[11] But statistics produced by investigation in French

---

[11] Colonel Paquier (Chief of the Historical Service of the Air Force), Chef de

war archives reveal that, if the question is considered simply in quantitative terms, the French command had at its disposal in May, 1940, a total of 2,262 modern tanks, 540 tanks of older models, and 743 armored cars while the Germans possessed 3,469 tanks.[12]   In addition, it seems as if there was near-parity in much of the other equipment utilized by the ground forces. Furthermore, postwar research, particularly by the United States Strategic Bombing Survey, has indicated that the western powers long overestimated German war production in the early years of the war and that the Nazi regime did not begin to think of a total economic mobilization until the failure of the Wehrmacht to crush the Russian Army in 1941-42.[13]   Consequently, revised estimates of the materiel available to the contending armies have changed opinions to such an extent that, as one contemporary French military writer has observed, "It does not seem possible that any one can retain as an explanation for our

---

Bataillon Pierre Lyet, and Lt. Colonel Charles de Cossé-Brissac, "Combien d'avions allemands contre combien d'avions français le 10 mai 1940," *Revue de défense nationale,* VI (Jun., 1948), 741-59. A German superiority of at least three-to-one, or even higher, has been established, in addition to which, the qualitative weaknesses of French aircraft must be considered.

[12] Commandant A. Wauquier, "Les Forces cuirassées dans la bataille," *Revue d'histoire de la deuxième guerre mondiale,* Nos. 10 and 11 (Jun., 1953), 151-52. Other studies which give approximately the same figures and which indicate that the German armored superiority was far less than was imagined at the time are Colonel Georges Ferré, *Le Défaut de l'armure* (Paris: Charles-Lavauzelle, 1948), and Lt. Colonel Charles de Cossé-Brissac, "Combien de chars français contre combien de chars allemands le 10 mai 1940?" *Revue de défense nationale,* V (Jul., 1947), 75-89. See also Gamelin, *Servir,* I, 160 and III, 448-49. None of these studies provide identical figures, but their net effect is to destroy the legend that there was an overwhelming German superiority in numbers of armored vehicles. It should be noted, too, that there were also 600 British tanks available for the fighting in Belgium and Holland and that these have not been included in the total.

[13] United States, Strategic Bombing Survey, *The Effects of Strategic Bombing on the German War Economy* (Washington: Government Printing Office, 1945), p. 6. "The outstanding feature of the German war effort is the suprisingly low output of armaments in the first three years of the war—surprisingly low as measured not only by Germany's later achievement, but also by the general expectations of the time and by the level of production of her enemy, Britain. In aircraft, trucks, tanks, self-propelled guns, and several other types of armaments, British production was greater than Germany's in 1940, 1941, and 1942."

1940 defeat the sole argument of the crushing inferiority of our mechanized calvalry and tank forces." [14]

As a result, the question of French war doctrine has become more significant. It is, of course, still true that much French equipment was inferior to the weapons of the invading Germans; but this qualitative deficiency was, in turn, the consequence of the military theories of the High Command. To take but one example: because French war doctrine called for the utilization of tanks in the defensive and for their employment as auxiliaries of the infantry, French armor was clumsy and heavy, had a limited range of action, and was not highly maneuverable. Tanks were employed not in mass but broken up into small units of company size and smaller. The result was that German tanks, integrated into self-contained units and supported by air power, won easy victories. [15] A second result, incidentally, was that most observers, for this reason, received the impression that the French were hopelessly inferior in quantity of armor as well as in quality. But these qualitative weaknesses in French mechanized equipment arose in large measure from the tendency of the General Staff to envisage the primary role for the tank as one of assisting the defense. [16] Hence, one is led to the logical conclusion that the French theory of war was

---

[14] Lt. Colonel Charles de Cossé-Brissac, "Combien de chars français contre combien de chars allemands le 10 mai 1940?" *Revue de défense nationale*, V (Jul., 1947), 88.

[15] Ferré, *Défaut*, pp. 104, 116 ff., and 193.

[16] The question of the extent to which the French had considered the offensive use of the tank is still widely debated. For strong criticism of the prevailing theories for their defensive orientation and their effect upon the quality of French armor, see the testimony of General Bruneau (the 1940 commander of the 1st Armored Division) and of General Dassault (former chief of the Technical Cabinet of the General Staff), in *Commission d'enquête, Témoignages et documents*, V, 1187 ff. and 1466 ff. It is true that in the years immediately prior to 1939 the French command did begin to pay some attention to the formation of armored divisions and to the offensive potentialities of tanks. But, at the same time, little was done to spread such ideas throughout the army, and most commanders continued to think of their armor in terms of the accompaniment of infantry. See Commandant A. Wauquier, "Les Forces cuirassées dans la bataille," *Revue de l'histoire de la deuxième guerre mondiale*, Nos. 10 and 11 (Jun., 1953), 153, 161-162.

as important a cause of defeat as material considerations or quantities of armament. As one writer succinctly phrased his conclusion, "The defeat of 1940 has its roots . . . in an eclipse of French military thought during the twenty years between the two world conflicts." [17]

Although the general theory of the nation in arms prescribed no set military forms, certainly the concepts which became dominant after 1918 were in large measure responsible for the creation of an army unable to act in an emergency. The laws passed in the twenties had clearly recognized that no military operation, even a limited or "police" action, could be undertaken unless at least a sizable portion of the reserves were recalled to duty. Far more than in 1914, as the postwar investigating commission has expressly noted, the French system rested upon the reserves, and there was no division which could attain a war strength without their recall to duty. "We could no longer do anything to fulfill our international obligations without making an appeal to the ensemble of the mobilized nation." And, the report continues, "Our military system required recourse to the nation in arms." How was it possible, the post-Liberation deputies have asked, for the responsible ministers of government not to know these facts or to be surprised when they learned that "to chase three regiments of the *Wehrmacht*, it would have been necessary to put all the French army on a war footing?" [18]

When, in March of 1936 Hitler occupied the Rhineland with his new army, the French failure to respond was as much due to military unpreparedness as to political weakness. There were, as a note to the *Conseil Supérieur* by Gamelin made clear, no troops immediately available for use as an expeditionary force in the Rhineland—"Our military system does not give us this possibility," for the active units are but "the nucleus of the mobilized national army." Any rapid military operation in

[17] Tony Albord, "Appel à l'imagination," *Revue de dèfense nationale*, IX (Aug.-Sept., 1949), 159.

[18] *Commission d'enquête, Rapport*, I, 80, 87.

the Rhineland, Gamelin advised, "even in a more or less symbolic form is fantastic." [19] Hence, he and the Minister of War, General Maurin, informed the cabinet that, if a military reply was contemplated, it would be necessary to put the entire *couverture* upon a war footing—a demand which meant that, at the very least, a considerable number of the reservists and of the frontier troops would have to be called up. All in all, over one million young men would have to be mobilized. In addition, Air and Navy Ministers insisted upon total mobilization of their branches, and Gamelin warned that, if Germany resisted, it might be necessary to order a total mobilization of all French forces. These considerations, in turn, raised the specter of economic disorganization and political repercussions; the weak Sarraut regime, at best a caretaker government, could not find the courage to call the German bluff.[20]

Even at the moment of the final outbreak of war in 1939, the fact that the French army was so dependent upon the untroubled and uninterrupted recall of its reserves was apparent. One of the reasons why Gamelin approved a declaration of war at that time was that the German involvement in Poland would provide him with the opportunity to mobilize his forces without interference from the enemy. On the other hand, he pointed out, if the French permitted their Polish ally to be defeated without themselves declaring war, then, if and when Germany opened hostilities against France, it might be impossible to mobilize and concentrate the armies in time to wage an effective defense.[21] Here, in both instances, were examples of

[19] *Ibid.*, I, 54-55.

[20] *Ibid.*, I, 30 ff., 51-56. For the reaction of Premier Sarraut, *ibid.*, *Témoignages et documents*, III, 583, 604 ff. Sarraut claimed he was surprised to learn that France's army was a purely defensive instrument and that War Minister Maurin demanded a full mobilization, a contention which is not valid. P.-E. Flandin has also made the same claim, see his *Politique française, 1919-1940* (Paris: Les Éditions nouvelles, 1947), pp. 195-99, 205. For other versions, see Gamelin, *Servir*, I, 199-219 and Paul Reynaud, *La France a sauvé l'Europe* (2 vols., Paris: Flammarion, 1947), I, 353-56.

[21] Gamelin, *Servir*, I, 29-30. On the basis of such remarks a recent student of French military affairs has concluded that France went to war in 1939 not to aid

the heavy price which the French paid for adopting a military organization in which the role of the reservists was so crucial.

Equally serious was the fact that the French military institutions of the thirties provided aid and comfort to the men who made Munich. The defeatists, the appeasers, and the men who wished to avoid war at any price could argue with considerable force that their foreign policies were based upon the realities of the military situation and that the defensive orientation of the French military organization made appeasement necessary. Since our army is a defensive army, they said, how can we dream of military intervention anywhere on the Continent of Europe? Maurin's remark in the 1935 conscription debates that to advance beyond the Maginot Line would be tantamount to beginning an "adventure" typified this attitude. And so did the statement of the Right-wing publicist, Raymond Recouly, who announced shortly after the Rhineland crisis:

If . . . we look at our military preparations, we are obliged to state that the army we have forged since the war has an almost exclusively defensive character. [Even with the two-year service] our army is scarcely in a state to undertake the day after tomorrow, an offensive action.[22]

The conclusion might be the same as that reached by General Gamelin, but the purpose of a Recouly was to limit France's obligations to her treaty partners.

Particularly after 1935-36, when the French Right began to lose much of its traditional hatred of Germany, its spokesmen reiterated time and time again that it was a tragic mistake to maintain a defensive army and a foreign policy of mutual assistance to Continental allies. The conservatives, to be sure, were not the only ones to recognize this anomaly. In 1936, for

Poland or to force the Nazis to fight on a second front but simply to guarantee an uninterrupted mobilization. See Fred M. Greene, *French Security and Military Leadership against Germany, 1919-1939* (Unpublished dissertation, Yale University, 1950), p. 227.

[22] Raymond Recouly, "Les Leçons d'une crise," *Revue de France,* XVI (Apr., 1936), 538-39.

instance, General Gamelin observed that the form of the French army was "a trifle too defensive," and he argued that if the country wished to preserve its alliances, French military forces must be made capable of intervention beyond the frontiers.[23] Similarly, an ardent patriot like Paul Reynaud recognized the fact that France no longer had "the army of her policy," and his plea for armored divisions was in large measure based upon his desire to provide the nation with a military arm that would be able to support its foreign policies. But the disillusioned conservatives, fearing Socialism at home, did not draw the same conclusions from the dichotomy between the capabilities of the army and the demands of treaty obligations. In the succinct phrase of Recouly: "When one doesn't have the army of his policies, it is absolutely necessary to have the policies of his army." Hence, to the fear-ridden conservatives and the children of appeasement the *mot du jour* became retrenchment in foreign policy, abandonment of Continental allies and retirement behind the sure fortress of the Maginot Line.[24]

Another of the basic assumptions of these same men was that, in an age in which war had become total, France simply did not possess the economic and industrial resources to engage in such a conflict. Pierre-Étienne Flandin, one of the foremost of the appeasers, has attempted to justify his pre-1939 policies on the grounds that the world had entered an era in which warfare had become both technical and scientific and in which the "élan of 1792" no longer sufficed and that, in such a world, France could not hope to fight the Germans on equal terms. In fact, Flandin

---

[23] *Commission d'enquête, Rapport,* I, 129-30.

[24] See such secondary sources as Arnold Wolfers, *Britain and France between Two Wars* (New York: Harcourt, Brace, 1940), pp. 103 ff. and Charles Micaud, *The French Right and Nazi Germany, 1933-1939* (Durham: Duke University Press, 1943), pp. 137 ff. Both point out in detail how many disillusioned French conservatives believed that the condition of the French army made it essential for France to curtail her international commitments and to retire to a Gallic version of "splendid isolation." Particular offenders were such men as Flandin, Bonnet, Recouly, Montigny, and the well-known jurist, Professor Joseph Barthélemy. A large number of speeches of this nature are cited in Alexander Werth, *The Twilight of France* (New York: Harper, 1942), particularly pp. 140 ff.

has claimed that his country possessed the resources to fight Germany only during the brief and unnatural period which followed immediately after the Armistice when the Weimar Republic did not have an overwhelming industrial potential for war. Hence, to Flandin, the Rhineland—Austria—Czechoslovakia—were events France could not counter by force of arms, and his policies were not only justifiable but inevitable.[25] None, of course, will deny that the French war potential was less than the German, but here, in such arguments, was an unexpected twist: the basic assumption of the post-1918 nation in arms—the idea that war had become total and involved all the resources of the nation—provided the ammunition for those who wished to avoid war at any cost.

Of greater significance, however, than the pessimistic conclusions of the appeasers were the ideas about the nature of modern warfare which both the French military and political leaders developed during the years between the two world conflicts. These ideas, closely bound up with the prevailing concept of the nation in arms, had the effect of strengthening the intention of the French to wage defensive war and at the same time of giving them the unjustified confidence that, whatever else might happen, their nation could not easily be defeated in a new war. These, and not the views of the Recoulys or the Flandins, were the official, prevailing opinions, and it is in the French acceptance of this credo of defensive warfare that one finds the principal reasons for believing that the military defeat of 1940 was particularly related to "an eclipse of French military thought."

It has already been noted on innumerable occasions—in this as well as in countless other studies—that the French military establishment of the interwar years had a primarily defensive orientation. This was, as previously discussed, as much due to political as to military factors, for the dominant groups in the Chamber and the Senate had sought to create and maintain a short-service army dependent on the reserves, and the general

[25] Flandin, *Politique,* pp. 291, 363.

public had been apathetic toward military reform. This defensive orientation was, of course, also due to the very nature of the army's organization. But at the military level there was the belief that, as the events of 1914-1918 had apparently indicated, a strong defensive line was easier to maintain than to breach. The logic of the top army commanders, founded upon many purely military considerations, rested on the basic assumption that the firepower of modern weapons made it almost an impossibility for any frontal assault upon prepared positions to be successful. Moreover, men like Pétain, who had fought in the First World War and who could never forget Verdun, long continued to set the styles of French military thought and to believe that an entrenched army, backed by the firepower of contemporary weapons, was capable of an almost indefinite defense.[26]

Moreover, the weight of the evidence indicates that this faith in the defensive was as prevalent at the top echelons in 1939 as it was immediately after Versailles. Maurice Gamelin, who claims to have known better, has confessed that if he made any errors of judgment, his greatest was to believe that it was unnecessary to make a special effort to change the "Maginot Line complex" of his officer corps.[27] Moreover, when in 1936 the military command rewrote the basic manual which laid down the principles governing the employment of large units, the authors stated that the technical progress in armaments since 1918 had not been sufficient to make the original manual of 1921 obsolete. They

---

[26] The best, over-all survey of French military thought, as previously noted, is still Irving Gibson, "Maginot and Liddell Hart: The Doctrine of Defense," in E. M. Earle, ed., *Makers of Modern Strategy* (Princeton: Princeton University Press, 1943), pp. 365-87. For an unfair yet interesting analysis of the continuing influence of Pétain and his followers, see Reynaud, *La France*, I, 191 ff.

[27] Gamelin, *Servir*, I, 237, 373-74. In retrospect, Gamelin's role appears doubly tragic. He was, of course, charged with the responsibility for the military defeat, and yet he seems to have been aware, prior to 1939, of the weaknesses of the French army although either unwilling or unable to do anything about them. Furthermore, Maxime Weygand, although he claims to have warned against accepting the idea of a static defense, also admits that faith in linear defenses was widespread in the ranks of the army. While insisting that the army did not have sufficient material for battle, Weygand likewise indicates. that the strategic doctrines of the High Command were faulty. See Weygand, *Rappelé au service*, pp. 143-46, 561 ff.

insisted that the principles proclaimed in 1921 were still valid fifteen years later—and it is worth noting that these *Instructions* not only expressed the opinions of the highest military echelons but also were the most authoritative and official statements of military doctrine in the French army.   The 1936 document stated,

The value of defensive organizations has followed, it is true, a parallel development [to that of armaments and weapons], and this synchronization of progress in the domain of firepower and in that of protection has had the effect of preserving the fundamental characteristics ... of operations and of maintaining the respective tasks in battle of the different large units.[28]

As evidence, the *Instructions* went on to point out that new defensive weapons had effectively countered improvements in offensive arms—every improvement in mechanized vehicles had been matched by new antitank guns, and, therefore, the tank should be employed in battle only with heavy artillery support and only after the enemy's defensive system had been ruptured.[29]

Neither the Spanish nor the Polish campaigns appear to have done much to modify these views.[30]   To be sure, the French had long planned to move into Belgium with their main forces in the event of war with Germany, but this operation was essentially a part of an over-all defensive campaign.   The objective, after all, was to establish a linear defense based upon Belgian rivers and fortifications and not to secure a springboard for an

---

[28] Ministère de la Guerre, *Instructions sur l'emploi tactique des grandes unités* (Paris: Charles-Lavauzelle, ed. of 1940), pp. 19-20.

[29] *Ibid.*, pp. 17-18.   As noted earlier, there were "instructions" issued after this which pertained to tanks and which did indicate a wider role for armor, but these seem to have had little effect.

[30] See, for instance, General A. Niessel, "Chars, antichars et motorisation dans la guerre d'Espagne," *Revue militaire générale*, II (Dec., 1938), 759-60.   Paul Bénazet, an important member of Chamber and Senate military commissions since before the First World War, wrote that the Spanish war had provided positive proof that unaided tanks could never breach a line and leave the infantry with the sole task of exploiting the gap.   Because of the tremendous power of antitank guns it was, on the contrary, necessary to employ armor only in conjunction with infantry.   Paul Bénazet, *Défense nationale, notre sécurité* (Paris: Grasset, 1938), pp. 32-44.

immediate attack upon Germany. With some modifications this was the plan that was put into effect in May of 1940. There are, to be sure, some indications that the French in 1939 did consider a limited offensive to aid the Poles; but these plans suggest only the first faint stirrings along different lines of strategy and seem not to have produced any appreciable modifications in the broad intention to wage a defensive war or to have indicated any lessening of the French faith in the defensive.[31]

But this misplaced faith in the defensive arose from other considerations than those which pertained to the effect and supremacy of firepower. Of considerable importance was the belief that in any future war the mass armies of each side would occupy all the space that was available for maneuver and would, therefore, re-establish the stalemated conditions of 1914-1918. Gamelin at the time of the Rhineland occupation in 1936 envisaged such an outcome if the French army challenged the German move and if Hitler decided to resist. Despite the pessimistic tone of Gamelin's statement, it was characteristic of the French belief that the very nature of mass armies automatically created a situation in which the defense would be predominant:

But, on a closed battlefield and in a relatively restricted area, the French and German armies would be in a position, almost immediately, to saturate the terrain. However, the experience of the last war indicates that, even if the empty regions initially permitted maneuver, the saturation of the front rapidly led to an equilibrium between the

---

[31] See Theodore Draper, *The Six Weeks' War* (New York: Viking, 1944), pp. 4-11, 21 ff. for accounts of the plan to move into Belgium. See Lt. Colonel Lugand, "Les Forces en présence au 10 mai 1940," *Revue d'histoire de la deuxième guerre mondiale,* Nos. 10 and 11 (Jun., 1953), 19, on the plans to aid the Poles. Even these, however, suggest how much the French trusted in the defensive, for their ideas on helping Poland were based on the assumption that the Polish army could hold out for at least several months of fighting. The French plans to defend the Meuse—the point of the main German breakthrough in 1940—provide further proof that established ideas had not changed. Here, it seems, the command had made all its arrangements on the assumption that operations would follow the pattern of 1914-1918, that any attack would necessitate long delays, and that, therefore, there would always be time to rush up reserves after the nature of the enemy threat was exactly known. See Colonel Fox, and Chef d'Escadron d'Ornano, "La Percée des Ardennes," *ibid.,* 117.

opposing forces—an equilibrium which could not be broken until after a long attrition of German power. It is quite probable that an operation between the Rhine and the Moselle, in terrain difficult for the offensive, would similarly lead rather quickly to an equilibrium of the contending forces; what we may reasonably hope, given the respective value of the existing armies, is that this equilibrium will probably result in the establishment of a front beyond our national border.[32]

Thus to Gamelin in 1936—at a time when German rearmament was incomplete and the German staff aghast at Hitler's move in the Rhineland—it appeared that military operations by mass armies could only lead to a stalemate. His memorandum is a salient example of how the concept of the nation in arms led the French to think in terms of defensive warfare.

But, at the same time, virtually the same logic made the French confident that they themselves would be able to prevent the invasion of their nation. This confidence arose not only from their faith in defensive armaments and in the virtues of the short-service army but also from their ideas about the nature of twentieth-century warfare. And it was also the logical outcome of the assumption that in modern war each belligerent must make the maximum use of his total resources in manpower and materiel and that the post-1918 nation in arms implied such a total effort. In the hands of a logician like General, Debeney, the one-time Chief of Staff, the basic argument was as follows: modern weapons had given the upper hand to the defense, and it was consequently possible to maintain an unbroken front. But behind the armies were the factories, and each army had at its disposal the fully developed and fully organized capacity of the industrial system of its country. Furthermore, experience had indicated that the potentialities of industry were practically limitless and that each belligerent would use his economic resources to the utmost. Under these circumstances, then, the stage was set for wars of long duration. The front lines would remain stationary as long as the war factories continued to turn

[32] *Commission d'enquête, Rapport,* I, 55-56.

out their endless stream of weapons, and a war could not end until the industrial and economic system of one nation was exhausted. The only limitation on the length of a future European war was the limitation imposed by the strength and capacity of the economies of the belligerents.[33]

Writers like Debeney pushed this argument to its logical conclusion. It followed, for instance, that no sudden attack by Germany could succeed in knocking out or capturing all French war industry, certainly not as long as the weapons of the defense maintained their superiority. It followed, too, that since war industries would be safe and production guaranteed, any future war with Germany would of necessity become a war of attrition. Arguments of this nature were, as previously noted, used against the men like de Gaulle who believed it possible to wage short or "limited" wars, but they also led to the all too comforting feeling that the very nature of the modern nation in arms was a guarantee that France could not easily be conquered.

These were opinions held by political leaders as well as the military hierarchy. In April of 1938, shortly before the Munich crisis, Édouard Daladier held a conference with the British Prime Minister, Neville Chamberlain, in which he indicated how completely he accepted the prevailing military concepts. Daladier told Chamberlain that although France and Britain might have to bear the brunt of a German attack, it was unlikely that any modern nation could be put out of action by a single, sudden assault. This, he said, was confirmed by the events of the Spanish war in which a weak screen of machine gunners, protected only by barbed wire, had frequently thwarted the attacks of more numerous and better armed soldiers. Furthermore, Daladier doubted if any single military factor—such as an air force—could produce decisive results in modern war. After all, whatever importance might be attached to any one particular

[33] General Marie Eugène Debeney, *Sur la sécurité militaire de la France* (Paris: Payot, 1930), pp. 46-51.

weapon, it was still true that war was a single, complex problem which required that all the resources of a nation come into play before victory could be achieved.[34]

The theory of the nation in arms, with its emphasis upon material factors and national war production, also led the French to confuse their actual war strength with their potential strength. Perhaps, for instance, one of the principal reasons why Daladier consistently opposed creating an Armaments Ministry in 1938 lay in his conviction that any war with Germany would be a long one and that there would be sufficient time to produce the necessary war material after the conflict had opened.[35] But, in any event, once the war had begun in 1939 there was certainly a pronounced tendency to make plans upon this confident assumption. Paul Reynaud, the Minister of Finance, drew up plans to purchase raw materials from foreign countries rather than already finished goods and indicated that overseas purchases should be spaced out over an extensive period of time in order to protect the French gold reserves; Raoul Dautry, the newly created Minister of Armaments, drew up a program to purchase machine tools in preference to completed war materiel; and Daladier, the Premier, hesitated to make a full application of his power to assign workers to industrial jobs.[36] These men know full well that the war potential of Germany

[34] Great Britain, Foreign Office, *Documents on British Foreign Policy, 1919-1939,* ed. E. L. Woodward and Rohan Butler, (14 vols., London: H. M. Stationery Office, 1946-52), 3rd series, I, (1938), 205-07. See also the evidence about Daladier's military ideas which Paul Reynaud collected and presented in *La France,* I, 402 ff. and in *Commission d'enquête, Témoignages et documents,* I, 103 ff. Daladier appears to have been convinced that modern weapons would prevent movement and maneuver on the battlefield and that it was foolish to envisage any sort of war except a war of attrition.

[35] See the testimony of Robert Jacomet, *Commission d'enquête, Témoignages et documents,* I, 190. Jacomet confirmed the fact that the French felt confident there would be time to carry out industrial mobilization after the outbreak of war, but—to defend himself and Daladier—he tried to shift the blame to the military hierarchy.

[36] See, for instance, the reasoning in Paul Reynaud, *La Guerre: notre plan économique et financier* (Paris: Imprimerie nationale, 1939), pp. 17-18, 45.

was far superior to that of metropolitan France, but at the same time they took heart in their knowledge that the war potential of the combined empires of England and France was, in turn, overwhelmingly greater than that of the enemy. And, feeling secure behind the Maginot Line and confident in the defensive power of French armaments, they believed that they had sufficient time to organize their own military might. For, as the very nature of the modern nation in arms seemed to proclaim, if economic capacity was of decisive importance in war, then, the superior potential of the Allies was bound to triumph.

These assumptions led the French to believe in a long war. They envisaged a conflict in which naval and air blockade would so weaken Germany that—almost like the classic Marxist state—German power would slowly wither away. They were confident that, secure in their defenses, they could over a period of several years accumulate such an overwhelming superiority in armaments that offensive military action would finally be feasible. The Germans, weakened not only by blockade but also by futile attacks of their own against the impregnable Allied defenses, would be unable to sustain resistance. Hence, on the basis of such assumptions, General Gamelin, in the autumn of 1939, believed the French would wage a successful defensive battle in the spring of the following year and that, after a period of several years, his armies would at last be able to undertake the offensive.[37] In the confident words of one military writer of the same year: "Germany has no chance to win a war in which her enemies put their economic superiority into operation in all its amplitude." [38]

---

[37] Gamelin, *Servir*, I, 33.

[38] André Labarthe, *La France devant la guerre* (Paris: Grasset, 1939), preface by General Prételat, in which the latter officer argued that the French must prepare for a long war so that their ultimately superior war potential could be brought to bear. See also a book by General Bernard Serrigny, then in retirement, *L'Allemagne face à la guerre totale* (Paris: Grasset, 1940), pp. 140 ff. Serrigny maintained that the Germans must lose since their war potential could only decrease while, on the contrary, that of the Allies was steadily bound to increase.

Thus it appears that the particular theory of the nation in arms held by the military and political leaders was a contributing factor to the defeat of the French armies in 1940. French faith in the short-term soldier and the reservist led to the creation of an army which could not stop aggression and which could not, by its very nature, assume any role except the defensive. Yet despite the inability of the army to win decisive victories, the French leaders had not lost confidence—indeed, they had deliberately chosen the defensive. The postwar concept of the nation in arms had, after all, led them to assume that the very nature of the modern industrial system provided them with advantages in defending the nation. Consequently, when the entire French military organization crumbled in the first days of the German attack, the psychological shock was even greater and defeat, because so unexpected, even more bitter.

Yet, the over-all French failure was, as it was in 1914, essentially a failure to envisage alternatives. Frenchmen were certainly not wrong in believing that a full-scale twentieth-century war between major powers required the organization of all human and material resources into a vast nation in arms. Though men may still hope for "limited" war, in 1954 they prepare for total war. And, indeed, the post-Liberation French writers seem to believe that at least one of the lessons of the Second World War is the need to devote even more attention to war materiel and production. But in 1939-40 French theories of the nation in arms were too inflexible. The French, forgetting the many warnings expressed in the twenties, became too confident in the thirties that they had learned the lessons of the first world conflict and that the war against Hitler would follow a predetermined pattern. Had they thought, for instance, that industrial power might not prevent defeat, or that a war could be short, or that the tank and airplane had especial virtues, then the outcome might have differed. But instead their theorists and leaders were too doctrinaire and too logical. They rationalized their ideas into the assumption that the proper organization of manpower and resources—backed by the "defensive" weapons they trusted too much—was a virtual gage of victory. They might well have remembered the words of Clausewitz who observed, with appropriate scepticism, that "Activity in war is movement in a resistant medium. Just as a man in water is unable to perform with ease and regularity the most natural and simple movement, that of walking, so in war one cannot, with ordinary powers, keep even the line of mediocrity."

Bibliography

NOTE ON ABBREVIATIONS

THE FOLLOWING ABBREVIATIONS have been used for references to
French parliamentary debates and documents: *J.O.* = *Journal officiel de
la République française*; *C.* = *Chambre des Députés*; *S.* = *Sénat*; *Deb.* =
Débats; *Doc.* = *Documents.* Thus, *J.O.C. Deb.* will refer to a volume
of the debates of the Chamber of Deputies, while *J.O.S. Doc.* will refer
to a volume of the documents of the Senate. Many volumes of the
parliamentary record for the years immediately after 1871 are titled,
simply, *Journal officiel,* and debates, documents, and decrees of both
legislative houses are bound within a single cover; the abbreviation
J.O. is used to refer to these volumes. Finally, the abbreviation *AAN*
is used to refer to the *Annales de l'Assemblée nationale,* the separately
published record of the National Assembly of 1871-75.

I. BIBLIOGRAPHIES

Lauterbach, Albert T.   Modern War, Its Economic and Social Aspects.
   Princeton: Institute for Advanced Study, 1941.
Probobysz, A. Favitski de.   Répertoire bibliographique de la littérature
   militaire et coloniale française depuis cent ans.   Paris: Berger-
   Levrault, 1935.
Shanahan, William O.   "The Literature on War," *Review of Politics,*
   IV (Apr. and Jul., 1942), 206-22 and 327-46.

II. PRIMARY SOURCES: OFFICIAL DOCUMENTS, LETTERS, MEMOIRS, AND SPEECHES

Adam, Juliette.   Mes Sentiments et nos idées avant 1870.   Paris:
   A. Lemerre, 1905.
André, General Louis.   Cinq Ans de ministère.   Paris: Louis-Michaud,
   1907.

Auriol, Vincent. Hier . . . demain. 2 vols., Tunis: Charlot, 1944.

Baquet, General Louis Henry. Souvenirs d'un directeur d'artillerie. Paris: Charles-Lavauzelle, 1921.

Caillaux, Joseph. Mes Mémoires. 3 vols., Paris: Plon, 1942-47.

Castellane, Esprit V. Le Journal du Maréchal Castellane, 1804-1862. 5 vols., Paris: Plon, 1897-1930.

Chesnelong, Charles. Les Derniers Jours de l'Empire et le gouvernement de M. Thiers. Paris: Librairie Académique Perrin, 1932.

Cot, Pierre. The Triumph of Treason. Trans. Sybille and Milton Crane. Chicago: Ziff-Davis, 1944.

Documents on British Foreign Policy, 1919-1939. Ed. E. L. Woodward and Rohan Butler. 44 vols., London: H. M. Stationery Office, 1949-53.

Du Barail, General François-Charles. Mes Souvenirs. 3 vols., Paris: Plon, 1894-96.

Ferry, Jules. Discours et opinions de Jules Ferry. Ed. Paul Robiquet. 7 vols., Paris: Colin, 1893-98.

Fix, Colonel Nathanaël. Souvenirs d'un officier d'état-major (1846-70). Paris: Juven, n.d.

———— Souvenirs d'un officier d'état-major (1870-94). Paris: Juven, n.d.

Flandin, P.-E. Politique française, 1919-1940. Paris: Les Éditions nouvelles, 1947.

Foch, Ferdinand. The Memoirs of Marshal Foch. Trans. Colonel T. Bentley Mott. New York: Doubleday, Doran, 1931.

France, Assemblée Nationale. Commission d'enquête parlementaire: Les Événements survenus en France de 1933 à 1945. Rapport de M. Charles Serre (2 vols.). Témoignages et documents (9 vols.). Paris: Presses universitaires de France, 1951. (Assembly Doc. No. 2344, *annexe* to the session of August 8, 1947).

France, Chambre des Députés. Procès-verbal de la commission d'enquête sur le rôle et la situation de la métallurgie en France. Paris: Imprimerie de la Chambre des Députés, 1919. (Chamber Doc. No. 6026, *annexe* to the session of April 16, 1919).

France, Ministère des Affaires Étrangères. Documents diplomatiques français (1871-1914). 32 vols., Paris: Imprimerie nationale, 1929 ————.

France, Ministère de la Guerre. État-major de l'Armée. Instruction provisoire du 6 octobre 1921 sur l'emploi tactique des grandes unités. Paris: Charles-Lavauzelle, 1925.

———— Instruction sur l'emploi tactique des grandes unités. Paris: Charles-Lavauzelle, 1940. (Issued August 12, 1936).

———— Les Armées françaises dans la grande guerre. 10 vols. in 66, Paris: Imprimerie nationale, 1922-36.

Freycinet, Charles de. Souvenirs, 1848-1878. Paris: Delagrave, 1912.

———— Souvenirs, 1878-1893. Paris: Delagrave, 1914.

Gambetta, Léon. Lettres de Gambetta (1868-1882). Ed. Émile Pillias and Daniel Halévy. Paris: Grasset, 1938.

Gamelin, General Maurice. Servir. 3 vols., Paris: Plon, 1946-47.

Herriot, Édouard. The French Plan. London: New Commonwealth Pamphlets, 1934. (Proposal for the organization of Peace presented by the Herriot government to the Geneva Conference for the Reduction and Limitation of Armaments).

———— In Those Days. Trans. Adolphe de Milly. New York: Old and New World Publishing Company, 1952.

Historique des diverses lois sur le recrutement depuis la Révolution jusqu'à nos jours. Paris: Imprimerie nationale, 1902. (Extracts from Chamber and Senate documents and debates).

Jarras, General Hugues-Louis. Souvenirs du Général Jarras. Paris: Plon, 1892.

Joffre, Joseph. Mémoires du Maréchal Joffre. 2 vols., Paris: Plon, 1932.

Journal officiel de la République française, 1871-1940.

League of Nations. Documents of the Preparatory Commission for the Disarmament Convention. Series II, IX, Armaments, 1926. IX. 7. Geneva: Imprimerie d'Ambilly, 1926.

Messimy, General Adolphe. Mes Souvenirs. Paris: Plon, 1937.

Millerand, Alexandre. Pour la défense nationale. Paris: Charpentier, 1913.

Moniteur universel, 1866-68.

Painlevé, Paul. Paul Painlevé, paroles et écrits. Paris: Rieder, 1936.

Paul-Boncour, Joseph. Entre deux guerres. 3 vols., Paris: Plon, 1945-46.

Poincaré, Raymond. Au service de la France. 10 vols., Paris: Plon, 1926-33.

Randon, Jacques Louis. Mémoires du Maréchal Randon. 2 vols., Lahure, 1875-77.

Reinach, Joseph. Mes Comptes rendus. 4 vols., Paris: Alcan, 1911-18.

Reynaud, Paul. La France a sauvé l'Europe. 2 vols., Paris: Flammarion, 1947.

——— La Guerre, notre plan économique et financier. Paris: Imprimerie nationale, 1939.

Senior, Nassau. Conversations with Distinguished Persons during the Second Empire. 2 vols., London: Hurst and Blackett, 1880.

——— Conversations with M. Thiers, M. Guizot and Other Distinguished Persons during the Second Empire. 2 vols., London: Hurst and Blackett, 1878.

Simon, Jules. La Politique radicale. Paris: Librairie Internationale, 1868.

Stoffel, Colonel Baron Eugène. Rapports militaires écrits de Berlin, 1866-1870. Paris: Garnier Frères, 1871.

Taufflieb, General Émile. Souvenirs d'un enfant d'Alsace. Strasbourg: Imprimerie Alsacienne, 1934.

Thiers, Adolphe. Memoirs of M. Thiers. Trans. F. M. Atkinson. London: Allen and Unwin, 1915.

United States, Department of State. Conference on the Limitation of Armament, Washington, November 12, 1921-February 6, 1922. Washington: Government Printing Office, 1922.

United States, Department of the Army. Second Section, General Staff. Monthly Reports of Important Military Events, France. (File 6167, Unpublished reports of the U. S. military attachés in France, 1912-1914; in the National Archives, Washington, D. C.).

United States, Strategic Bombing Survey. The Effects of Strategic Bombing on the German War Economy. Washington: Government Printing Office, 1945.

Weygand, General Maxime. Mémoires. 2 vols., Paris: Flammarion, 1950-53.

III. SECONDARY SOURCES

Acomb, Evelyn. The French Laic Laws. New York: Columbia University Press, 1941.

Ailleret, Lt. Charles. "Mobilisation industrielle," *Revue militaire française*, LIX (Feb., 1936), 145-206.

——— L'Organisation économique de la nation en temps de guerre. Paris: Librairie technique et économique, 1935.

Albord, Tony. "Appel à l'imagination," *Revue de défense nationale*, IX (Aug.-Sept., 1949), 145-60.

Alléhaut, General Émile. Être prêts. Paris: Berger-Levrault, 1935.

——— La Guerre n'est pas une industrie. Paris: Berger-Levrault, 1925.

G. André, "L'Armée: Les Formes et les forces," *Nouvelle Revue*, CXV (Nov., 1898), 234-44.

L'Armée française vivra, by J.I.R.G.I. Paris: Librairie de la *Revue française*, 1929.

L'Armée nouvelle et le service d'un an, by B.A.R. Paris: Plon, 1921.

Aubry, Octave. Le Second Empire. Paris: Fayard, 1938.

Augé-Laribé, Michel. L'Agriculture pendant la guerre. Paris: Presses universitaires de France, 1925.

Aumale, le Duc Henri d'. Les Institutions militaires de la France. Paris: Levy Frères, 1867.

Azan, General Paul. "L'Organisation de la défense nationale," *Revue militaire générale*, II (Mar., 1938), 1-9.

Bapst, Germain. Le Maréchal Canrobert. 4 vols., Paris: Plon, 1898-1909.

Barrès, Maurice. Scènes et doctrines du nationalisme. Paris: Émile-Paul, n.d.

Barrès, Philippe. Charles de Gaulle. New York: Brentano's, 1941.

Bauer, Major Édouard. La Guerre des blindés. Lausanne: Payot, 1947.

Belperron, Pierre. Maginot of the Line. Trans. H. Stenning. London: Williams and Morgate, 1940.

Bénazet, Paul. Défense nationale, notre sécurité. Paris: Grasset, 1938.

Bernier, Paul. La Loi d'un an. Paris: Charles-Lavauzelle, 1931.

Berthaut, General Henri. Principes de stratégie. Paris: Dumaine, 1881.

Bertillon, Jacques. La Dépopulation de la France. Paris: Alcan, 1911.

Bidault, Colonel Frédéric-Léopold. L'Armée française et le service de deux ans. Paris: Charles-Lavauzelle, 1898.

Bigant, A. La Nationalisation et le contrôle des usines de guerre. Paris: Domat-Montchrestien, 1939.

Bloch, Jean de. The Future of War. Trans. R. C. Long. Boston: Ginn and Company, 1899.

Bonaparte, Louis Napoléon. Oeuvres de Louis-Napoléon Bonaparte, Ed. Charles Temolaire. 2 vols., Paris: Librairie Napoléonienne, 1848.

———— Oeuvres de Napoleon III. 5 vols., Paris: Plon, 1856-69.

Bonnal, General Henri. Les Conditions de la guerre moderne. Paris: Boccard, 1916.

———— La Première Bataille. Paris: Chapelot, 1908.

———— La Prochaine Guerre. Paris: Chapelot, 1906.

Boucher, General Arthur. Les Doctrines dans la préparation de la grande guerre. Paris: Berger-Levrault, 1925.

Boudenoot, Louis. "L'Armée en 1899," *Revue politique et parlementaire*, XXII (Nov., 1899), 251-91.

Bourelly, General Jules. "L'Armée est-elle et doit-elle être la nation?" *Correspondant*, CLXXI (Apr. 25, 1902), 193-220.

———— "L'Armée française au commencement de 1904—l'oeuvre du Général André," *Correspondant*, CLXXVIII (Feb. 10 and 25, 1904), 402-26 and 686-713.

Bourgeois, Émile. Manuel de politique étrangère. 4 vols., Paris: Belin, 1900-26.

Brindel, General. "La Nouvelle Organisation militaire," *Revue des deux mondes*, LI (Jun. 1, 1929), 481-501.

Brisson, Andre. Deux Ministres de la guerre: Général André et Général Gallifet. (Trans. from an article in *Nouvelle Presse libre de Vienne*, April 26, 1903: copy available in the New York Public Library).

Brocade, Lucien. "Le Développement économique de la Lorraine française," *La Réforme sociale* (Jun. 1913), 727-45.

Brogan, D. W. French Personalities and Problems. New York: Knopf, 1947.

Brossé, Colonel Julien. "Notre théorie de 1914 sur la conduite des opérations et les leçons de la guerre," *Revue militaire française*, X (Nov., 1923), 245-61.

Bruneau, Pierre. Le Rôle du haut commandement au point de vue économique de 1914 à 1921. Paris: Berger-Levrault, 1924.

Bury, J. P. T. Gambetta and the National Defense. London: Longmans, Green, 1936.

Buthmann, William. The Rise of Integral Nationalism in France. New York: Columbia University Press, 1939.

Camon, General Hubert. La Motorisation de l'armée. Paris: Berger-Levrault, 1926.

Cauwès, Paul. Cours d'économie politique. 4 vols., Paris: Larose, 1893.

Chambers, Frank P. The War behind the War, 1914-1918. New York: Harcourt, Brace, 1939.

Changarnier, General Nicolas. "Un Mot sur le projet de réorganisation militaire," *Revue des deux mondes*, LXVIII (Apr. 15, 1867), 874-90.

Chapuis, Commandant Félix. Manuel de la préparation militaire. Paris: Berger-Levrault, 1910.

Chareton, General Jean. Projet motivé de réorganisation de l'état militaire de France. Paris: Plon, 1871.

Chassin, General L.-M. Histoire de la deuxième guerre mondiale. Paris: Payot, 1947.

Chauvineau, Narcisse. *Cours de fortification.* École Supérieure de Guerre, 1925. (Unpublished text, available at the National War College, Washington, D. C.).

———— Une Invasion: Est-elle encore possible? Paris: Berger-Levrault, 1939.

Choppin, Captain Henri. L'Armée française, 1870-1890. Paris: Albert Savene, 1890.

Clough, Shepard B. France: A History of National Economics. New York: Scribners, 1939.

Colin, Commandant Jean. France and the Next War. Trans. Major L. H. R. Pope-Hennesey. London: Hodder and Stoughton, 1914.

Colson, Léon. Cours d'économie politique. 6 vols., Paris: Gauthier-Villars, 1907-09.

Condamy, Captain Charles. La Loi de deux ans et la leçon du conflit franco-allemand à propos du Maroc. Paris: Charles-Lavauzelle, 1905.

"Le Conseil Supérieur de la Défense Nationale et la 'guerre totale,'" by Commandant, A. L., *Revue politique et parlementaire*, CXX (Aug. 10, 1924), 199-218.

Cossé-Brissac, Lt. Colonel Charles de. "Combien de chars français contre combien de chars allemands le 10 mai 1940?" *Revue de défense nationale*, V (Jul., 1947), 75-89.

Cours d'art militaire—Notions de droit international . . . législation . . . organisation de l'armée . . . mobilisation. École Polytechnique, 1911.

(Unpublished text, available at the National War College, Washington, D. C.).

Créhange, André. Chômage et placement. Paris: Presses universitaires de France, 1927.

Culmann, General Frédéric. Reichsheer et milices. Paris: Charles-Lavauzelle, 1933.

———— Tactique d'artillerie. Paris: Charles-Lavauzelle, 1937.

Davis, Shelby C. The French War Machine. London: Allen and Unwin, 1937.

———— Reservoirs of Men. Chambéry: Imprimeries Réunies, 1934.

Debeney, General Marie Eugène. "Encore l'armée de métier," *Revue des deux mondes*, XXVIII (Jul. 15, 1935), 279-95.

———— La Guerre et les hommes. Paris: Plon, 1937.

———— "La Motorisation des armées modernes," *Revue des deux mondes*, XXXII (Mar. 15, 1936), 273-91.

———— Sur la sécurité militaire de la France. Paris: Payot, 1930.

Delaperrierre, Eugène. La France économique et l'armée. Paris: Charles-Lavauzelle, 1893.

Delavallée, Lt. Colonel. Cours de fabrications de guerre. Paris: Imprimerie nationale, 1922. (Text used at the École Supérieure de Guerre).

———— Mobilisation industrielle. Centre d'Études Tactiques d'Artillerie de Metz, 1920. (Unpublished text, available at National War College, Washington, D. C.).

———— Quelques Considérations sur la mobilisation industrielle. Centre d'Études Tactiques d'Artillerie de Metz, 1923. (Unpublished text, available at the National War College, Washington, D. C.).

Dietz, Jean. "Les Débuts de Jules Ferry," *Revue de France*, XII (Oct. 15, 1932), 608-27.

Doukas, Kimon A. "Armaments and the French Experience," *American Political Science Review*, XXXIII (Apr. 1939), 279-91.

———— The French Railroads and the State. New York: Columbia University Press, 1945.

Draper, Theodore. The Six Weeks' War. New York: Viking, 1944.

Dreyfus, Robert. "Les Premières Armes de Gambetta," *Revue de France*, XII (Dec. 15, 1932), 674-92.

Duchemin, Commandant. "Poudres et explosifs, 1914-1918," *Revue militaire française,* XVIII (Oct., 1925), 119-31.

Ducrot, General Auguste. *La Défense de Paris.* 4 vols., Paris: Dentu, 1877-83.

Du Picq, Ardant. Études sur le combat. Paris: Chapelot, ed. of 1904.

Dupuy, Charles. "Le Service de deux ans et les dispenses," *Revue politique et parlementaire,* XXXIV (Feb., 1903), 229-46.

Duruy, Georges. L'Officier éducateur. Paris: Chapelot, 1904. (Text used at the École Polytechnique).

Duval, General Maurice. "La Crise de notre organisation militaire," *Revue de Paris,* II (Apr. 15, 1926).

Earle, Edward Meade, ed. Makers of Modern Strategy. Princeton: Princeton University Press, 1943.

Ebener, Lt. Colonel Charles. Conférences sur le rôle social de l'officier. Paris: Charles-Lavauzelle, 1901. (Text used at the École Spéciale Militaire de Saint-Cyr).

Ehrmann, Henry W. French Labor from Popular Front to Liberation. New York: Oxford University Press, 1947.

Engels, Friedrich. Notes on the War. Ed. Friedrich Adler. Vienna: Wiener Volksbuchshandlung, 1923.

Engerand, Fernand. La Bataille de la frontière. Paris: Éditions Bossard, 1920.

Fabry, Jean. "La Défense nationale," *Revue militaire générale,* II (Jan., 1938), 15-24.

Farre, General Jean-Joseph. Observations sur les réformes militaires à l'étude. Paris: Baudoin, 1882.

Favé, General Ildephonse. Cours d'art militaire professé a l'École Polytechnique. Paris: Dumaine, 1877.

Ferré, Colonel Georges. Le Défaut de l'armure. Paris: Charles-Lavauzelle, 1948.

Fin de la nation armée. Paris: Berger-Levrault, 1934.

Foch, Ferdinand. Des Principes de la guerre. Paris: Berger-Levrault, ed. of 1917.

Fontaine, Arthur. L'Industrie française pendant la guerre. Paris: Presses universitaires de France, 1924.

Fox, Colonel and Chef d'escadron d'Ornano. "La Percée des Ardennes," *Revue d'histoire de la deuxième guerre mondiale,* Nos. 10 and 11 (Jun., 1953), 77-118.

French Economic Effort in the World War, The. (Unidentified paper, translated for the Military Intelligence Division, U. S. Army; available in the National War College, Washington, D. C.).

Freycinet, Charles de. La Guerre en province pendant le siège de Paris, 1870-71. Paris: Michel Lèvy, 1871.

Froment, Lieutenant A. La Mobilisation et la préparation à la guerre. Paris: Librairie illustrée, 1887.

Fuller, Major General J. F. C. Armament and History. New York: Scribners, 1945.

Gachot, Édouard. "Histoire du tirage au sort," *Nouvelle Revue*, XXVI (Jan.-Feb., 1904), 21-34.

Gaulle, Charles de. Vers l'armée de métier. Paris: Berger-Levrault, 1934.

——— Trois Études (suivies du Memorandum du 26 janvier 1940). Paris: Berger-Levrault, 1945.

——— La France et son armée. Paris: Plon, 1945.

Géraud, André (Pertinax). The Gravediggers of France. New York: Doubleday, Doran, 1944.

Gervais, A. "La Question des effectifs," *Revue politique et parlementaire*, XXXIV (Dec., 1902), 454-81.

Gidel, Gilbert. "L'Organisation de la nation pour le temps de guerre et le droit international," *Revue politique et parlementaire*, CXXXI (Jun. 10, 1927), 314-29.

Gilbert, Captain Georges. Lois et institutions militaires. Paris: Librairie de la *Nouvelle Revue*, 1895.

——— "Le Service de deux ans," *Nouvelle Revue*, CXIII (Jul.-Aug., 1898), 385-401.

Goguel, François. La Politique des partis sous la Troisième République. Paris: Éditions du Seuil, 1946.

Gohier, Urbain. L'Armée nouvelle. Paris: Stock, 1897.

Golob, Eugene. The Méline Tariff: French Agriculture and Nationalist Economic Policy. New York: Columbia University Press, 1944.

Gorce, Pierre de la. Histoire du Second Empire. 7 vols., Paris: Plon, 1899-1905.

Greene, Fred M. French Military Leadership and Security against Germany, 1919-1940. (Unpublished dissertation, Yale University, 1950).

Grosche, Eberhard. Der Einfluss des Weltkrieges auf die seitherige Entwicklung der französischen Wehrwirtschaft. Hamburg: Hanseatische Verlagsanstalt, 1937.

Guesde, Jules. État, politique et morale de classe. Paris: Giard and Brière, 1901.

Halévy, Élie. L'Ère des tyrannies. Paris: Gallimard, 1938.

———— Histoire du socialisme européen. Paris: Gallimard, 1948.

Hanotaux, Gabriel *et al.* Histoire militaire et navale (L'Histoire de la nation française, ed. Gabriel Hanotaux, Part II, Vol. VIII). 15 vols., Paris: Plon, 1920-29.

Harvey, Donald J. French Concepts of Military Strategy, 1919-1939. (Unpublished dissertation, Columbia University, 1953).

Hayes, Carleton J. H. France: A Nation of Patriots. New York: Columbia University Press, 1930.

Herr, General Frédéric. L'Artillerie. Paris: Berger-Levrault, 1924.

Hittle, James D. The Military Staff—Its History and Development. Harrisburg, Pa.: The Telegraph Press, 1949.

Humbert, Senator Charles. Les Voeux de l'armée. Paris: Librairie universelle, n.d.

Irvine, Dallas D. "The French Discovery of Clausewitz and Napoleon," *Journal of the American Military Institute*, IV (Summer, 1940), 143-61.

———— "The Origin of Capital Staffs," *Journal of Modern History*, X (Jun., 1938), 161-79.

Iung, General Théodore, La République et l'armée. Paris: Bibliothèque Charpentier, 1892.

Jacomet, Robert. L'Armement de la France, 1936-1939. Paris: Éditions Lajeunesse, 1945.

Jaurès, Jean. L'Armée nouvelle. Paris: L'Humanité, ed. of 1915.

———— Democracy and Military Service. Trans. G. G. Coulton. London: Simpkin, 1916. (Abbreviated version of L'Armée nouvelle).

Jellinek, Frank. The Paris Commune of 1871. New York: Oxford University Press, 1937.

Joffre, Marshal Joseph, 1914-1915—la préparation de la guerre et la conduite des opérations. Paris: Chiron, 1920.

Jordan, W. M. Great Britain, France, and the German Problem, 1918-1939. London: Oxford University Press, 1943.

Katzenbach, Edward L., Jr. Charles-Louis de Soulces de Freycinet and the Army of Metropolitan France. (Unpublished dissertation, Princeton University, 1953).

Kerviler, Georges. La Navigation intérieure en France pendant la guerre. Paris: Presses universitaires de France, 1926.

Kessler, General Charles. La Guerre. Paris: Berger-Levrault, 1909.

———— "La Loi du service de deux ans," *Correspondant*, CLXXVII (Nov. 10, 1903), 483-500.

Kovacs, Arpad. "French Military Institutions before the Franco-Prussian War," *American Historical Review*, LI (Jan., 1946), 217-35.

———— "French Military Legislation in the Third Republic, 1871-1940," *Military Affairs*, XIII (Spring, 1949), 1-13.

Kraehe, Enno A. "Motives behind the Maginot Line," *Military Affairs*, VIII (Summer, 1944), 138-52.

Labarthe, André. La France devant la guerre. Paris: Grasset, 1939.

Lafon, Gabriel. Les Chemins de fer français pendant la guerre. Paris: Rousseau, 1922.

Lamy, Étienne. "L'Armée et la démocratie," *Revue des deux mondes*, LXIX (Jun. 15, 1885), 835-84.

———— "Les Ennemis de l'armée," *Revue des deux mondes*, CXXII (Mar. 15, 1894), 425-55.

Lanessan, Jean-Joseph de. Nos Forces militaires. Paris: Alcan, 1913.

Langlois, General Hippolyte. Lessons from Two Recent Wars. Trans. For the General Staff, War Office. London: His Majesty's Stationery Office, 1909.

———— Questions de défaut. Paris: Berger-Levrault, 1906.

———— Tactical Changes Resulting from Improvements in Armament. (Unpublished trans. for the U. S. Army available in the National War College, Washington, D. C.).

Lanrezac, General Charles. Le Plan de campagne français et le premier mois de la guerre. Paris: Payot, 1921.

La Panousse, Colonel de. "L'Organisation militaire—le service de deux ans: Les Finances, la population, le nombre," *Revue des deux mondes*, XXI (May 15, 1904), 318-52.

Laporte, Intendant General Ferdinand. Mobilisation économique et intendance militaire. Paris: Charles-Lavauzelle, 1931.

Lavisse, Ernest, ed. L'Armée à travers les âges. Paris: Chapelot, 1904. (Lectures given at the École Spéciale Militaire de Saint-Cyr in 1898).

Leaman, Bertha R. "The Influence of Domestic Policy on Foreign Affairs in France, 1898-1905," *Journal of Modern History*, XIV (Dec., 1942), 449-79.

Lefebvre, Georges. The Coming of the French Revolution. Trans. R. R. Palmer. Princeton: Princeton University Press, 1947.

Lehautcourt, Pierre. Histoire de la guerre de 1870-71. 7 vols., Paris: Berger-Levrault, 1901-08.

———— "La Réorganisation de l'armée avant 1870," *Revue de Paris*, IV (Aug., 1901), 525-52.

Le Hénaff, Joseph. Conférence sur les chemins de fer. Centre des Hautes Études Militaires, 1919. (Unpublished text, available at the National War College, Washington, D. C.).

———— The Preparation and Execution of a Plan of Transportation for Concentration. (Unpublished trans. for the U. S. Army, available in the National War College, Washington, D. C.).

———— Le Rôle militaire des chemins de fer. Paris: Berger-Levrault, 1923.

Le Hénaff, General Joseph, and Captain Henri Bornecque. Les Chemins de fer français et la guerre. Paris: Chapelot, 1922.

Leroy-Beaulieu, Paul. La Guerre de 1914, vue en son cours chaque semaine. Paris: Delagrave, 1915.

———— La Question de la population. Paris: Alcan, 1913.

———— "Les Ressources de la France et de la Prusse dans la guerre," *Revue des deux mondes*, LXXXIX (Sept. 1, 1870), 135-55.

———— Traité théorique et pratique d'économie politique. 4 vols., Paris: Guillaumin, 1896.

Lestien, General. "La Campagne de France devant la commission d'enquête parlementaire," *Revue d'histoire de la deuxième guerre mondiale*, Nos. 10 and 11 (Jun., 1953), 184-91.

Levasseur, Émile. La Population française. 3 vols., Paris: Rousseau, 1889-92.

Lewal, General Jules. Études de guerre. 2 vols., Paris: Baudoin, 1889.

Lugand, Lt. Colonel. "Les Forces en présence au 10 mai 1940," *Revue d'histoire de la deuxième guerre mondiale*, Nos. 10 and 11 (Jun., 1953), 5-48.

Lyautey, Colonel Louis. "Du Rôle social de l'officier," *Revue des deux mondes*, CIV (Mar. 15, 1891), 443-58.

Maitrot, General Charles. Le Nouvel État militaire de la France. Paris: Berger-Levrault, 1919.

Mangin, Charles. La Force noire. Paris: Hachette, 1911.

———— Des Hommes et des faits. Paris: Plon, 1923.

Mason, Edward S. The Paris Commune: An Episode in the History of the Socialist Movement. New York: MacMillan, 1930.

Maurin, General Joseph-Léon-Marie. L'Armée moderne. Paris: Flammarion, 1938.

Maurras, Charles. Enquête sur la monarchie. Paris: Nouvelle Librairie nationale, ed. of 1925.

Mayer, Lt. Colonel Émile. La Guerre de hier et l'armée de demain. Paris: Garnier Frères, 1921.

Menu, Lt. Colonel Charles. Applications de l'industrie. 2 vols., École Supérieure de Guerre, 1928-31. (Unpublished text, available at the Industrial College of the Armed Forces, Washington, D. C.).

———— Influence of Industrial Production on Military Operations. (Translation of a speech given at the Centre des Hautes Études Militaires, available at the National War College, Washington, D. C.).

Micaud, Charles. The French Right and Nazi Germany, 1933-1939. Durham, N. C.: Duke University Press, 1943.

Michon, Georges. La Préparation à la guerre; la loi de trois ans. Paris: Rivière, 1935.

Modiano, Héléne. Les Militaires contre la nation. Paris: Éditions du Parti SFIO, 1936.

Monteilhet, Joseph. Des Armées permanentes à la nation armée. Paris: Giard and Brière, 1903.

———— Les Institutions militaires de la France (1814-1932). Paris: Alcan, 1932.

Mordacq, Henri. La Défense nationale en danger. Paris: Les Éditions de la France, 1938.

———— La Guerre au vingtième siècle. Paris: Berger-Levrault, 1914.

Namier, L. B. Europe in Decay. London: Macmillan, 1950.

Négrier, General François de. "Le Moral des troupes," *Revue des deux mondes*, XXV (Feb. 1, 1905), 481-505.

Nickerson, Hoffman. The Armed Horde, 1793-1939. New York: Putnam, 1940.

Niessel, General A. "Chars, antichars et motorisation dans la guerre d'Espagne," *Revue militaire générale*, II (Dec., 1938), 742-63.

Ollivier, Émile. L'Empire libéral. 18 vols., Paris: Garnier Frères, 1895-1918.

Oncken, Herman. Napoleon III and the Rhine. Trans. Edwin H. Zeydel. New York: Knopf, 1928.

"L'Organisation de la nation pour le temps de guerre," by Commandant, A. P., *Revue politique et parlementaire*, CXXVII (Jun. 10, 1926), 348-63.

"Organisation militaire," by B. A. R., *Correspondant*, CCLXXXII (Jan. 25 and Feb. 10, 1921), 193-222 and 385-424.

Oualid, William and Charles Picquemard. Salaires et tarifs pendant la guerre. Paris: Presses universitaires de France, 1927.

Padover, Saul K. "France Today," *Social Research*, XVI (Dec., 1949), 485-98.

Paixhans, J. "La Loi militaire et le service militaire," *Correspondant*, LI (May 10, 1872), 393-444.

Paléologue, Maurice. " Comment le service de trois ans fut rétabli en 1913," *Revue des deux mondes*, XXVII (May 1 and 15, 1935), 67-94 and 307-44.

Paquier, Colonel, Chef de bataillon Pierre Lyet, and Lt. Colonel Charles de Cossé-Brissac. "Combien d'avions allemands contre combien d'avions français le 10 mai 1940," *Revue de défense nationale*, VI (Jun., 1948), 741-59.

Percin, General Alexandre. L'Armée de demain. Paris: Bibliothèque socialiste, 1920.

———— 1914-les erreurs du haut commandement. Paris: Michel, 1920.

Peschaud, Marcel. Politique et fonctionnement de transports par chemin de fer pendant la guerre. Paris: Presses universitaires de France, 1926.

Pétain, Philippe. "La Sécurité française pendant les années creuses," *Revue des deux mondes*, XXVI (Mar., 1, 1935), 1-20.

Picard, Roger. Le Mouvement syndical durant la guerre. Paris: Presses universitaires de France, 1927.

Pierce, Watson. Industrial Mobilization in France. Washington, 1945. (Unpublished study for the Army Industrial College, Department of Research; available at the Industrial College of the Armed Forces, Washington, D. C.).

Pinot, Robert. Le Comité des Forges de France au service de la nation. Paris: Colin, 1919.

Pont, Charles. Les Réquisitions militaires. Paris: Berger-Levrault, 1905.

Popper, D. H. and J. C. de Wilde. "The Wartime Economy of Britain and France," *Foreign Policy Reports*, XVI (Jul. 15, 1940), 110-24.

Potez, Captain Émile. Le Moral de nos soldats. Paris: Charles-Lavauzelle, 1904.

Pratt, Edwin A. The Rise of Rail Power in War and Conquest, 1833-1914. London: King, 1915.

Raoult, Major S. "The Fourth Bureau of the French General Staff." (Translation from an article in the *Revue militaire générale* [Oct.-Nov., 1924], available in the National War College, Washington, D. C.).

Razouls, Jacques. La Responsabilité des chemins de fer en temps de guerre. Paris: Sirey, 1942.

Reboul, Lt. Colonel Frédéric. "Le Malaise de l'armée," *Revue des deux mondes*, XXVI (Mar. 15, 1925), 378-95.

——— Mobilisation industrielle. Paris: Berger-Levrault, 1925.

Recouly, Raymond. "Les Leçons d'une crise," *Revue de France*, XVI (Apr., 1936), 535-40.

Renan, Ernest. Oeuvres complètes d' Ernest Renan. 5 vols., Paris: Calmann-Lévy, 1947-52.

Renouvin, Pierre. The Forms of War Government in France. New Haven: Yale University Press, 1927.

Revol, Colonel Joseph. Histoire de l'armée française. Paris: Larousse, 1929.

Reynaud, Paul. Le Problème militaire français. Paris: Flammarion, 1937.

Rôle de l'officier de la nation armée. École Polytechnique, 1911-12. (Unpublished text, available at the National War College, Washington, D. C.).

Saposs, David J. The Labor Movement in Post-War France. New York: Columbia University Press, 1931.

Schuman, Frederick L. War and Diplomacy in the French Republic. New York: Whitesley House, 1931.

Sébe, Achille. La Conscription des indigènes d'Algérie. Paris: Larose, 1912.

Seeckt, Hans von. Thoughts of a Soldier. Trans. Gilbert Water-house. London: Ernest Benn, 1930.

Serrigny, Bernard. L'Allemagne face à la guerre totale. Paris: Grasset, 1940.

―――― Les Conséquences économiques et sociales de la prochaine guerre. Paris: Giard and Brière, 1909.

―――― La Guerre et le mouvement économique. Paris: Charles-Lavauzelle, 1905.

―――― "L'Organisation de la nation pour le temps de guerre," *Revue des deux mondes*, XVIII (Dec. 1, 1923), 583-601.

Shanahan, William O. Prussian Military Reforms, 1786-1813. New York: Columbia University Press, 1945.

Sheppard, Colonel E. W. "Two Generals―One Doctrine," *Army Quarterly*, XLI (1940), 105-18.

Silberner, Edmund. The Problem of War in Nineteenth Economic Thought. Princeton: Princeton University Press, 1946.

Simon, Jules. Le Gouvernement de M. Thiers (8 février 1871-24 mai 1873). 2 vols., Paris: Calmann-Lévy, 1879.

Souchon, Lucien. Feue l'armée française. Paris: Fayard, 1929.

Spengler, Joseph J. France Faces Depopulation. Durham, N. C.: Duke University Press, 1938.

Targe, General Antoine. La Garde de nos frontières. Paris: Charles-Lavauzelle, 1930.

Ténot, Eugène. Les Nouvelles Défenses de la France. 2 vols., Paris: Baillière, 1880.

Theil, Colonel de la Porte du. Cours d'artillerie. Courbevoie: P. Chenove, 1930. (Text used at the École Supérieure de Guerre, available at the National War College, Washington, D. C.).

Thomas, Albert. Le Second Empire, 1852-1870 (Histoire socialiste de la nation française, ed. Jean Jaurès, Vol. VIII). 12 vols., Paris: Rouff, 1901-08.

Tiffen, Charles. La Course aux armements et les finances publiques. Paris: Librairie Générale de Droit et de Jurisprudence, 1937.

Tissier, Lt. Colonel Pierre. The Riom Trial. London: Harrap, 1942.

Trentinian, General de. The General Staff in 1914. Trans. Lt. G. de Lagerberg. (Unpublished trans. available in the National War College, Washington, D. C.).

Trochu, General Louis. L'Armée française en 1867. Paris: Amyot, 1867.

──── Oeuvres posthumes. 2 vols. Tours: Alfred Mame, 1896.

Vagts, Alfred. Militarism: Romance and Realities of a Profession. New York: Norton, 1937.

Vallet, Albert. Le Problème militaire de la Quatrième République. Lyon: Éditions Seguila, 1947.

Vauthier, Colonel P. La Doctrine de guerre du Général Douhet. Paris: Berger-Levrault, 1935. (Preface by Marshal Pétain).

Villate, R. "L'Entrée des Français en Belgique," *Revue d'histoire de la deuxième guerre mondiale*, Nos. 10 and 11 (Jun., 1953), 60-76.

Villenoisy, General Cosseron de. "La Nation armée à propos de l'ouvrage du Baron von der Goltz," *Revue des deux mondes*, LXIV (Aug. 1, 1884), 513-50.

Vinoy, General Joseph. L'Armée française en 1873. Paris: Plon, 1873.

Vuillemin, Louis. Les S. A. G. dans la nation. 2 vols., Charles-Lavauzelle, 1914.

Wauquier, Colonel A. "Les Forces cuirassées dans la bataille," *Revue d'histoire de la deuxième guerre mondiale*, Nos. 10 and 11 (Jun., 1953), 150-62.

Weinstein, Harold. Jean Jaurès: A Study of Patriotism in the French Socialist Movement. New York: Columbia University Press, 1936.

Werth, Alexander. The Twilight of France, 1933-1940. New York: Harper and Brothers, 1942.

Weygand, General Maxime. Histoire de l'armée française. Paris: Flammarion, 1938.

──── "L'Unité de l'armée," *Revue militaire générale*, I (Jan., 1937), 1-18.

Wheeler-Bennett, John W. The Pipe Dream of Peace. New York: William Morrow, 1935.

Wildenberg, Rodolphe de Planta de. Cauwès et l'économie nationale. Dijon: Belvet, 1938.

Winnacker, R. A. "The Délégation des Gauches: a Successful Attempt at Managing a Parliamentary Coalition," *Journal of Modern History*, IX (Dec., 1937), 449-70.

──── "The Influence of the Dreyfus Affairs on the Political Development of France," *Papers of the Michigan Academy of Science*,

Winnacker, R. A. (*continued*).

Art, and Letters, 1935, XXI (Ann Arbor, Michigan: University of Michigan Press, 1936).

Wise, Maurice K.   Requisition in France and Italy.   New York: Columbia University Press, 1944.

Wolfers, Arnold K.   Britain and France between Two Wars.   New York: Harcourt, Brace, 1940.

Wright, Gordon.   "Public Opinion and Conscription in France, 1866-70," *Journal of Modern History*, XIV (Mar., 1942), 26-45.

———— Raymond Poincaré and the French Presidency.   Stanford, California: Stanford University Press, 1942.

Zévaès, Alexandre.   Histoire du socialisme et du communisme en France de 1871 à 1947.   Paris: Éditions France-Empire, 1947.

Index

Supply services, pre-1914 organization, 123

Supreme commander, debate over appointment of, 237-38, 239-40, 244

Targe, General Antoine, 161

Thiers, Adolphe, approves post-Napoleonic recruitment practices, 13-14; role in establishment of compulsory service in 1872, 32-33, 39-41

Thomas, Albert, 150

"Total war," origins in French Revolution, 3; in World War I, 91; lack of preparation for, 91-94; post-1918 military thinking about, 143-46, 152-53, 184-85; Gaullist critique of, 250-51; High Command theories about, 254-55, 272-76; as justification for appeasement, 267-68; *see also* National Organization Bill, *Commission d'enquête sur . . . la situation de la métallurgie*, Industrial Mobilization, Economic Planning

Trochu, General Louis, 31*n*, 37

Villenoisy, General Cosseron de, 107*n*

Vinoy, General Joseph, 74

Viviani, René, 89

Waldeck-Rousseau, René, 63

War potential, discussed at League of Nations, 187-89; used as justification for appeasement, 267-68; in plans for World War II, 274-75

Wendell, Guy de, 99-100

Weygand, General Maxime, as admirer of Foch, 145*n*; on need for premilitary training, 177; defends existing military organization, 252-53; opinion on causes of 1940 defeat, 258, 269*n*

World War I, as first "total war," 91; munitions shortages during, 92-94; its "lessons," 142-46, 153-54; French war effort during, 186-87

World War II, divergent interpretations of French defeat in, 257-60; mobilization in 1939, 265-66; campaign plans for, 270-71; war effort during, 274-75; *see also* Defeat of 1940